P9-CET-629

Ellie Krieger

so easy

Ellie Krieger
so easy

Luscious, Healthy Recipes
for Every Meal of the Week

Photography by Alexandra Grablewski

John Wiley & Sons, Inc.

This book is printed on acid-free paper.

Copyright © 2009 by Ellie Krieger. All rights reserved

Photography copyright © 2009 by Alexandra Grablewski.
All rights reserved

Food styling by Mariana Velásquez

Prop styling by Lynda White

Author wardrobe styling by Nicole Gulotta

Author makeup by Kelley Quan at Kramer & Kramer, Inc.

Published by John Wiley & Sons, Inc., Hoboken, New Jersey

Published simultaneously in Canada

No part of this publication may be reproduced, stored in a retrieval
system, or transmitted in any form or by any means, electronic,
mechanical, photocopying, recording, scanning, or otherwise, except
as permitted under Section 107 or 108 of the 1976 United States
Copyright Act, without either the prior written permission
of the Publisher, or authorization through payment of the appropriate
per-copy fee to the Copyright Clearance Center, Inc., 222
Rosewood Drive, Danvers, MA 01923, (978) 750-8400,
fax (978) 646-8600, or on the web at www.copyright.com.
Requests to the Publisher for permission should be addressed
to the Permissions Department, John Wiley & Sons, Inc., 111 River
Street, Hoboken, NJ 07030, (201) 748-6011, fax (201) 748-6008,
or online at http://www.wiley.com/go/permissions.

Limit of Liability/Disclaimer of Warranty: While the publisher and
author have used their best efforts in preparing this book, they
make no representations or warranties with respect to the accuracy
or completeness of the contents of this book and specifically disclaim
any implied warranties of merchantability or fitness for a particular
purpose. No warranty may be created or extended by sales
representatives or written sales materials. The advice and strategies
contained herein may not be suitable for your situation. You should
consult with a professional where appropriate. Neither the publisher
nor author shall be liable for any loss of profit or any other
commercial damages, including but not limited to special,
incidental, consequential, or other damages.

For general information on our other products and services or for
technical support, please contact our Customer Care Department
within the United States at (800) 762-2974, outside the United States
at (317) 572-3993 or fax (317) 572-4002.

Wiley also publishes its books in a variety of electronic formats.
Some content that appears in print may not be available in electronic
books. For more information about Wiley products, visit our web
site at www.wiley.com.

Library of Congress Cataloging-in-Publication Data
Krieger, Ellie. So easy: Luscious, Healthy Recipes for Every Meal
of The Week / Ellie Krieger.
p. cm.
Includes index.
ISBN 978-0-470-42354-7 (cloth)
1. Cookery. 2. Nutrition. I. Title.
TX714.K76 2009
641.5--dc22   2008056026
Printed in the United States of America
10 9 8 7 6 5 4 3 2 1

For Thom and Isabella

ACKNOWLEDGMENTS

I am grateful to the many dedicated and talented
people who helped make this book possible.

THANK YOU:

- Thom and Isabella for the love and encouragement that keeps me going.
- Robert Flutie and Hilary Polk-Williams for pinning down all the details while keeping sight of the big picture. I am lucky to have such a creative, top-notch management team.
- Jane Dystel and Miriam Goderich, literary agents, and Marc Szafran, Esq., for your valuable guidance and expertise.
- Chefs Jacqueline Torren and Adeena Sussman for your culinary artistry and friendship.
- Elisabeth D'Alto, RD, and MaryEllen Conway, MS RD, my assistants, for helping pull together every last detail.
- Editor, Justin Schwartz, for your vision, incredible aesthetic sense, and easygoing professionalism. You are a joy to work with and you sure know how to put together a beautiful book!
- Alexandra Grablewski, photographer; Mariana Velásquez, food stylist; and Lynda White, prop stylist, for glorious photos that truly capture the food's lusciousness.
- Makeup artist Kelley Quan and stylist Nicole Gulotta for making me look like me, only better!
- Janell Vantrease, Carrie Bachman, and Gypsy Lovett, publicists, for spreading the word and getting this book into its place center stage.
- All the people at John Wiley and Sons who put so much into this project.
- Food Network, for all of your support.

*contents

INTRODUCTION

If you love food and want to eat well but struggle making it happen with life's hectic pace, keep reading. This book is full of solutions—solutions in the form of delicious, inspired recipes that answer the call of every meal of the week—all in the most effortless way possible. This is more than a collection of recipes, it is a little peace of mind and a lot of satisfaction. It is peace of mind knowing that no matter what life dishes out, or your level of confidence in the kitchen, you have the tools you need to nourish yourself and your family. And it is the ultimate satisfaction that comes from indulging in incredible, fortifying food each and every day.

EVERY MEAL OF THE WEEK: SOLVED

Here at your fingertips are over 150 delicious, doable recipes organized into chapters that tackle every possible mealtime situation. There are grab-and-go breakfasts for days when you are prone to skip this important meal, as well as easy breakfast options for when you have a little more time or want to impress guests. There are lunches to go, each road tested in a cooler pack, with simple packing instructions to ensure that lunch is something to look forward to wherever you are. And there are at-home lunches for when you have the luxury of eating in. There is a month's worth of different rush-hour dinners—fabulous meals you can whip up in less than thirty minutes without breaking a sweat—as well as dinners for days when you have a little more time to marinate or roast, but still want it all to be effortless. Finally, there are decadent desserts, some ready in minutes and others truly worth waiting for, all easily pulled together.

Every breakfast, lunch, and dinner recipe is put in the context of a complete meal, balanced in both taste and nutrition, so there is no guesswork to it. All you need to do is decide what meal you need to address and the easy answers are laid out for you. (Of course you can also mix and match if you want to!) The hardest part will be figuring out which enticing, accessible option you crave most that day.

There are also dozens of tips and ideas to take the stress out of meal planning and help you get the most out of every bite you take.

DELICIOUS-HEALTHY-EASY

Every recipe here hits the delicious-healthy-easy trifecta. Deliciousness is first and foremost. As a born food lover I am driven by great taste, and it is the most important factor in everything I make. But just tasting good isn't enough. As a nutritionist it's essential to me that food not only pleases your taste buds, but also fuels your body and soul, helping you feel great and get the most out of life. Luckily, I have found that elusive place where delicious and healthy meet, and I am thrilled to share it with you.

That incredible convergence is the inspiration for my tried-and-true, balanced food philosophy upon which all my recipes are founded. My golden rule: no food is ever off limits. Rather, I categorize food as Usually, Sometimes, or Rarely. Usually foods are those I use most plentifully and are the backbone of healthy eating: vegetables, fruit, beans, nuts, lean protein, low-fat dairy, and healthy oils. I sprinkle in Sometimes foods here and there for flavor and variety. They are a little more processed, like white flour, or higher in saturated fat, like chicken thighs. Rarely foods—like bacon, cream, full-fat cheese, and butter—are the foods that many nutritionists forbid and many cooks use with a heavy hand. I have found the ideal midpoint by using these foods strategically, in small amounts for maximum impact. So, for example, I serve my Herbed Mashed Potatoes (page 174) with a dab of butter right on top, to meltingly advertise to you how creamy and indulgent they are.

The idea is that there is no need to deprive yourself or go to extremes to be healthy. In fact, extremes are usually unhealthy and trap us into a diet mentality. Rather, balance is key. If you are eating mostly nutrient-rich whole foods, there is room for some butter in your mashed potatoes, some sugar on your strawberries, or even a slice of rich chocolate cake.

I also believe in using pure, minimally processed ingredients and steering clear of artificial additives. I will use reduced-fat foods only if they work taste-wise and are not laden with chemical additives. So I use low-fat milk and yogurt, for example, but you won't get me within a yard of fat-free whipped topping. (Have you ever read the ingredient list on that stuff?) I'll take a little good old-fashioned whipped cream any day.

And when it comes to cheeses like Parmesan, blue cheeses, and sharp cheddar, there is just no substitute. Besides, they are so flavorful that just a bit goes a long way. The truth is, sometimes, what's best is a little of the real thing.

The third part of the trifecta is the easy factor. Anyone who has all day and a culinary degree can make delicious, healthy food, but what about the rest of us? As a mom with a full-time job, I know how busy life is with a circus full of balls to keep in the air. The recipes here are specifically created to take the stress out of mealtime and be doable no matter what your time crunch or experience level in the kitchen. With life so complicated sometimes, isn't it nice to know that eating doesn't have to be? True to this book's title, after making and delighting in any meal in this book you should be compelled to say: "That was so easy!"

ABOUT THE NUTRITION FACTS

I don't cook with a calculator by my side to get a certain nutrient profile from a dish. That would take the love out of cooking for me and detract from the sensuous experience I think it should be. But amazingly, when I create recipes using my food philosophy the numbers tend to work out on their own. Because they can be a helpful guide, I have included the nutrition facts for each recipe, with the amount of calories, fat, protein, carbohydrate, fiber, cholesterol, and sodium in each serving. Since some fats are beneficial and others detrimental, I further break them down into saturated (bad fat), and monounsaturated and polyunsaturated (good fats).

I have also listed good and excellent sources of essential nutrients in each recipe. To qualify as a good source, a serving must contain at least 10% of the Daily Value (the standard daily recommended intake), and to be called an excellent source it needs to provide at least 20% of the Daily Value. I encourage you not to get hung up on these values, but factor them in when planning your meals and let them serve as a reminder that vitamins and minerals are not just found in powders and pills as so many marketers would have us believe. They are bountifully present in luscious, wholesome foods that are easy to prepare.

Keep in mind that the values provided are per serving for each complete meal. In cases where a meal has more than one recipe, I also noted the individual recipe values in the appendix. The nutrition information excludes optional ingredients or anything added to taste, and if there is a choice of ingredients, like "nonfat or low-fat yogurt," I always use the first option listed for the analysis.

To help put the nutrition breakdown in perspective, here are some daily total numbers to shoot for based on a 2,000-calorie diet (the calorie level for most moderately active women):

Total Fat: 65 g
(Saturated fat: 20 g or less, Monounsaturated fat: 25 g, Polyunsaturated fat: 20 g)
Protein: 90 g
Carbohydrate: 275 g
Fiber: 28 g or more
Cholesterol: 300 mg or less
Sodium: 2300 mg or less

Since everyone has different appetites and different calorie needs, there will always be a range of how many people a given recipe serves. But in order to do the nutrition analysis I had to pick one number. So I chose to base the serving sizes on portions that would satisfy and meet the daily calorie needs of most women. You'll see that most breakfast options range from 250 to 400 calories, lunches come in at 350 to 500, and dinners from 450 to 550. Most desserts are 100 to 200 calories. With one or two additional snacks a day and beverages, that puts you right in the zone. If you are serving a group of high school football players, you are training for a marathon, or you are not as active as you'd like to be, adjust the portions accordingly.

THE SO EASY PANTRY

A well-stocked pantry takes the stress out of meal planning and prep because it ensures that you have the tools you need to whip up a fantastic meal even if you are too busy to get to the store. This list covers all the nonperishable items you need to make any recipe in this book. Beyond the basics, it includes healthy convenience items that can help you get lots of flavor and nutrition effortlessly.

OILS AND VINEGARS

Canola oil

Cooking spray

Extra-virgin olive oil

Toasted sesame oil

Balsamic vinegar

Cider vinegar

Red wine vinegar

Rice vinegar

White wine vinegar

CONDIMENTS, SAUCES, AND OTHER FLAVOR BOOSTERS

Asian fish sauce

Capers

Chipotle chiles in adobo sauce

Cocoa powder, unsweetened, natural

Hot pepper sauce

Instant espresso

Jarred sauces (basil pesto, marinara, salsa)

Jarred roasted red peppers, in water

Liquid smoke

Mayonnaise

Mustard (grainy, Dijon)

Olives (green, Calamata)

Porcini mushrooms, dried

Soy sauce, low-sodium

Sun-dried tomatoes, not oil-packed

Thai red curry paste

Worcestershire sauce

Wine (dry red, dry white, sparkling, mirin)

ON THE SHELF

Applesauce, natural, unsweetened

Baking powder

Baking soda

Beans, canned, preferably low-sodium (black, cannellini, and navy beans; chickpeas)

Broth, low-sodium (chicken, beef, vegetable)

Chunk light tuna, packed in water

Chocolate (60% to 70% cocoa solids or bittersweet)

Coconut milk, unsweetened, light

Condensed milk, sweetened, fat-free

Evaporated milk

Gelatin

Hominy

Jams and preserves (apricot, raspberry)

Pineapple, packed in natural juice

Pumpkin, solid packed

Salmon, canned

Tomatoes, preferably no salt added (juice, diced, whole, tomato sauce, tomato paste)

SWEETENERS

Honey

Pure maple syrup

Sugar (granulated, brown [light and dark], turbinado, superfine, confectioners')

Unsulfured molasses

NUTS, SEEDS, AND DRIED FRUITS

Peanut butter, natural-style (chunky and creamy)

Tahini (sesame paste)

Variety of shelled, unsalted nuts and seeds (almonds, hazelnuts, peanuts, pecans, pine nuts, pistachios, pumpkin seeds, sesame seeds, sunflower seeds, walnuts)

Dried fruit (apricots, cherries, cranberries, dates, figs, crystallized ginger, raisins)

GRAINS

Bread crumbs, unseasoned, preferably whole-wheat

Breakfast cereals (crispy brown rice, Shredded Wheat, All-Bran)

Bulgur wheat

Cornmeal, yellow

Corn tortilla chips, baked

Couscous, whole wheat

Flour (whole-wheat, whole-wheat pastry, all-purpose)

Oats, old-fashioned rolled and quick-cooking

Pasta (whole-wheat or whole-wheat blend, in a variety of shapes)

Pre-cooked rice pouches, microwaveable

Quinoa

Rice (white, brown, wild, Arborio)

Soba noodles

Vanilla wafer cookies

Wheat berries

Wheat germ

Whole-grain graham crackers

IN THE FREEZER

Broccoli

Bread (whole-wheat baguettes, sliced bread, pita, buns)

Corn kernels

Edamame, shelled

Fruit, unsweetened (sliced peaches, mangos, berries, cherries)

Ice cream (light) or frozen yogurt, vanilla

Lima beans

Peas

Ravioli, cheese

Shrimp

Spinach, chopped

Sorbet, raspberry

Tortellini

Winter squash, pureed

Wonton wrappers

THE SPICE RACK

Almond extract

Caraway seeds

Cayenne pepper

Chili powder

Crushed red pepper flakes

Curry powder

Dried basil

Dried dill

Dried oregano

Dried thyme

Ground cinnamon

Ground coriander

Ground cumin

Ground ginger

Ground nutmeg

Ground oregano

Herbes de Provence

Peppercorns, black

Saffron

Salt

Turmeric

Vanilla extract

breakfast— at the ready

* **BREAKFAST IS THE MEAL OF FRESH STARTS** and new possibilities, a way of approaching the day with your best foot forward. It is remarkable how this first meal can set you on course, like a **COMPASS POINTING YOU** in the right direction. If you skip it you are passing up an opportunity to jumpstart your brain and give your body **THE FUEL IT NEEDS** to be at its peak. Unfortunately, the days we have the least time for breakfast are those when we need it most.

   The recipes in this chapter solve that conundrum. Each and every breakfast here is one you can **MAKE IN ADVANCE** to grab and go or whip up in minutes in the morning. They are all designed to be easy to **EAT ON THE FLY,** so you can enjoy this important meal without missing a beat. If you think you don't have time for breakfast, consider this your wake-up call.

start-right smoothie

This ultra-satisfying smoothie is the perfect morning jump start. The fruit and honey hit the sweet spot, and almonds and wheat germ make it nutty and substantial. Pour it in a to-go cup so you can drink it as you dash out the door.

MAKES 2 SERVINGS

SERVING SIZE
2½ CUPS

PER SERVING
CALORIES 410
TOTAL FAT 11 G
  SAT FAT 1 G
  MONO FAT 5.5 G
  POLY FAT 2 G
PROTEIN 17 G
CARB 62 G
FIBER 7 G
CHOLESTEROL 5 MG
SODIUM 135 MG

EXCELLENT SOURCE OF
CALCIUM, FIBER, FOLATE, IODINE, MAGNESIUM, MANGANESE, PHOSPHORUS, POTASSIUM, PROTEIN, THIAMIN, RIBOFLAVIN, VITAMIN C, ZINC

GOOD SOURCE OF
COPPER, IRON, PANTOTHENIC ACID, VITAMIN B6, VITAMIN B12

1	ripe banana, cut into chunks, frozen
6	medium (5 ounces) strawberries, fresh or thawed frozen ones
2	cups nonfat milk
¼	cup wheat germ
¼	cup unsalted almonds
2	tablespoons honey
½	teaspoon vanilla extract
1	cup ice water

Combine all of the ingredients in a blender and blend on high until smooth.

* EATING WELL TIP
Frozen fruit like strawberries is no compromise; it is actually one of the secrets to an extra-cool and frothy smoothie. Besides, it's handy and economical and has comparable nutrition to fresh. Just be sure to buy it unsweetened so you are in control of how much sweetener is added.

    Don't toss your overripe bananas. Cut them into chunks and freeze them in plastic bags. Their natural sweetness is perfect in smoothies, and sometimes it's all the sweetener you need.

peach pie smoothie

Pie for breakfast? Sure, especially when it is in the form of this luscious smoothie, with all the homey flavors of peach pie.

MAKES 2 SERVINGS

SERVING SIZE
2 CUPS

PER SERVING
CALORIES 260
TOTAL FAT 0 G
  SAT FAT 0 G
  MONO FAT 0 G
  POLY FAT 0 G
PROTEIN 12 G
CARB 52 G
FIBER 3 G
CHOLESTEROL 5 MG
SODIUM 150 MG

EXCELLENT SOURCE OF
CALCIUM, PROTEIN,
VITAMIN C

GOOD SOURCE OF
FIBER, IODINE, PHOSPHORUS,
RIBOFLAVIN, VITAMIN A

1	cup nonfat milk
1	cup nonfat or low-fat vanilla yogurt
2	cups frozen sliced peaches (unsweetened)
1	tablespoon honey, plus more to taste
½	teaspoon vanilla extract
⅛	teaspoon ground cinnamon
	Pinch of ground nutmeg
	Pinch of ground ginger
1	cup ice

Put all of the ingredients in a blender and blend on high until smooth.

cherry-vanilla smoothie

Cherry and vanilla form an all-American combo that never goes out of style. It really works in this thick, creamy shake that's candy pink and scented with vanilla. One sip and you'll feel like a kid again.

MAKES 2 SERVINGS

SERVING SIZE
2½ CUPS

PER SERVING
CALORIES 270
TOTAL FAT 0.5 G
  SAT FAT 0 G
  MONO FAT 0 G
  POLY FAT 0 G
PROTEIN 12 G
CARB 54 G
FIBER 3 G
CHOLESTEROL 5 MG
SODIUM 150 MG

EXCELLENT SOURCE OF
CALCIUM, PROTEIN,
VITAMIN C

GOOD SOURCE OF
FIBER, IODINE,
PHOSPHORUS,
RIBOFLAVIN

2   cups pitted sweet cherries (unsweetened), frozen
1   cup nonfat or low-fat vanilla yogurt
1   cup nonfat milk
2   teaspoons honey
½   teaspoon vanilla extract
1   cup ice

Combine all of the ingredients in a blender and blend on high until smooth.

* DID YOU KNOW?
Cherries could help you move more freely and sleep better thanks to their natural anti-inflammatory benefits and the sleep-regulating melatonin they contain.

mocha java smoothie

This decedent smoothie does double duty: it's your morning coffee and a filling breakfast, all in one frothy glass. Not to mention that it's a nice chocolate fix. What a way to rev up the day!

MAKES 2 SERVINGS

SERVING SIZE
2½ CUPS

PER SERVING
CALORIES 210
TOTAL FAT 1 G
  SAT FAT 0.5 G
  MONO FAT 0 G
  POLY FAT 0 G
PROTEIN 10 G
CARB 44 G
FIBER 4 G
CHOLESTEROL 5 MG
SODIUM 130 MG

EXCELLENT SOURCE OF
CALCIUM, IODINE,
PHOSPHORUS, POTASSIUM,
PROTEIN, RIBOFLAVIN,
VITAMIN B6, VITAMIN C

GOOD SOURCE OF
FIBER, MAGNESIUM,
MANGANESE,
PANTOTHENIC ACID,
VITAMIN B12

1   tablespoon sugar
2   rounded teaspoons instant espresso,
        or 2 shots of espresso
2   teaspoons unsweetened natural cocoa powder
¼   cup boiling water
2   cups nonfat milk
2   ripe bananas, peeled, cut into chunks, frozen
1   cup ice

In a small bowl, stir together the sugar, instant espresso, if using, and cocoa powder. Add the boiling water and stir until dissolved. (If using regular espresso, stir the sugar and cocoa into the coffee until dissolved.)
    Combine the coffee mixture in a blender with the milk, bananas, and ice, and blend on high until smooth.

* EATING WELL TIP
To help your morning go more smoothly, put all the smoothie ingredients, except the frozen bananas and ice, in the blender jug the night before. Cover and stash in the refrigerator. In the morning just add the frozen ingredients and whir.

cheddar-apple quesadilla

The combination of sharp, rich cheddar with sweet tart apples always wins me over. It's classic yet somehow unique, especially when grilled up in a flour tortilla, so the cheese melts and the apple softens slightly. This takes less than 5 minutes to whip up and will leave you feeling great all morning.

MAKES 4 SERVINGS

SERVING SIZE
1 QUESADILLA

PER SERVING
CALORIES 280
TOTAL FAT 12 G
    SAT FAT 6 G
    MONO FAT 3 G
    POLY FAT 0 G
PROTEIN 10 G
CARB 29 G
FIBER 3 G
CHOLESTEROL 25 MG
SODIUM 350 MG

EXCELLENT SOURCE OF
CALCIUM, PROTEIN

GOOD SOURCE OF
FIBER, PHOSPHORUS

1   Granny Smith apple, cored, thinly sliced
4   whole-wheat flour tortillas (9 inches in diameter)
1   cup shredded sharp cheddar cheese (4 ounces)

Preheat a large nonstick skillet over medium-high heat.
    Fan out the apple slices over the bottom half of each tortilla and top with the cheddar cheese. Fold the tortillas in half. Working in batches, place the quesadillas in the skillet and weigh them down with a smaller heavy skillet or an ovenproof plate topped with a heavy can. Cook until the cheese is melted and the tortillas are golden brown, about 1½ minutes per side. Cut in half and eat warm.

THERE'S NO "BUT" IN BREAKFAST

Want to be happier, brainier, thinner, and healthier? Breakfast just may be your ticket. Breakfast eaters tend to be mentally and emotionally better off, are leaner, and have better nutrition overall than those who pass on it. All that and you get to eat good food! Why wouldn't you? It turns out breakfast skippers have all sorts of reasons. Luckily, I have a solution for every breakfast "but" in the book.

BUT I HAVE NO TIME IN THE MORNING...

Two words: this chapter. Right now you are looking at more than a dozen delicious breakfast ideas that can be made in less than ten minutes and/or made ahead and eaten on the run.

BUT I AM NEVER HUNGRY FOR BREAKFAST...

I hear this one a lot and find that people who are not hungry for breakfast are often overeating the night before. If you keep dinner on the light side and avoid that 10 p.m. munch fest you will most likely wake up eager for breakfast. Also, once your body gets used to having breakfast, it starts to let you know.

BUT I AM TRYING TO CUT CALORIES...

Cutting calories by skipping breakfast usually backfires. Chances are you'll make up those calories, and then some, later that day. Eating breakfast, especially a healthy one including whole grain, fruit, and low-fat protein, is one of the key habits that keep you lean.

smoked salmon sandwich

This simple sandwich is a remarkably luxurious combination of tastes and textures—buttery smoked salmon, the cool crunch of cucumber, peppery radish, and a whisper of onion from fresh chives—all perfectly packaged between two slices of cream cheese–slathered pumpernickel. Make it the night before and stash it in the fridge for the morning rush.

MAKES 4 SERVINGS

SERVING SIZE
1 SANDWICH

PER SERVING
CALORIES 300
TOTAL FAT 9 G
  SAT FAT 3 G
  MONO FAT 3 G
  POLY FAT 2 G
PROTEIN 24 G
CARB 31 G
FIBER 4 G
CHOLESTEROL 55 MG
SODIUM 620 MG

EXCELLENT SOURCE OF
MANGANESE, NIACIN,
PHOSPHORUS, PROTEIN,
RIBOFLAVIN, SELENIUM,
THIAMIN, VITAMIN B12

GOOD SOURCE OF
COPPER, FIBER, FOLATE,
IRON, MAGNESIUM,
PANTOTHENIC ACID,
POTASSIUM, VITAMIN B6

¼   cup whipped cream cheese
8   slices pumpernickel bread
4   ounces sliced smoked salmon
⅛   English cucumber, thinly sliced
4   radishes, thinly sliced
¼   teaspoon salt
¼   teaspoon freshly ground black pepper
4   large or 8 small chives

Spread ½ tablespoon of the cream cheese on each slice of the bread. Top four of the bread slices with the salmon, then add the cucumber and radish slices and season with the salt and pepper. Fold 1 large chive or use 2 small chives and place on top. Cover with the remaining slices of bread. Cut each sandwich in half. Eat immediately or wrap in foil and refrigerate for up to 1 day.

spicy egg and avocado wrap

If, like me, you regularly spike your eggs with hot sauce, this one's for you. Chunks of egg, creamy avocado, and fresh crisp veggies are doused in tongue-tingling chili sauce, then tucked neatly into a hand-held wrap. It keeps well overnight so you can make it in advance.

MAKES 4 SERVINGS

SERVING SIZE
1 WRAP

PER SERVING
CALORIES 370
TOTAL FAT 14 G
 SAT FAT 3 G
 MONO FAT 7 G
 POLY FAT 2 G
PROTEIN 20 G
CARB 45 G
FIBER 9 G
CHOLESTEROL 210 MG
SODIUM 890 MG

EXCELLENT SOURCE OF
FIBER, FOLATE,
IODINE, MANGANESE,
PANTOTHENIC ACID,
PHOSPHORUS, PROTEIN,
RIBOFLAVIN, SELENIUM,
THIAMIN, VITAMIN A,
VITAMIN B6, VITAMIN K

GOOD SOURCE OF
COPPER, IRON,
MAGNESIUM, NIACIN,
POTASSIUM, VITAMIN B12,
VITAMIN C, ZINC

8	large eggs
4	large red-leaf lettuce leaves
4	whole-wheat wrap breads (about 9 inches in diameter)
1	avocado, pitted, peeled, sliced
1	medium tomato (about 4 ounces), sliced
⅛	English cucumber, thinly sliced
1	tablespoon prepared Thai chili sauce or hot sauce, divided
½	teaspoon salt
½	teaspoon freshly ground black pepper

Place the eggs in a 4-quart saucepan. Cover with water, bring to a boil, reduce the heat, and simmer for 9 minutes. Remove from the heat, rinse with cold water, and peel. Remove the yolks from 4 of the eggs and discard the yolks. Slice the remaining egg whites and whole eggs into ¼-inch slices.

Lay a lettuce leaf over the center of each wrap bread. Top each with the avocado, sliced eggs, tomato, and cucumber. Sprinkle with the chili sauce and season with the salt and pepper. Fold one side of the bread about 2 inches over the filling to form a pocket and roll into a wrap. Eat immediately or cover in foil and store in the refrigerator for up to 1 day.

✻ EATING WELL TIP
For easy, nutrient-rich, and inexpensive protein at your fingertips, cook up a few hard-boiled eggs and stash them in the fridge, where they will last up to a week.

peanut butter and fruit wrap

Succulent, sweet dates, a hint of cinnamon, and hearty whcle-wheat wrap bread give an exciting, exotic twist to your basic peanut butter sandwich. It's a grown-up sandwich that kids will love too. Put it together the night before so all you have to do in the a.m. is pluck it out of the fridge.

MAKES 4 SERVINGS

SERVING SIZE
1 WRAP

PER SERVING
CALORIES 450
TOTAL FAT 19 G
  SAT FAT 3.5 G
  MONO FAT 8 G
  POLY FAT 4.5 G
PROTEIN 13 G
CARB 60 G
FIBER 7 G
CHOLESTEROL 0 MG
SODIUM 320 MG

EXCELLENT SOURCE OF
FIBER, MANGANESE,
NIACIN, PROTEIN,
VITAMIN B6

GOOD SOURCE OF
COPPER, IRON, MAGNESIUM,
PHOSPHORUS, POTASSIUM

½ cup natural-style peanut butter
4 whole-wheat wrap breads (about 9 inches in diameter)
2 bananas, peeled, sliced
4 large pitted dates, chopped
1 teaspoon ground cinnamon

Spread 2 tablespoons of the peanut butter on each wrap. Evenly distribute the banana slices and dates among the wraps. Sprinkle with cinnamon. Roll the wraps and seal in aluminum foil for easy eating on the go.

BREAKFAST CHECKLIST

To get my gold standard seal of approval (which, naturally, all the recipes here have) a breakfast has to score at least 4 out of 5 on this breakfast checklist.

☐ **PROTEIN**

Including protein insures that you won't be hungry again an hour after eating, since it is digested more gradually than carbohydrates. Breakfast-friendly protein foods include egg, ham, low-fat milk or yogurt, cheese, smoked fish, and nuts.

☐ **FRUIT AND/OR VEGETABLE**

A colorful fruit or vegetable is a must-have in every meal. Breakfast is an especially good opportunity to work in some fruit, which gives our bodies a quick burst of energy. Try varying your fresh fruit and vegetables with the seasons. Use frozen fruit in smoothies and dried fruit as a sweet, chewy option.

☐ **WHOLE GRAIN**

Most Americans don't get a single serving of whole grain daily, much less the 3 daily servings recommended. Whole grains provide essential minerals, fiber, and protective antioxidants, and there are lots of breakfast-friendly choices, from hot and cold cereals to breads and pancakes.

☐ **LOW IN ADDED SUGAR AND SATURATED FAT**

No problem adding a little honey to your smoothie, putting a touch of brown sugar on your oatmeal, or spreading a pat of butter on your toast. But too much sugar (pastries and sugary cereals) and saturated fat (sausage and biscuits), while fine once in a while, is a disqualifier in my Ideal Breakfast category.

☐ **DELICIOUS**

Who cares if it has all the right numbers if it doesn't taste great? To be a perfect breakfast, it has to make me want to eat it!

cinnamon raisin toast
with honey-walnut spread

The smell of toasting cinnamon raisin bread somehow reassures me that all is well with the world. Spreading that warm bread with a creamy, honey-sweetened walnut spread, then topping it with slices of fresh fruit drives the point home further. It's a deliciously comforting start to the day. Make the spread up to three days ahead of time and refrigerate it so it's ready when you want it.

MAKES 4 SERVINGS

SERVING SIZE
2 PIECES

PER SERVING
CALORIES 250
TOTAL FAT 8 G
    SAT FAT 0.5 G
    MONO FAT 0.5 G
    POLY FAT 3.5 G
PROTEIN 10 G
CARB 37 G
FIBER 3 G
CHOLESTEROL 0 MG
SODIUM 220 MG

EXCELLENT SOURCE OF
IRON, PROTEIN

GOOD SOURCE OF
FIBER, MANGANESE

½   cup walnut pieces
½   cup plain Greek-style nonfat yogurt
2   teaspoons honey
8   slices cinnamon raisin bread
1   peach (or apple or pear), pitted (or cored)

Toast the walnuts in a dry skillet over medium-high heat, stirring frequently, until fragrant, 3 to 5 minutes. Allow them to cool slightly, then chop them finely.

In a small bowl, add the chopped walnuts to the yogurt and honey and stir until well combined. The spread will keep in the refrigerator in an airtight container for up to 3 days. Just stir well before using.

When ready to serve, toast the bread and cut the fruit into ¼-inch slices. Spread about 1 tablespoon of the walnut spread onto each piece of bread. Top each piece with a few slices of fruit. Eat immediately.

muesli parfaits

Muesli (pronounced moose-ly) is a traditional Swiss breakfast that's a mixture of oats, nuts, and fruit. The oats soften and plump up, becoming like a pudding as they soak in a vanilla-laced honey and milk mixture. Topped with juicy berries and crunchy almonds, these parfaits are so delicious and satisfying you might just start yodeling. Prepare a batch in to-go cups for a true grab-and-go breakfast that will keep in the refrigerator for a few days, or make them in fancy glasses for company.

MAKES 4 SERVINGS

SERVING SIZE
¾ CUP MUESLI
½ CUP BERRIES
2 TABLESPOONS ALMONDS

PER SERVING
CALORIES 300
TOTAL FAT 10 G
　SAT FAT 1 G
　MONO FAT 6 G
　POLY FAT 2 G
PROTEIN 13 G
CARB 41 G
FIBER 6 G
CHOLESTEROL 0 MG
SODIUM 75 MG

EXCELLENT SOURCE OF
CALCIUM, FIBER,
MANGANESE, PROTEIN,
VITAMIN C

GOOD SOURCE OF
COPPER, IODINE,
IRON, MAGNESIUM,
PHOSPHORUS, RIBOFLAVIN

½	cup unsalted raw almonds
1	cup nonfat milk
1	cup nonfat plain yogurt
1	cup old-fashioned rolled oats
2	tablespoons honey
¼	teaspoon vanilla extract
2	cups mixed berries, fresh or frozen (strawberries hulled and halved)

Toast the almonds in a dry skillet over medium-high heat, stirring frequently, until golden and fragrant, about 3 minutes. Chop them coarsely.

In a medium bowl, stir together the milk, yogurt, oats, honey, and vanilla. Divide the oat mixture evenly among 4 small dishes or parfait glasses. Top each with ½ cup of berries, then 2 tablespoons of the chopped almonds. Cover tightly and refrigerate overnight. The parfaits will keep up to 3 days in the refrigerator.

vanilla spice oatmeal

I love oatmeal cookies so much I thought it would be fun to have all those heartwarming flavors in my morning oatmeal. Fragrant with cinnamon, nutmeg, and vanilla, sweetened with rich brown sugar and juicy raisins, and topped with a buttery crunch of pecans, a bowl of this oatmeal is the very essence of comfort. And it's comforting to know you can have it on the table—or in a to-go hot cup—in less than 10 minutes.

MAKES 4 SERVINGS

SERVING SIZE
1¼ CUPS

PER SERVING
CALORIES 370
TOTAL FAT 13 G
  SAT FAT 1 G
  MONO FAT 5.5 G
  POLY FAT 3 G
PROTEIN 11 G
CARB 54 G
FIBER 6 G
CHOLESTEROL 5 MG
SODIUM 190 MG

EXCELLENT SOURCE OF
FIBER, MANGANESE, PROTEIN

GOOD SOURCE OF
CALCIUM, IRON

½	cup pecans
3½	cups water
2	cups old-fashioned rolled oats
½	cup raisins
¼	teaspoon salt (optional)
¼	teaspoon vanilla extract
	Pinch of ground nutmeg
2	tablespoons firmly packed dark brown sugar, plus more to taste
1	cup low-fat milk, or to taste
⅛	teaspoon ground cinnamon

Toast the pecans in a dry skillet over medium-high heat, stirring frequently, until golden and fragrant, 3 to 5 minutes. Chop them coarsely.

Combine the water, oats, raisins, and salt, if using, in a medium saucepan. Bring to a boil, reduce the heat to low, and simmer, stirring a few times, until the oats are tender, about 5 minutes.

Remove the pan from the heat and stir in the vanilla and nutmeg. Swirl in the brown sugar and place the oatmeal in serving bowls. Pour ¼ cup of milk on top of each bowl, sprinkle with the toasted pecans and cinnamon, and serve.

walnut and dried cherry bars

There are so many breakfast bars on the market but none come close to tasting this good. These are tender, cakey, and perfectly sweetened with a great nutty crunch and fruity chewiness. All that and they're a cinch to make.

MAKES 12 SERVINGS

SERVING SIZE
1 BAR

PER SERVING
CALORIES 230
TOTAL FAT 9 G
  SAT FAT 1 G
  MONO FAT 3 G
  POLY FAT 4 G
PROTEIN 4 G
CARB 34 G
FIBER 2 G
CHOLESTEROL 20 MG
SODIUM 60 MG

EXCELLENT SOURCE OF
MANGANESE

GOOD SOURCE OF
THIAMIN

1	cup quick-cooking rolled oats
¾	cup whole-wheat pastry flour or regular whole-wheat flour
¼	cup toasted wheat germ
1	teaspoon ground cinnamon
¼	teaspoon salt
½	cup honey
⅓	cup unsweetened applesauce
¼	cup canola oil
1	large egg, beaten to blend
1	large egg white
¾	cup chopped dried tart cherries
½	cup finely chopped walnuts
	Cooking spray
¼	cup "fruit only" apricot preserves

Preheat the oven to 350°F. In a medium bowl, whisk together the oats, flour, wheat germ, cinnamon, and salt.

In another bowl, whisk together the honey, applesauce, oil, egg, and egg white until well combined. Stir in the oat mixture until well combined. Add the dried cherries and walnuts.

Coat an 8-inch square baking pan with cooking spray. Spread the mixture in the prepared pan and bake until a toothpick inserted in the center comes out clean, 30 to 35 minutes. When the bars are nearly done, put the preserves in a small saucepan and bring to a boil. As soon as the bars come out of the oven, brush with the preserves. Cool completely and cut into 12 bars, about 4x1½ inches each.

fig bran muffins

These moist, tender muffins will erase any memories of the rubbery, leaden low-fat muffins you have had before. One of the secrets is the applesauce, which adds extra tenderness and sweet fruity flavor. The figs lend a deep-flavored, sophisticated touch. It's maximum muffin satisfaction with minimal effort.

MAKES 12 MUFFINS

SERVING SIZE
1 MUFFIN

PER SERVING
CALORIES 230
TOTAL FAT 8 G
   SAT FAT 1 G
   MONO FAT 4 G
   POLY FAT 2 G
PROTEIN 5 G
CARB 42 G
FIBER 6 G
CHOLESTEROL 20 MG
SODIUM 135 MG

EXCELLENT SOURCE OF
FIBER, FOLATE,
MANGANESE, PHOSPHORUS,
VITAMIN B6, VITAMIN B12

GOOD SOURCE OF
CALCIUM, IRON, MAGNESIUM,
NIACIN, POTASSIUM,
RIBOFLAVIN, SELENIUM,
THIAMIN, ZINC

Cooking spray
1½ cups bran cereal, such as All-Bran
1   cup low-fat milk
1½ cups whole-wheat flour
1   tablespoon baking powder
½   teaspoon salt
¾   cup natural applesauce
½   cup honey
⅓   cup canola oil
2   tablespoons unsulfured molasses
1   large egg, beaten to blend
1   cup chopped dried figs, plus 3 whole
       dried figs, thinly sliced

Preheat the oven to 400°F. Coat a 12-capacity muffin pan with cooking spray.

In a large bowl, combine the cereal and milk. Let sit until softened, about 5 minutes. Meanwhile, whisk together the flour, baking powder, and salt in a separate bowl.

Add the applesauce, honey, oil, molasses, and egg to the cereal mixture and stir until combined. Add the flour mixture and stir until just combined. Gently stir in the chopped figs. Spoon the batter into the prepared pan and top each muffin with a fig slice. Tap the pan on the counter a few times to remove any air bubbles.

Bake for about 20 minutes or until a wooden toothpick inserted in the center of a muffin comes out clean. Let cool in the pan on a wire rack for 15 minutes. If necessary, run a knife around the muffins to loosen from the tin. Unmold the muffins and cool completely on a rack.

* EATING WELL TIP
Make a batch of these muffins on the weekend, wrap them individually in wax paper, and freeze them in a plastic bag. Take one out the night before to defrost at room temperature for a perfect start to a busy day.

breakfast—
at leisure

* **MY FAVORITE BREAKFASTS** are those lingered over in my pajamas with the newspaper spread out around me and a bottomless mug of steaming coffee in my hand. These relaxed **BREAKFASTS ARE LIKE A BUFFER ZONE, TIME TO REV UP GRADUALLY** before the day's active pace takes hold. They are usually warm meals that fill my kitchen with homey aromas, but to be truly leisurely they **HAVE TO BE FUSS-FREE.** The recipes here are perfect for easing into a day off. They are impressive and special enough for company—not something you'd make if you had to rush out the door—but they don't take much effort at all, **LEAVING YOU MORE TIME TO RELAX AND ENJOY.**

egg muffin sandwich

This sandwich takes the classic comfort bacon-egg-and-cheese sandwich to new heights. Fluffy herb-spiked eggs, smoky bacon, melting cheddar, and a juicy slice of tomato are all piled onto a crunchy English muffin. It's nice to wake up knowing you are just one pan and ten minutes away from total contentment.

MAKES 4 SERVINGS

SERVING SIZE
1 SANDWICH

PER SERVING
CALORIES 330
TOTAL FAT 13 G
  SAT FAT 5 G
  MONO FAT 3 G
  POLY FAT 1 G
PROTEIN 25 G
CARB 31 G
FIBER 5 G
CHOLESTEROL 245 MG
SODIUM 920 MG

EXCELLENT SOURCE OF
CALCIUM, FIBER,
MANGANESE, NIACIN,
PHOSPHORUS, PROTEIN
RIBOFLAVIN, SELENIUM,
THIAMIN, VITAMIN A,
VITAMIN C, VITAMIN K

GOOD SOURCE OF
COPPER, FOLATE,
IODINE, IRON,
MAGNESIUM, POTASSIUM,
VITAMIN B6, ZINC

4	large eggs
4	large egg whites
¼	cup minced fresh chives
¼	cup minced fresh parsley
	Cooking spray
4	½-inch-thick round slices Canadian bacon
4	whole-wheat English muffins
4	thin slices sharp cheddar cheese (½ ounce each)
1	large beefsteak tomato, sliced into ½-inch-thick slices

Crack the eggs and egg whites into a bowl and whisk. Add the chives and parsley and stir to incorporate.

Spray a large nonstick skillet with cooking spray. Ladle ¼ of the egg mixture into the skillet and cook, omelet style, until the eggs are cooked through, 1 to 2 minutes per side. Slide the omelet onto a plate and cover with foil to keep warm. Repeat with remaining eggs.

In the same skillet, heat the Canadian bacon until warm, 1 to 2 minutes per side. Toast the English muffins. Fold each omelet to fit in an English muffin, then place the omelet on one muffin half. Top with the cheese slice, then the bacon slice, and then a tomato slice. Top with the other muffin half and serve.

YOLKS: MORE THAN THEY'RE CRACKED UP TO BE

If you have been sworn to egg-white omelets, you may be missing out on more than you think. True, egg yolks contain all of an egg's fat (5 grams) and cholesterol (212 mg). That's not so much fat, but it is most of the 300 mg daily cholesterol limit.

But surprisingly, yolks also contain most of the egg's nutrients: lots of protein plus rich amounts of over a dozen vitamins and minerals including hard-to-get vitamins D and B12, iron, zinc, brain-protective choline, and the eye-health antioxidants lutein and zeaxanthin. Not to mention that yolks make your egg dishes sunny yellow, rich, and flavorful.

What's a healthy food lover to do? I say split the difference and get the best of both worlds. You can eat up to one yolk a day without overdoing cholesterol. So when serving eggs, include one whole egg and one or two whites per person.

egg in a basket with
smoked turkey and asparagus

Egg in a Basket is one of those simple pleasures you probably remember from childhood—an over-easy egg cooked inside a hole cut out of a piece of bread. This version builds on that fun basic with an easy yet inspired smoked turkey and asparagus topping. It's still simple and still kid friendly but definitely good enough for company.

MAKES 4 SERVINGS

SERVING SIZE
1 EGG IN A BASKET WITH
½ CUP ASPARAGUS-TURKEY
TOPPING AND 1 BREAD
CUTOUT

PER SERVING
CALORIES 270
TOTAL FAT 11 G
  SAT FAT 5 G
  MONO FAT 1.5 G
  POLY FAT 0.5 G
PROTEIN 21 G
CARB 25 G
FIBER 5 G
CHOLESTEROL 250 MG
SODIUM 630 MG

EXCELLENT SOURCE OF
MANGANESE, PROTEIN,
SELENIUM, VITAMIN A,
VITAMIN K

GOOD SOURCE OF
COPPER, FIBER, FOLATE,
IRON, MAGNESIUM,
NIACIN, PHOSPHORUS,
RIBOFLAVIN, THIAMIN

¾ pound asparagus stalks (about ¾ bunch), woody bottoms removed)
4 pieces whole-wheat sandwich bread
4 teaspoons butter, melted
   Cooking spray
6 ounces sliced smoked turkey, sliced again into thin ribbons
¼ teaspoon freshly ground black pepper
4 large eggs

Place the asparagus in a steamer basket over a pot of boiling water. Cover and steam until crisp-tender, about 3 minutes. Chop the asparagus into ½-inch pieces.

Brush both sides of each slice of bread with the melted butter. Using a 3-inch cookie cutter, cut a hole in the center of each slice of bread; reserve the cutouts.

Spray a large nonstick skillet with cooking spray and set over medium-high heat. Cook the turkey slices until they are browned around the edges, about 3 minutes. Add the asparagus and cook until it is heated through, about 2 minutes, then season with the pepper. Transfer the mixture to a plate and cover with foil to keep warm.

Place 2 of the bread slices and cutouts in the same skillet and crack one egg into the hole of each slice. Cook until the egg whites are set and the bread is toasted on the underside, about 3 minutes. Using a spatula, flip the bread/egg slices and cutouts and cook an additional 1 minute. Transfer the bread/egg pieces to individual plates. Repeat with the remaining bread slices and cutouts. Top each one with ¼ of the turkey-asparagus mixture. Arrange the cutouts on each plate.

big breakfast burrito

Everything about this breakfast is big—big tastes, big portion, and big satisfaction. The only small thing is the effort you need to make it. This soft flour tortilla stuffed with goodies—savory beans, scrambled eggs, spicy salsa, melting cheese, rich avocado, and tangy sour cream—is just the right size to keep you going all morning without weighing you down.

MAKES 4 SERVINGS

SERVING SIZE
1 BURRITO

PER SERVING
CALORIES 460
TOTAL FAT 20 G
   SAT FAT 6 G
   MONO FAT 4 G
   POLY FAT 1 G
PROTEIN 23 G
CARB 51 G
FIBER 12 G
CHOLESTEROL 235 MG
SODIUM 860 MG

EXCELLENT SOURCE OF
FIBER, PROTEIN,
VITAMIN A, VITAMIN C

GOOD SOURCE OF
CALCIUM, FOLATE,
IODINE, IRON,
POTASSIUM, RIBOFLAVIN,
SELENIUM, VITAMIN B6,
VITAMIN K

2	teaspoons canola oil
½	small red onion, diced (1 cup)
1	red bell pepper, seeded and diced
1	cup canned black beans, preferably low-sodium, drained and rinsed
¼	teaspoon crushed red pepper flakes
	Salt and freshly ground black pepper to taste
4	large eggs
4	large egg whites
⅓	cup (about 1½ ounces) shredded pepper Jack cheese
	Cooking spray
4	whole-wheat flour tortillas (10 inches in diameter; burrito-size)
¼	cup reduced-fat sour cream
¼	cup salsa
1	large tomato (4 ounces), seeded and diced
1	small avocado (4 ounces), pitted, peeled, and cubed
	Hot pepper sauce, to taste

Heat the oil in a large nonstick skillet over medium-high heat. Add the onion and red bell pepper and cook, stirring, until softened, about 5 minutes. Add the black beans and red pepper flakes and cook, stirring occasionally, another 3 minutes. Season with salt and pepper, and then transfer the mixture to a bowl.

Whisk the eggs and egg whites together in a medium-size bowl, then add the cheese. Spray the skillet with cooking spray and reheat it over medium heat. Reduce the heat to low, add the eggs, and scramble until cooked through, about 3 minutes.

Spread each tortilla with 1 tablespoon each of sour cream and salsa, then layer with ¼ of the black bean mixture, ¼ of the scrambled eggs, some diced tomato, and ¼ of the avocado. Season to taste with the hot pepper sauce. Roll up burrito-style.

grilled portobello benedict

Here's a fresh take on a classic Benedict. The base is a savory, juicy grilled portobello mushroom that's layered with Canadian bacon and eggs, then topped with a rich pesto sauce, aromatic basil leaves, and a sprinkle of Parmesan. The taste of each layer amplifies the others for maximum flavor impact.

MAKES 4 SERVINGS

SERVING SIZE
1 ASSEMBLED MUSHROOM
CAP

PER SERVING
CALORIES 240
TOTAL FAT 14 G
  SAT FAT 3.5 G
  MONO FAT 5 G
  POLY FAT 1 G
PROTEIN 20 G
CARB 7 G
FIBER 2 G
CHOLESTEROL 230 MG
SODIUM 720 MG

EXCELLENT SOURCE OF
COPPER, IODINE, NIACIN,
PANTOTHENIC ACID,
POTASSIUM, PROTEIN,
RIBOFLAVIN, SELENIUM,
THIAMIN

GOOD SOURCE OF
FOLATE, IRON, MANGANESE,
PHOSPHORUS, VITAMIN B6,
VITAMIN B12, ZINC

Cooking spray
4 portobello mushroom caps (about 4 ounces each)
1 tablespoon olive oil
¼ teaspoon salt, plus more to taste
4 slices Canadian bacon
4 large eggs
4 large egg whites
2 tablespoons water
  Freshly ground black pepper to taste
4 teaspoons store-bought basil pesto
8 fresh basil leaves, cut into ribbons
4 teaspoons freshly grated Parmesan cheese

Preheat a grill or grill pan sprayed with cooking spray.

With a spoon, gently scrape out the dark inside of the mushroom caps (the gills), being careful not to break the cap. Brush both sides of the mushroom caps with oil and sprinkle with ¼ teaspoon of salt. Grill the mushrooms over medium-high heat until they are tender and their juices begin to release, about 7 minutes per side. Transfer each mushroom to a plate, top side down.

On the same grill pan or grill, cook the Canadian bacon slices over medium-high heat until they are warm and grill marks have formed, about 30 seconds per side. Place 1 slice of bacon in each of the mushroom caps.

In a medium-size bowl, whisk the eggs, egg whites, and water together until well combined. Spray a medium-size nonstick skillet with cooking spray and heat over medium-low heat. Add the eggs and scramble until cooked through, about 3 minutes. Season with salt and pepper.

Spoon ¼ of the scrambled eggs on top of the Canadian bacon in each of the mushroom caps. Drizzle 1 teaspoon of pesto over each and top each with some basil ribbons and 1 teaspoon of Parmesan cheese.

salmon, eggs, and onion with pumpernickel crisps

For this native New Yorker, an ideal weekend day includes an indulgent lox (smoked salmon) and bagel breakfast with a cup of strong coffee and a fat Sunday paper. An afternoon nap and a TV football game don't hurt either. This savory scramble of eggs and smoky salmon with golden caramelized onion is a perfect start. Served with crisp pumpernickel rounds made from sliced bagels, it is all the decadent breakfast I crave with no downsides.

MAKES 4 SERVINGS

SERVING SIZE
¾ CUP EGG MIXTURE
2 SLICES PUMPERNICKEL
CRISPS
AND 1 THICK TOMATO SLICE

PER SERVING
CALORIES 370
TOTAL FAT 10 G
  SAT FAT 2.5 G
  MONO FAT 2 G
  POLY FAT 1.5 G
PROTEIN 33 G
CARB 37 G
FIBER 3 G
CHOLESTEROL 260 MG
SODIUM 420 MG

EXCELLENT SOURCE OF
NIACIN, PHOSPHORUS,
PROTEIN, RIBOFLAVIN,
SELENIUM, THIAMIN,
VITAMIN B12, VITAMIN D

GOOD SOURCE OF
FIBER, IODINE,
IRON, POTASSIUM,
VITAMIN A, VITAMIN B6,
VITAMIN C, VITAMIN K

4	large eggs
4	large egg whites
1	teaspoon canola oil
1	large onion, thinly sliced (about 3 cups)
4	ounces thinly sliced smoked salmon
½	teaspoon cracked black pepper
¼	cup thinly sliced chives
1	recipe Pumpernickel Crisps (recipe follows)
	Beefsteak tomato slices

In a medium bowl, whisk the eggs and egg whites. Heat the oil in a large nonstick skillet over medium-high heat. Add the onions and cook, stirring occasionally, until soft and golden brown, 15 to 20 minutes, adding 2 to 3 tablespoons of water after the first 10 minutes to keep the onions moistened. Reduce the heat to medium and add the eggs, smoked salmon, and pepper. Cook, stirring, until the eggs are set, about 5 minutes. Stir in the chives.

Serve with the Pumpernickel Crisps and sliced tomato.

✳ **PUMPERNICKEL CRISPS**
MAKES 4 SERVINGS • SERVING SIZE: 2 SLICES

2	pumpernickel bagels

Slice each of the bagels into 4 rounds so you wind up with 8 bagel rounds. Toast the bagel rounds in a toaster until crisp, 7 to 8 minutes.

broccoli-cheddar breakfast bake

This dish and the Blueberry-Almond French Toast Bake on page 55 let you serve something extraordinary for breakfast while keeping your morning totally fuss-free. You whip them up the night before so all you have to do when you wake up is pull the dish out of the refrigerator and bake. They puff up beautifully and golden brown, almost like a soufflé. This bake elevates the crowd-pleasing broccoli-cheddar duo to something glorious.

MAKES 8 SERVINGS

SERVING SIZE
ONE 4X3-INCH PIECE

PER SERVING
CALORIES 310
TOTAL FAT 15 G
  SAT FAT 8 G
  MONO FAT 3.5 G
  POLY FAT 1 G
PROTEIN 21 G
CARB 19 G
FIBER 3 G
CHOLESTEROL 235 MG
SODIUM 580 MG

EXCELLENT SOURCE OF
CALCIUM, IODINE,
MANGANESE, PHOSPHORUS,
PROTEIN, RIBOFLAVIN,
SELENIUM, VITAMIN C

GOOD SOURCE OF
FIBER, FOLATE,
MAGNESIUM,
PANTOTHENIC ACID,
POTASSIUM, THIAMIN,
VITAMIN A, VITAMIN B6,
VITAMIN B12, VITAMIN D

2 teaspoons olive oil
1 large onion, diced (about 2 cups)
   Cooking spray
1 whole-wheat baguette (about 18 inches long, 8 ounces), cut into 1-inch cubes
8 large eggs
8 large egg whites
2 cups low-fat (1%) milk
1 10-ounce package frozen chopped broccoli, thawed
1½ cups shredded extra-sharp cheddar cheese (6 ounces)
¾ teaspoon ground nutmeg
½ teaspoon salt
½ teaspoon freshly ground black pepper

Heat the oil in a nonstick skillet over medium-high heat. Add the onions and cook, stirring, until translucent and beginning to brown, about 4 minutes. Set aside to cool.

Spray a 9x13-inch baking dish with cooking spray. Arrange the bread cubes in the dish. In a large bowl, beat the eggs, egg whites, and milk until incorporated. Add the onions, broccoli, cheese, nutmeg, salt, and pepper and stir to incorporate. Pour the egg mixture over the bread, spreading it around so the liquid saturates the bread. Cover with plastic wrap and refrigerate for at least 8 hours or overnight.

Preheat the oven to 350°F. Remove the plastic wrap and bake until the top forms a light brown crust, 50 to 60 minutes. Serve hot.

chocolate and strawberry stuffed french toast

Special days call for special breakfasts, and nothing does the trick better than chocolate. It instantly turns the morning into a celebration. This decadent French toast seems so sinful, stuffed with creamy cheese and melted chocolate and dusted with sugar. But with whole grain, fruit, and fat-free milk, it definitely gets a nod from this nutritionist.

MAKES 4 SERVINGS

SERVING SIZE
1 "SANDWICH"

PER SERVING
CALORIES 270
TOTAL FAT 8 G
   SAT FAT 3 G
   MONO FAT 2 G
   POLY FAT 0 G
PROTEIN 15 G
CARB 38 G
FIBER 5 G
CHOLESTEROL 165 MG
SODIUM 390 MG

EXCELLENT SOURCE OF
FIBER, IODINE,
PHOSPHORUS,
PROTEIN, RIBOFLAVIN,
SELENIUM, VITAMIN C

GOOD SOURCE OF
CALCIUM, IRON,
MANGANESE, THIAMIN,
VITAMIN B12

1¼	cups nonfat milk
3	large eggs
½	teaspoon vanilla extract
¼	cup part-skim ricotta cheese
8	slices whole-wheat sandwich bread, crusts removed
1	8-ounce container fresh strawberries, hulled and sliced
4	teaspoons bittersweet chocolate chips
	Cooking spray
2	teaspoons confectioners' sugar

In a large bowl, whisk together the milk, eggs, and vanilla. Set aside.

Place 1 tablespoon of the ricotta cheese in the center of 4 of the slices of bread and spread around slightly. Top each with about 6 slices of strawberries and 1 teaspoon of chocolate chips. Cover each with another piece of bread to make a "sandwich."

Spray a large nonstick skillet or griddle with cooking spray and preheat over medium heat. Carefully dip each of the "sandwiches" into the egg mixture until completely moistened. Then place on the skillet and cook until the outside is golden brown, the center is warm and the chocolate is melted, 3 to 4 minutes per side.

Transfer to serving dishes. Top with the remaining strawberries and sprinkle with the confectioners' sugar.

blueberry-almond french toast bake

The hardest thing about this dish is waiting for it to come out of the oven, because as it is baking it fills your kitchen with the most enticing, heartwarming, vanilla-cinnamon aroma. Its looks and taste hold up their end of the bargain too. Inside, it is eggy, perfectly sweetened, and studded with bursting warm blueberries. Outside, it is crisp and crowned with sugared toasted almonds.

MAKES 8 SERVINGS

SERVING SIZE
1 4X3-INCH PIECE

PER SERVING
CALORIES 270
TOTAL FAT 8 G
  SAT FAT 2.5 G
  MONO FAT 2 G
  POLY FAT 0.75 G
PROTEIN 16 G
CARB 35 G
FIBER 3 G
CHOLESTEROL 220 MG
SODIUM 280 MG

EXCELLENT SOURCE OF
IODINE, MANGANESE,
PROTEIN, RIBOFLAVIN,
SELENIUM

GOOD SOURCE OF
CALCIUM, FIBER,
IRON, MAGNESIUM,
PHOSPHORUS,
VITAMIN K, ZINC

Cooking spray
1 whole-wheat baguette (about 18 inches long, 8 ounces), cut into 1-inch cubes
2 cups low-fat (1%) milk
8 large eggs
8 large egg whites
⅓ cup pure maple syrup
1 teaspoon vanilla extract
½ teaspoon ground cinnamon
2 cups fresh blueberries
⅓ cup sliced almonds
2 tablespoons dark brown sugar

Spray a 9x13-inch baking pan with cooking spray. Arrange the bread in a single layer in the baking pan. Whisk together the milk, eggs, egg whites, maple syrup, vanilla, and cinnamon. Pour the egg mixture over the bread in the pan, spreading it around so the liquid saturates the bread. Scatter the blueberries evenly on top. Sprinkle with the almonds and brown sugar. Cover and refrigerate for at least 8 hours or overnight.

Preheat the oven to 350°F. Uncover and bake for 50 to 60 minutes. Serve hot.

dutch baby pancake with peach compote

When this pancake comes out of the oven in its dramatic puffed and golden splendor, your guests will think you really went out of your way for them. Let them think that. Only you'll know that all you did was mix a few simple ingredients together and pour them into a skillet.

MAKES 4 SERVINGS

SERVING SIZE
¼ DUTCH BABY AND
⅓ CUP PEACH COMPOTE

PER SERVING
CALORIES 310
TOTAL FAT 7 G
  SAT FAT 3.5 G
  MONO FAT 1.25 G
  POLY FAT 0 G
PROTEIN 11 G
CARB 53 G
FIBER 3 G
CHOLESTEROL 120 MG
SODIUM 530 MG

EXCELLENT SOURCE OF
MANGANESE, PROTEIN,
THIAMIN

GOOD SOURCE OF
CALCIUM, FIBER, IODINE,
IRON, NIACIN,
POTASSIUM, RIBOFLAVIN,
VITAMIN A, VITAMIN C

½	cup all-purpose flour
½	cup whole-wheat pastry flour or regular whole-wheat flour
4	teaspoons sugar
½	teaspoon salt
1	cup low-fat (1%) milk
2	large eggs
2	large egg whites
	Grated zest of 1 lemon
4	teaspoons butter
1	recipe Peach Compote (recipe follows)

Preheat the oven to 450°F.

In a medium bowl, whisk together the flours, sugar, and salt. In another bowl, whisk the milk, eggs, egg whites, and lemon zest. Add the wet ingredients to the dry ingredients and mix until just combined.

In a heavy 10-inch cast-iron or ovenproof nonstick skillet, heat the butter until very hot but not smoking. Pour the batter into the skillet and quickly transfer it to the oven. Bake for 25 minutes, until golden brown and puffed; do not open oven during baking. Serve immediately with the Peach Compote.

* peach compote

This delightful peachy topping is a perfect accompaniment for the Dutch Baby Pancake. In fact, it's delicious with just about any pancake, French toast, or waffle. It's also fantastic with yogurt or ice cream.

MAKES 4 SERVINGS

SERVING SIZE
⅓ CUP

3	large ripe peaches or 4 cups (about 15 ounces) unsweetened frozen sliced peaches
¼	cup pure maple syrup
1	tablespoon fresh lemon juice
1	tablespoon water
½	teaspoon ground cinnamon
½	teaspoon vanilla extract
¼	teaspoon salt

If using fresh peaches, bring a 4-quart pot of water to a boil and fill a large bowl with ice water. With a paring knife, slice through each peach skin all the way around the fruit, but leave the peach intact. Gently place the peaches into the boiling water and boil for 30 seconds. Transfer the peaches into the ice water for 30 seconds, then remove them using a slotted spoon. Gently remove the skins from the peaches, then split the peaches in half and remove the pits. Cut each peach into 8 slices.

Place the peach slices, maple syrup, lemon juice, water, cinnamon, vanilla, and salt in a saucepan and bring to a boil. Reduce the heat and simmer until the mixture has thickened slightly, about 5 minutes. The compote will keep for up to 3 days in an airtight container in the refrigerator.

LOCAL, ORGANIC, BETTER.

Delicious, healthy food starts with great ingredients. Since those ingredients are literally made from the ground up, buying the best means considering where your food comes from and how it is produced.

GO ORGANIC

Organic food is produced without synthetic pesticides, antibiotics, or added hormones. That makes it better for the earth, better for the animals and farm workers involved, and better for you. While no one fully understands the impact these pesticides have on our long-term health, everyone agrees the less you consume the better. What's more, organic packaged goods are generally lower in sodium and free of trans fats and artificial additives.

KEEP IT LOCAL

Local food gets to your table soon after it is harvested, so it often tastes better and has a higher nutrient content. Also, when you focus on local produce you wind up with a natural variety to your diet; you're eating foods as they come into season. Since local food doesn't have to travel far, it uses fewer natural resources, making it more earth-friendly. And buying local helps support local economies, and helps to keep small farmers in business.

HAVE TO CHOOSE? DON'T STRESS.

It is one of the most daunting decisions of the ingredient-conscious: you are in the store and have to choose between the organic apples from New Zealand or the conventionally-grown (non-organic) apples from a local farm. What do you do? Recognize that simply buying health-ful, unprocessed food is a good choice even if it is neither organic nor local. I choose what looks fresher, and that is usually the local one.

whole-wheat apple pancakes with nutty topping

Pancakes are my daughter Bella's favorite food to make and eat. She knows the recipe for this apple-laced version by heart. The batter lasts in the fridge for up to two days, so we whip up a double batch on a Sunday to have it on hand for the beginning of the week. It sure makes Monday mornings a lot easier to face!

MAKES 6 SERVINGS

SERVING SIZE
2 PANCAKES WITH TOPPING
AND 1 TABLESPOON SYRUP

PER SERVING
CALORIES 400
TOTAL FAT 11 G
　SAT FAT 2.5 G
　MONO FAT 3 G
　POLY FAT 2.5 G
PROTEIN 15 G
CARB 63 G
FIBER 5 G
CHOLESTEROL 75 MG
SODIUM 450 MG

EXCELLENT SOURCE OF
CALCIUM, FIBER, IRON,
MAGNESIUM, MANGANESE,
PHOSPHORUS, PROTEIN,
SELENIUM, ZINC

GOOD SOURCE OF
COPPER, FOLATE,
NIACIN, POTASSIUM,
RIBOFLAVIN, THIAMIN

1	medium apple (such as Golden Delicious), cored and diced (about 2 cups)
¾	cup all-purpose flour
¾	cup whole-wheat flour
2	teaspoons baking powder
½	teaspoon baking soda
¼	teaspoon salt
1	cup low-fat (1%) buttermilk
¾	cup nonfat milk
2	large eggs
1	tablespoon honey
1	recipe Nutty Topping (recipe follows)
6	tablespoons pure maple syrup, plus more to taste

Put the apple in a microwave-safe bowl, tightly cover with plastic wrap, and microwave on high until softened, about 2 minutes.

In a large bowl, whisk the flours, baking powder, baking soda, and salt. In a small bowl, whisk together the buttermilk, milk, eggs, and honey. Slowly add the egg mixture to the dry ingredients, stirring until just combined.

Heat a large nonstick griddle over medium heat. Spoon about ¼ cup of the batter per pancake onto the griddle and distribute about a heaping tablespoon of the cooked apple on top. Drizzle a little more batter on top to coat the apple. Flip when the pancake tops are covered with bubbles and the edges look cooked, about 2 minutes. Cook until the pancakes are golden brown and cooked through, an additional 1 to 2 minutes. Serve immediately, or transfer the cooked pancakes to an ovenproof dish and keep warm in a 250°F oven while making the rest.

To serve, arrange 2 pancakes on each plate and sprinkle each serving with about 2 heaping tablespoons of the Nutty Topping. Serve with maple syrup.

* nutty topping

The apple pancakes are great on their own, but this ambrosial nutty topping brings them to the next level. The topping is also incredible in hot or cold cereal, stirred into yogurt, with fruit salad, or as a snack on its own. Consider yourself fairly warned, though: it's addictive.

MAKES 6 SERVINGS

SERVING SIZE
2 HEAPING TABLESPOONS

¼ cup hulled (green) pumpkin seeds
¼ cup sliced almonds
¼ cup shelled sunflower seeds
1 tablespoon sesame seeds
¼ cup toasted wheat germ
¼ cup pure maple syrup
   Salt to taste

In a large skillet, toast the pumpkin seeds and almonds over medium-high heat, stirring, for about 1 minute. Add the sunflower seeds and cook, stirring, for 1 minute more. Add the sesame seeds to the pan. Cover and cook, shaking the pan, until the seeds are toasted, about 30 seconds more. Transfer the toasted nuts and seeds to a medium-size bowl. Add the wheat germ. Stir in the syrup and season with salt. The topping will keep for a week in an airtight container.

honey harvest quinoa

I always thought of quinoa as a savory side dish until my Peruvian friend told me that there they eat it for breakfast cooked with apples and honey. So I tried it, tossing in some chewy dried cranberries and crunchy pecans for good measure, and discovered my new favorite hot breakfast cereal.

MAKES 4 SERVINGS

SERVING SIZE
1¼ CUPS

PER SERVING
CALORIES 380
TOTAL FAT 14 G
 SAT FAT 1.5 G
 MONO FAT 6.5 G
 POLY FAT 5 G
PROTEIN 10 G
CARB 57 G
FIBER 6 G
CHOLESTEROL 0 MG
SODIUM 25 MG

EXCELLENT SOURCE OF
COPPER, FIBER, FOLATE,
MAGNESIUM, MANGANESE,
PROTEIN, THIAMIN

GOOD SOURCE OF
IRON, POTASSIUM,
RIBOFLAVIN,
VITAMIN B6, ZINC

1⅓	cups quinoa
2⅔	cups water
1	small Golden Delicious apple, cored and cut into chunks
¼	cup dried cranberries
½	cup pecans
½	cup low-fat (1%) milk, plus more for serving
2	tablespoons honey, plus more for serving
½	teaspoon ground cinnamon
4	teaspoons unsalted butter, optional

Put the quinoa in a fine-mesh strainer and rinse under the tap. Put the rinsed quinoa in a saucepan with the water. Bring to a boil, then reduce the heat to a simmer, cover and cook for 5 minutes. Add the apple chunks and cranberries and continue to cook, covered over low heat, until the water is absorbed, about 10 minutes more.

In the meantime, toast the pecans in a dry skillet over medium-high heat, stirring frequently, until fragrant, about 2 minutes. Allow to cool, then coarsely chop.

When the quinoa is cooked, stir in ½ cup of milk, 2 tablespoons of honey, and the cinnamon, and cook until the milk is heated through, about 1 more minute.

Spoon the cereal into serving bowls and top with the toasted pecans and butter, if using. Serve with additional honey and milk to taste.

* EATING WELL TIP
Quinoa (pronounced keen-wah—yes, that's how you say it!), is one of the best plant sources of protein and was a staple for the ancient Incas. It's perfect for modern survival, too, since it cooks up, tender and mildly flavored, in about 15 minutes. Use it just as you would rice, in soups, salads, pilafs, and such. Although most commercially available quinoa is pre-washed to remove its natural, slightly bitter coating, it's a good idea to give it a quick rinse before cooking.

lunch—to go

* Now that the lunch hour is more like the twenty-minute lunch, it is harder than ever to eat right at midday. In fact, **WITH LIFE'S HECTIC PACE, IT IS EASY TO FORGET ABOUT LUNCH ALTOGETHER.** That is until you are about to pass out from hunger at 3 p.m., at which point you grab the first thing you can find—something that's probably not very good or good for you. But there is **ONE SURE WAY TO HAVE A FANTASTIC MEAL** whenever and wherever you need it: bring it with you.

   EVERY LUNCH HERE IS AN ABSOLUTELY DELICIOUS, nutritionally balanced, make-ahead, fully travel-tested meal. Forget about that boring turkey sandwich or soggy salads—I am talking about truly inspired, perfectly-packed food that will **TURN YOUR LUNCH BOX INTO A TREASURE CHEST** you will look forward to digging into all morning and that will energize your afternoon.

YOU CAN TAKE IT WITH YOU

CHILL

Perishable food is not safe to eat when left at room temperature for more than two hours. So unless you plan to eat your packed lunch before 10 a.m., you need to keep it cold. Get yourself a stylin' insulated lunch box and a freezer pack to keep things fresh, and keep your lunch box in a cool place once you get to your destination. If you are packing a hot lunch like soup or chili, pack it in a tightly sealed thermal container designed for hot food.

SEPARATE

Lettuce gets soggy if it sits after being dressed, so always pack dressing separately and put it on the salad right before eating. Check out some of the neat salad containers on the market now that have a separate dressing chamber. Crunchy items like breadsticks, crackers, and chips should be packed separately, too.

ADD ON

Don't forget a drink. Water is best. Flavor it with a slice of citrus and some cucumber for a twist. You can also freeze it so you have extra chill in your lunch box. And for a juicy sweet finish, add some fresh fruit to your lunch box as well.

curried chicken salad

This salad is one of my favorites to bring to a party, so it always puts me in a festive mood when I have it for lunch on a work day. With chunks of chicken in a gorgeous yellow, creamy curry sauce, juicy grapes, and crunchy almonds, it somehow manages to be exotic and comfortably familiar at the same time.

MAKES 4 SERVINGS

SERVING SIZE
1 CUP CHICKEN SALAD,
1¼ CUPS MIXED GREENS,
1 LEMON WEDGE, AND
1 OUNCE PITA CHIPS

PER SERVING
CALORIES 400
TOTAL FAT 16 G
  SAT FAT 2 G
  MONO FAT 4 G
  POLY FAT 4.5 G
PROTEIN 36 G
CARB 26 G
FIBER 4 G
CHOLESTEROL 80 MG
SODIUM 460 MG

EXCELLENT SOURCE OF
NIACIN, PHOSPHORUS,
PROTEIN, SELENIUM,
VITAMIN A, VITAMIN B6,
VITAMIN C

GOOD SOURCE OF
CALCIUM, FIBER, IRON,
MAGNESIUM, MANGANESE,
POTASSIUM, RIBOFLAVIN

¼	cup sliced almonds
½	cup nonfat plain yogurt
2	tablespoons mayonnaise
1	teaspoon curry powder
2½	cups cubed cooked chicken breasts (about 1¼ pounds)
1	cup halved red grapes
¼	cup chopped cilantro
	Salt and freshly ground black pepper to taste
5	ounces mixed greens (about 5 cups lightly packed)
4	lemon wedges
4	ounces pita chips

Toast the almonds in a small dry skillet over medium-high heat, stirring occasionally, until fragrant and beginning to turn golden, 2 to 3 minutes.

In a large bowl, stir together the yogurt, mayonnaise, and curry powder. Fold in the chicken, grapes, and cilantro and season with salt and pepper. This salad will keep in an airtight container in the refrigerator for up to 3 days.

To serve, put a scoop of the chicken salad on a bed of greens on a plate or in a to-go container and sprinkle with the toasted almonds. Add a lemon wedge to squeeze over the greens just before eating. Serve with pita chips, stored in a separate container, if packing.

* DID YOU KNOW?
Curry powder is a blend of many different spices like turmeric, ginger, coriander, cumin, and peppers, which gives you much more than great flavor and brilliant color. Research shows that curry may help aid digestion, protect against cancer, and stimulate the immune system.

wheat berry salad with lemon-cumin grilled chicken

This hearty salad is bursting with harvest flavors and chock-full of exciting textures—chewy yet tender wheat berries, sweet-tart dried cherries, crunchy walnuts, and crisp celery. Served over leafy spinach and topped with cumin-scented chicken, this is a power lunch that will fill you up without slowing you down.

MAKES 4 SERVINGS

SERVING SIZE
¾ CUP WHEAT BERRY SALAD,
1 CUP SPINACH, AND
7 SLICES CHICKEN

PER SERVING
CALORIES 550
TOTAL FAT 23 G
  SAT FAT 3 G
  MONO FAT 9 G
  POLY FAT 8.5 G
PROTEIN 39 G
CARB 48 G
FIBER 8 G
CHOLESTEROL 80 MG
SODIUM 420 MG

EXCELLENT SOURCE OF
FIBER, IRON, MANGANESE,
NIACIN, PHOSPHORUS,
PROTEIN, SELENIUM,
VITAMIN A, VITAMIN B,
VITAMIN C, VITAMIN K

GOOD SOURCE OF
COPPER, MAGNESIUM,
PANTOTHENIC ACID,
POTASSIUM

1   cup hard wheat berries
½   cup chopped walnuts
2   stalks celery, finely chopped
⅓   cup finely chopped parsley
⅓   cup tart dried cherries, chopped
1   small scallion (white and green parts), chopped
2   tablespoons olive oil
1   tablespoon plus 1 teaspoon fresh lemon juice, plus 4 lemon wedges for serving
     Salt and freshly ground black pepper to taste
4   cups lightly packed baby spinach leaves
1   recipe Lemon-Cumin Grilled Chicken Breast (recipe follows)

In a medium-size pot, combine the wheat berries and enough water to come 2 inches above the wheat berries. Bring to a boil, then reduce the heat to a simmer. Cook, uncovered, until tender, about 1 hour. Drain and let cool.

Meanwhile, toast the walnuts in a medium-size dry skillet over medium-high heat, stirring occasionally, until fragrant, 2 to 3 minutes.

In a large bowl, combine the wheat berries, toasted walnuts, celery, parsley, dried cherries, scallions, olive oil, and lemon juice. Season with salt and pepper. This salad will keep up to 5 days in an airtight container in the refrigerator.

To serve, place 1 cup of spinach leaves on each plate or in to-go containers. Mound ¾ cup of the wheat berry salad on top of each serving and top that with slices of the Lemon-Cumin Grilled Chicken. Place a lemon wedge on the side of each serving. Right before eating, squeeze the lemon wedges on top.

* DID YOU KNOW?
Studies show that the act of chewing can help relieve stress, so go for a chewy-crunchy lunch, like this wheat berry salad, to help take the edge off midday.

*lemon-cumin grilled chicken breast

A touch of aromatic cumin and a citrus punch take basic grilled chicken to the next level.

MAKES 4 SERVINGS

SERVING SIZE
ABOUT 7 SLICES CHICKEN

1¼	pounds skinless boneless chicken breasts
1	teaspoon ground cumin
½	teaspoon salt
¼	teaspoon freshly ground black pepper
2	teaspoons olive oil
	Cooking spray
2	tablespoons fresh lemon juice

Put the chicken between 2 pieces of plastic wrap and pound it slightly with a mallet or rolling pin so it is an even thickness of about ½ inch.

In a small bowl, combine the cumin, salt, and pepper. Rub the chicken breasts on both sides with olive oil and then rub the spice mixture on both sides.

Spray a grill or nonstick grill pan with cooking spray and heat over medium-high heat. Grill the chicken until grill marks have formed and the chicken is cooked through, 3 to 4 minutes per side. Remove from the heat, let rest for 5 minutes, then slice into ½-inch-thick slices and drizzle with the lemon juice. The chicken will keep for up to 3 days in an airtight container in the refrigerator.

A CHICKEN IN EVERY FRIDGE

Having pre-cooked chicken on hand is one of my key tactics for whipping up quick, healthy meals. It is a lean, versatile, crowd-pleasing protein that will keep up to three days in the fridge. There is more than one way to get it there.

ROTISSERIE

Rotisserie chicken is a weekly staple for me. It is so easy to get a delicious one at the market these days, and I can always get at least two meals out of it. I use the thighs and legs (skin off) for dinner the first night and then use the breast meat for salads and sandwiches over the next couple of days.

DELI COUNTER

The fresh grilled chicken breasts at the prepared-food counter can be a good choice, but they are sometimes heavily seasoned. Stick to the simplest preparations available so the flavors work with a variety of recipes.

PACKAGED

Cooked chicken options abound in the refrigerator section at the grocery store—diced chicken, tenders, grilled and sliced breasts… They sure are convenient and they taste pretty good. But they can be very high in sodium–two to ten times more than homemade. Look for brands that have less than 400 mg sodium per serving.

DIY

The most delicious and economical way to get cooked chicken in your fridge is to do it yourself. Before you cook it I recommend pounding it out a little to a uniform thickness so it cooks evenly. To get around that step you can ask your butcher to do it for you or you can buy thin-sliced chicken breast. Keep in mind that because the thin cut is so thin, it will cook up faster. Following are two no-fail basic chicken preparations.

* basic poached chicken breast

MAKES 4 SERVINGS

PER SERVING
CALORIES 150
TOTAL FAT 3.5 G
  SAT FAT 1 G
  MONO FAT 1 G
  POLY FAT .75 G
PROTEIN 29 G
CARB 0 G
FIBER 0 G
CHOLESTEROL 80 MG
SODIUM 70 MG

EXCELLENT SOURCE OF
NIACIN, PHOSPHORUS,
PROTEIN, SELENIUM,
VITAMIN B6

1 cup low-sodium chicken broth
1 cup water
1¼ pounds skinless boneless chicken breasts

Bring the broth and water to a boil in a medium sauce-pan. Put the chicken between 2 pieces of plastic wrap and pound it slightly with a mallet or rolling pin so it is an even thickness of about ½ inch. Add the chicken to the broth and simmer, covered, for 8 minutes. Turn the heat off and let chicken stand in the cooking liquid, covered, until cooked through, about 20 minutes. Remove the chicken from the broth and serve or chill.

* basic grilled chicken breast

MAKES 4 SERVINGS

PER SERVING
CALORIES 150
TOTAL FAT 4.5 G
  SAT FAT 1 G
  MONO FAT 2 G
  POLY FAT 1 G
PROTEIN 29 G
CARB 0 G
FIBER 0 G
CHOLESTEROL 80 MG
SODIUM 360 MG

EXCELLENT SOURCE OF
NIACIN, PHOSPHORUS,
PROTEIN, SELENIUM,
VITAMIN B6

1¼   pounds skinless boneless chicken breasts
1   teaspoon canola or olive oil
½   teaspoon salt

Put the chicken between 2 pieces of plastic wrap and pound it slightly with a mallet or rolling pin so it is an even thickness of about ½ inch. Spray a grill or nonstick grill pan with cooking spray and heat over medium-high heat. Rub the chicken with oil on both sides and season with the salt. Grill until the chicken is just done, 3 to 4 minutes per side.

pasta salad with salmon, peas, and herbs

Imagine a decadently rich creamy pasta salad that's actually good for you. Well, here you have it. The secret is in the dressing, which has a base of tangy thickened yogurt that's the ideal foil for the rich salmon. Sweet peas stud the dish with beautiful color, and dill and scallion make it delightfully fragrant and flavorful.

MAKES 4 SERVINGS

SERVING SIZE
1¾ CUPS PASTA SALAD AND
2 CUPS LETTUCE

PER SERVING
CALORIES 490
TOTAL FAT 14 G
  SAT FAT 2 G
  MONO FAT 1.75 G
  POLY FAT 1.5 G
PROTEIN 35 G
CARB 56 G
FIBER 6 G
CHOLESTEROL 55 MG
SODIUM 730 MG

EXCELLENT SOURCE OF
FIBER, FOLATE, IRON,
MAGNESIUM, MANGANESE,
NIACIN, PHOSPHORUS,
PROTEIN, RIBOFLAVIN,
SELENIUM, THIAMIN,
VITAMIN A, VITAMIN B12,
VITAMIN C, VITAMIN D,
VITAMIN K

GOOD SOURCE OF
COPPER, POTASSIUM,
VITAMIN B6, ZINC

⅔ cup plain Greek-style nonfat yogurt
3 tablespoons fresh lemon juice
3 tablespoons mayonnaise
2 teaspoons finely grated lemon zest
1 teaspoon minced fresh dill, or 2 teaspoons dried
½ teaspoon salt
½ teaspoon freshly ground black pepper
1 (14-ounce) can wild red salmon, drained, skinned and boned, and cut into chunks
1 10-ounce package frozen peas, defrosted
½ pound bowtie or corkscrew pasta, cooked according to package directions and cooled
2 scallions (white and green parts), minced (about ¼ cup)
8 cups chopped red-leaf lettuce

Combine the yogurt, lemon juice, mayonnaise, lemon zest, dill, salt, and pepper in a bowl and whisk to incorporate. Add the salmon, peas, pasta, and scallions and toss to incorporate. The pasta salad will keep up to 2 days in an airtight container in the refrigerator.

To serve, mound 2 cups of the lettuce onto each plate or into to-go containers and scoop about 1¾ cups of the pasta salad on top.

* EATING WELL TIP
Greek-style yogurt is simply yogurt that has been strained so it is ultra thick and creamy. It is perfect as a base for creamy dressings, dips, and spreads. It's now in major markets nationwide. If you can't find it, don't worry. It is simple to make. Just put plain, nonfat yogurt into a strainer lined with a paper towel. Set the strainer over a bowl and let it sit in the refrigerator for at least 30 minutes and up to 4 hours depending on how thick you want it. You need about 1⅓ cups of regular yogurt to make 1 cup strained. It keeps for about a week in the refrigerator.

salmon niçoise salad
with lemon dijon dressing

This classic salad from Nice, France, is usually made with tuna, but salmon makes it richer and more luxurious. The zesty lemon Dijon dressing balances that richness perfectly. You can make this any time of the year, but it is especially lovely in the summer when you can get the produce freshly picked from the farm stand.

MAKES 4 SERVINGS

SERVING SIZE
4 OUNCES COOKED SALMON, 5 LETTUCE LEAVES, 10 GREEN BEANS, ½ CUP POTATOES, 1½ TABLESPOONS OLIVES, AND 2 TABLESPOONS DRESSING

PER SERVING
CALORIES 430
TOTAL FAT 24 G
  SAT FAT 3.5 G
  MONO FAT 13.5 G
  POLY FAT 5.5 G
PROTEIN 30 G
CARB 26 G
FIBER 6 G
CHOLESTEROL 70 MG
SODIUM 510 MG

EXCELLENT SOURCE OF
COPPER, FIBER, FOLATE, MAGNESIUM, MANGANESE, NIACIN, PANTOTHENIC ACID, PHOSPHORUS, POTASSIUM, PROTEIN, RIBOFLAVIN, SELENIUM, THIAMIN, VITAMIN A, VITAMIN B6, VITAMIN B12, VITAMIN C, VITAMIN D, VITAMIN K

GOOD SOURCE OF
IRON, ZINC

¾   pound red new potatoes, quartered
½   pound green beans, trimmed
2   9-ounce skinless salmon fillets
½   teaspoon salt
½   teaspoon freshly ground black pepper
1   head Boston or Bibb lettuce, leaves separated
½   pint grape tomatoes
⅓   cup Niçoise, Calamata, or other black olives
¼   cup extra-virgin olive oil
1   tablespoon plus 1 teaspoon fresh lemon juice
1   tablespoon Dijon mustard

Place the potatoes in a steamer basket over a pot of boiling water. Cover and steam for 6 minutes. Add the green beans to the steamer and continue cooking for 4 minutes more. Transfer the potatoes and green beans to a bowl and set aside to cool.

Preheat a grill or grill pan over medium-high heat. Season the salmon with ¼ teaspoon of salt and ¼ teaspoon of pepper. Grill the salmon, turning once, for 3 to 5 minutes per side for medium doneness. Cut each piece of salmon in half crosswise. Set aside to cool.

Make a bed of about 5 lettuce leaves on each serving plate or in to-go serving containers. Top with a piece of the salmon. Divide the green beans, potatoes, tomatoes, and olives among the servings, arranging each vegetable in a separate pile on the plate.

In a small bowl, whisk together the oil, lemon juice, Dijon mustard, and the remaining ¼ teaspoon each of salt and pepper. For lunch on the go, put 2 tablespoons of dressing in a small separate container. Drizzle the salad with dressing right before serving.

beef taco salad
with chunky tomato dressing

There's nothing dainty about this salad. With mounds of chili-spiced beef and sharp cheddar cheese over a bed of crisp greens, all doused with a chunky tomato-lime dressing and topped with shards of corn chips, it has high-impact flavor and heartiness to satisfy even the biggest appetites.

MAKES 4 SERVINGS

SERVING SIZE
2 CUPS LETTUCE,
1 CUP BEEF MIXTURE,
2 TABLESPOONS CHEESE,
¾ CUP CHUNKY TOMATO
DRESSING, AND
ABOUT 8 CRUSHED
TORTILLA CHIPS

PER SERVING
CALORIES 430
TOTAL FAT 22 G
  SAT FAT 8 G
  MONO FAT 10 G
  POLY FAT 2 G
PROTEIN 29 G
CARB 36 G
FIBER 9 G
CHOLESTEROL 70 MG
SODIUM 770 MG

EXCELLENT SOURCE OF
CALCIUM, FIBER, IRON,
NIACIN, PHOSPHORUS,
POTASSIUM, PROTEIN,
SELENIUM, VITAMIN A,
VITAMIN B6, VITAMIN B12,
VITAMIN C, ZINC

GOOD SOURCE OF
MANGANESE, RIBOFLAVIN,
VITAMIN K

FOR THE MEAT

¾ pound lean ground beef (90% lean or higher)
1   15.5-ounce can black beans, preferably
       low-sodium, drained and rinsed
2   cloves garlic, minced
⅓   cup water
1   tablespoon chili powder
⅛   teaspoon cayenne pepper, plus more to taste

FOR THE DRESSING

4   medium tomatoes, chopped
2   tablespoons extra-virgin olive oil
2   tablespoons fresh lime juice
½   teaspoon salt
¼   teaspoon freshly ground black pepper

FOR THE SALAD

2   hearts of romaine lettuce, chopped
½   cup grated cheddar cheese (2 ounces)
2   ounces baked corn tortilla chips (about 32 chips)

Heat a large skillet over medium-high heat. Add the beef and cook until no longer pink, breaking up the meat with a spoon. Add the beans and garlic and cook for 2 minutes more. Add the water, chili powder, and cayenne and stir until well combined. Remove from the heat and allow the mixture to cool slightly.

In a medium bowl, combine the tomatoes (with their juices), oil, lime juice, salt, and pepper. The dressing and meat mixture may be prepared up to 2 days ahead and stored in airtight containers in the refrigerator.

To serve, place 2 cups of lettuce on each plate or in lunch containers. Top each serving with 1 cup of the beef mixture, then sprinkle with 2 tablespoons of cheese. If making to go, pack ¾ cup of the chunky tomato dressing in a separate sealable container and put about 8 chips in a separate bag. Right before eating, top each salad with dressing, and crush the tortilla chips on top.

5-minute salad: tricolor salad with white beans and parmesan

This trio of lettuces is an irresistible balance of peppery robust tastes, crisp and tender textures, and beautiful colors. The balsamic vinegar adds just the right sweet acidity to bring it all together and white beans and cheese make it a complete, satisfying meal. It's a whole lot of goodness for very little effort.

MAKES 4 SERVINGS

SERVING SIZE
3 CUPS SALAD,
1½ TABLESPOONS DRESSING,
2 BREADSTICKS

PER SERVING
CALORIES 350
TOTAL FAT 20 G
  SAT FAT 4 G
  MONO FAT 10 G
  POLY FAT 2 G
PROTEIN 15 G
CARB 29 G
FIBER 7 G
CHOLESTEROL 10 MG
SODIUM 540 MG

EXCELLENT SOURCE OF
CALCIUM, FIBER, FOLATE,
MAGNESIUM, MANGANESE,
PROTEIN, THIAMIN, VITAMIN A,
VITAMIN C, VITAMIN K

GOOD SOURCE OF
COPPER, IRON,
PHOSPHORUS, POTASSIUM,
RIBOFLAVIN, ZINC

5	cups lightly packed arugula (about 5 ounces)
1	head radicchio, core removed, sliced
2	Belgian endives, bottom ½ inch removed, sliced
1	15-ounce can white beans (such as cannellini; preferably low-sodium), drained and rinsed
½	cup shaved Parmesan cheese (about 2 ounces)
¼	cup extra-virgin olive oil
2	tablespoons balsamic vinegar
¼	teaspoon salt
8	Italian bread sticks

In a large bowl, toss together the arugula, radicchio, endive, beans, and Parmesan. In a small bowl, whisk together the oil, vinegar, and salt.

To serve, place 3 cups of the salad in a large bowl or lunch container. If preparing a salad to go, put 1½ tablespoons of the dressing into a small container. Toss with the dressing right before eating. Serve with breadsticks on the side.

greek salad pitas with feta spread and turkey

Here all the mouthwatering Greek salad essentials are stuffed into portable pita pockets. Be sure to include the fresh mint—it really lights up the sandwich. As a bonus, the lemony feta spread doubles as a dip that's fantastic with cool, crisp veggies, like cucumber, celery, or red bell pepper.

MAKES 4 SERVINGS

SERVING SIZE
2 POCKETS

PER SERVING
CALORIES 360
TOTAL FAT 9 G
   SAT FAT 5 G
   MONO FAT 1.5 G
   POLY FAT 1 G
PROTEIN 32 G
CARB 40 G
FIBER 6 G
CHOLESTEROL 80 MG
SODIUM 700 MG

EXCELLENT SOURCE OF
CALCIUM, FIBER, IRON,
MAGNESIUM, MANGANESE,
NIACIN, PHOSPHORUS,
PROTEIN, RIBOFLAVIN,
SELENIUM, THIAMIN,
VITAMIN B6, ZINC

GOOD SOURCE OF
COPPER, FOLATE,
PANTOTHENIC ACID,
POTASSIUM,
VITAMIN B12, VITAMIN K

FOR THE SPREAD
¾   cup crumbled feta cheese (4 ounces)
3   tablespoons nonfat plain yogurt
1   tablespoon fresh lemon juice
2   teaspoons dried oregano
1   teaspoon finely grated lemon zest
¼   teaspoon freshly ground black pepper

FOR THE SANDWICH
4   whole-wheat pita breads
4   large pieces romaine lettuce, torn in half
1   English cucumber, sliced into half moons
¼   cup lightly packed fresh mint leaves
¾   pound thinly sliced roasted turkey breast

In a medium bowl, combine the feta cheese and yogurt with a fork, mashing any large chunks of cheese. Stir in the lemon juice, oregano, lemon zest, and pepper. The spread will keep for up to 5 days in an airtight container in the refrigerator.

   To make a sandwich, cut a pita in half to form 2 pockets. Line each pocket with half a lettuce leaf. Spread 2 heaping tablespoons of feta spread into each pocket. Then fill each pocket with about 6 cucumber slices, 4 or 5 mint leaves, and 2 or 3 slices of turkey. Serve immediately or wrap in foil to go.

asian chicken wrap

Bring this sandwich for lunch and you'll be thinking about it all morning. You'll yearn for the sweet-spicy-creamy-sesame sauce and you'll anticipate the perfect balance between the crunch of the vegetables and the savory tenderness of the chicken. You might not be able to hold out till noon, but when you do dig in you will love every bite.

MAKES 4 SERVINGS

SERVING SIZE
1 WRAP

PER SERVING
CALORIES 380
TOTAL FAT 12 G
  SAT FAT 2 G
  MONO FAT 2.5 G
  POLY FAT 4 G
PROTEIN 35
CARB 29 G
FIBER 3 G
CHOLESTEROL 80 MG
SODIUM 420 MG

EXCELLENT SOURCE OF
NIACIN, PHOSPHORUS,
PROTEIN, SELENIUM,
VITAMIN A, VITAMIN B6,
VITAMIN C

GOOD SOURCE OF
FIBER, IRON

FOR THE SAUCE

3	tablespoons plain Greek-style nonfat yogurt
2	tablespoons mayonnaise
1	tablespoon brown sugar
1	tablespoon low-sodium soy sauce
1	teaspoon Dijon mustard
½	teaspoon toasted sesame oil
¼	teaspoon Thai-style chili sauce (such as Sriracha), optional

FOR THE SANDWICH

12	napa cabbage leaves, white center ribs removed
4	whole-wheat wrap breads (about 9 inches in diameter)
4	cooked chicken breast halves (about 5 ounces each), sliced into ½-inch-thick slices
1	red bell pepper, sliced into thin strips

To make the sauce, combine the yogurt, mayonnaise, brown sugar, soy sauce, mustard, sesame oil, and chili sauce, if using, and stir until well blended. The sauce will keep up to 5 days in an airtight container in the refrigerator.

To make each wrap, place 2 cabbage leaves on 1 wrap bread, then layer with a quarter of the chicken and peppers. Drizzle with 2 tablespoons of the sauce. Top with an additional cabbage leaf. Fold the bread about an inch over each end of the filling, then roll up. Serve or wrap in foil to go.

waldorf chicken wrap

Meaty chunks of chicken, crisp juicy apple, and the rich crunch of walnuts folded into a thick, creamy dressing form an indulgent combination of flavors and textures that, when tucked into a wrap, is satisfaction you can hold in your hand.

MAKES 4 SERVINGS

SERVING SIZE
1 WRAP

PER SERVING:
CALORIES 290
TOTAL FAT 11 G
  SAT FAT 1 G
  MONO FAT 1.5 G
  POLY FAT 5 G
PROTEIN 19 G
CARB 29 G
FIBER 3 G
CHOLESTEROL 35 MG
SODIUM 240 MG

EXCELLENT SOURCE OF
NIACIN, PROTEIN

GOOD SOURCE OF
FIBER, MANGANESE, PHOSPHORUS, SELENIUM, VITAMIN B6

¼ cup walnuts
⅓ cup plain Greek-style nonfat yogurt
1 tablespoon mayonnaise
2 teaspoons fresh lemon juice
1 teaspoon Dijon mustard
1 teaspoon minced fresh thyme
1 cup cubed cooked chicken breast (about ½ pound)
1 medium apple, unpeeled and diced (about ¾ cup)
Salt and freshly ground black pepper to taste
4 large leaves romaine lettuce, rinsed and patted dry
4 whole-wheat wrap breads (about 9 inches in diameter)

Toast the walnuts in a dry skillet over medium-high heat, stirring frequently, until fragrant, 3 to 5 minutes.

In a medium bowl, stir the yogurt, mayonnaise, lemon juice, mustard, and thyme until smooth. Fold in the chicken, toasted walnuts, and apples. Season with salt and pepper.

To make each wrap, place 1 lettuce leaf on 1 wrap bread, then spoon about ¾ cup of the chicken mixture on top. Fold the bread about an inch over each end of the filling, then roll up. Serve or wrap in foil to go.

mediterranean tuna wrap

Oceans away from your typical mayonnaise-y tuna salad, this one is inspired by the way canned tuna is prepared in the Mediterranean. You'll commonly find it there tossed with olives, onion, and fresh parsley in a lemon and olive oil dressing. Bursting with flavor, it brings out the absolute best in the fish. Once you try tuna this way, you might never go back.

MAKES 4 SERVINGS

SERVING SIZE
1 WRAP

PER SERVING
CALORIES 340
TOTAL FAT 11 G
  SAT FAT 1 G
  MONO FAT 6 G
  POLY FAT 1 G
PROTEIN 28 G
CARB 27 G
FIBER 4 G
CHOLESTEROL 0 MG
SODIUM 50 MG

EXCELLENT SOURCE OF
PROTEIN, VITAMIN A,
VITAMIN C, VITAMIN D,
VITAMIN K

GOOD SOURCE OF
FIBER, IRON

2	6-ounce cans chunk light tuna in water, drained well
¼	cup chopped fresh parsley
¼	cup chopped pitted Calamata olives
¼	cup finely diced red onion
2	tablespoons extra-virgin olive oil
1	tablespoon fresh lemon juice
½	teaspoon finely grated lemon zest
	Salt and freshly ground black pepper to taste
12	leaves romaine lettuce, thick ribs removed
4	whole-wheat wrap breads (about 9 inches in diameter)
1	large ripe tomato, sliced into half moons

In a medium bowl, combine the tuna, parsley, olives, onion, oil, lemon juice, and zest. Add salt and pepper to taste.

To make each sandwich, place 3 lettuce leaves on a wrap bread. Top with ⅓ cup of the tuna salad and a few tomato slices. Fold the bread about an inch over each end of the filling, then roll up. Serve or wrap in foil to go.

roast beef sandwich
with watercress and horseradish sauce

Why settle for the same old roast beef sandwich when you can have one that's truly extraordinary with so little effort? What makes this one a standout are the zingy horseradish sauce that takes seconds to make, the peppery watercress that stands up so well to it, and pumpernickel bread that gives an unmistakable depth of flavor. Together they bring out the best in each other and the savory beef.

MAKES 4 SERVINGS

SERVING SIZE
1 SANDWICH

PER SERVING
CALORIES 330
TOTAL FAT 9 G
 SAT FAT 2 G
 MONO FAT 0.5 G
 POLY FAT 1 G
PROTEIN 23 G
CARB 38 G
FIBER 5 G
CHOLESTEROL 30 MG
SODIUM 1290 MG

EXCELLENT SOURCE OF
FIBER, MANGANESE,
PROTEIN, SELENIUM,
VITAMIN C, VITAMIN K

GOOD SOURCE OF
CALCIUM, COPPER,
FOLATE, IRON,
MAGNESIUM, NIACIN,
PHOSPHORUS, RIBOFLAVIN,
THIAMIN, VITAMIN A

FOR THE SAUCE
- ¼ cup plain Greek-style nonfat yogurt
- ¼ cup prepared white horseradish, squeezed of excess juice (about 3 tablespoons)
- 2 tablespoons mayonnaise
- ¼ teaspoon salt
- ⅛ teaspoon freshly ground black pepper

FOR THE SANDWICH
- 1 bunch watercress, thick stems removed
- 8 slices pumpernickel bread
- ¾ pound lean roast beef, thinly sliced
- 2 medium tomatoes, sliced
- ½ small red onion, thinly sliced

To make the sauce, combine the yogurt, horseradish, mayonnaise, salt, and pepper in a small bowl and stir to incorporate. The sauce will keep for up to 5 days in an airtight container in the refrigerator.

To make each sandwich, place ¼ cup of watercress on a slice of bread and drizzle with 2 tablespoons of the sauce. Layer with a few slices of roast beef, then some of the tomato and onion slices. Top with another slice of bread and serve or wrap in foil to go.

herbed tuna–stuffed peppers

Sweet, crisp red peppers make the perfect edible serving cups for lemony tuna salad piled with fresh herbs. It will bring an energizing burst of garden freshness to you wherever you choose to eat it.

MAKES 4 SERVINGS

SERVING SIZE
2 FILLED PEPPER HALVES

PER SERVING
CALORIES 380
TOTAL FAT 15 G
  SAT FAT 2 G
  MONO FAT 10 G
  POLY FAT 2 G
PROTEIN 47 G
CARB 9 G
FIBER 3 G
CHOLESTEROL 105 MG
SODIUM 1020 MG

EXCELLENT SOURCE OF
PROTEIN, VITAMIN A,
VITAMIN C, VITAMIN K

GOOD SOURCE OF
FIBER, FOLATE, MANGANESE,
POTASSIUM, VITAMIN B6

4	red bell peppers, stemmed and sliced in half crosswise
¼	cup extra-virgin olive oil
3	tablespoons fresh lemon juice
2	teaspoons Dijon mustard
½	teaspoon salt
¼	teaspoon freshly ground black pepper
4	6-ounce cans chunk light tuna in water, drained
1½	cups lightly packed baby arugula leaves, roughly chopped
1	cup lightly packed fresh basil leaves, minced
1	cup lightly packed fresh parsley leaves, minced
3	tablespoons loosely packed fresh tarragon, minced

Using a paring knife, remove the seeds and white membrane from inside the pepper halves.

In a large bowl, combine the olive oil, lemon juice, mustard, salt, and pepper and whisk to incorporate. Add the tuna, arugula, and minced herbs and stir to incorporate. Spoon about ½ cup of the tuna mixture into each pepper half and serve, or place 2 filled peppers in each to-go container. Filled peppers will keep up to 2 days in an airtight container in the refrigerator.

★ EATING WELL TIP

Canned tuna is a delicious, convenient lean protein that is rich in omega-3 fats. Trouble is, some varieties can have high levels of mercury, a toxic environmental pollutant. Stick with light tuna, which has about a third the mercury of albacore or chunk white, and you can safely have up to three cans a week.

gazpacho with shrimp

This refreshing, zesty, cold tomato soup couldn't be simpler to make. All you do is take garden fresh ingredients, whir them in the blender, and voilà! Plump bites of shrimp and some crusty bread make it a satisfying meal. It is as good in a packed lunch as it is served in large cocktail glasses as an elegant appetizer.

MAKES 4 SERVINGS

SERVING SIZE
2 CUPS PLUS 2 SLICES BREAD

PER SERVING
CALORIES 360
TOTAL FAT 10 G
　SAT FAT 1 G
　MONO FAT 5 G
　POLY FAT 1.5 G
PROTEIN 22 G
CARB 49 G
FIBER 10 G
CHOLESTEROL 110 MG
SODIUM 630 MG

EXCELLENT SOURCE OF
COPPER, FIBER, FOLATE,
IRON, NIACIN, POTASSIUM,
PROTEIN, SELENIUM,
THIAMIN, VITAMIN A,
VITAMIN B6, VITAMIN C,
VITAMIN D, VITAMIN K,

GOOD SOURCE OF
MAGNESIUM, MANGANESE,
PHOSPHORUS, RIBOFLAVIN,
VITAMIN B12, ZINC

2　scallions
1　English cucumber (about 1 pound), seeded
　　and cut into chunks
1　large red or orange bell pepper, cored,
　　seeded and cut into chunks
¼　teaspoon finely chopped garlic
1　quart low-sodium tomato juice
4　medium tomatoes (about 1 pound), diced
2　tablespoons extra-virgin olive oil
4　teaspoons red wine vinegar, or more to taste
　　Salt and freshly ground black pepper to taste
　　Hot sauce, to taste
½　pound cooked peeled shrimp, cut into
　　½-inch pieces
　　Crusty whole-wheat bread

Thinly slice the green portion of 1 scallion and reserve for garnish. Cut the remaining white portion and whole scallion into chunks. In the bowl of a food processor, combine the scallion, cucumber, bell pepper, and garlic. Pulse until the vegetables are coarsely chopped. Add the tomato juice and pulse until the vegetables are finely chopped. Transfer to a large bowl and stir in the diced tomatoes, olive oil, and vinegar. Season to taste with salt, pepper, and hot sauce. Gazpacho will keep for up to 5 days in an airtight container in the refrigerator.

To serve, transfer the soup to individual bowls or to-go containers. Right before eating, top with the chopped shrimp and scallion greens. Serve with the bread.

tortellini-spinach soup

Who says a meal on the go has to be cold? Get yourself a good wide-mouthed thermos and you can have a belly-warming lunch anytime. This simple recipe is soup-er satisfying thanks to the plump cheese-filled pasta.

MAKES 4 SERVINGS

SERVING SIZE
3 CUPS SOUP
PLUS 2 TABLESPOONS
PARMESAN CHEESE

PER SERVING
CALORIES 380
TOTAL FAT 12 G
  SAT FAT 5 G
  MONO FAT 1.75 G
  POLY FAT 1 G
PROTEIN 24 G
CARB 45 G
FIBER 5 G
CHOLESTEROL 45 MG
SODIUM 770 MG

EXCELLENT SOURCE OF
CALCIUM, FIBER, IRON,
NIACIN, PROTEIN, VITAMIN A,
VITAMIN C, VITAMIN K

GOOD SOURCE OF
COPPER, PHOSPHORUS,
POTASSIUM

1	teaspoon canola oil
1	medium onion, chopped (about 2 cups)
2	cloves garlic, thinly sliced
1	large carrot, peeled and sliced (1½ cups)
2	ribs celery, chopped (1 cup)
1	teaspoon dried oregano
1	teaspoon dried thyme
½	teaspoon crushed red pepper flakes
1	14-ounce can low-sodium diced tomatoes, with juice
6	cups low-sodium chicken broth or vegetable broth
3	ounces baby spinach, sliced into ribbons (3 cups)
1	9-ounce package fresh store-bought spinach-and-cheese tortellini (2 cups)
½	cup grated Parmesan cheese (1½ ounces)

Heat the oil in a 4- or 6-quart saucepan over medium-high heat. Add the onions and cook, stirring, until softened, about 5 minutes. Add the garlic and cook, stirring, until the onions are translucent and the garlic is softened, another 3 minutes. Add the carrot, celery, oregano, thyme, and red pepper flakes and cook, stirring, until softened, 5 to 6 minutes.

Add the tomatoes with their juices and the broth and bring to a boil; reduce the heat and simmer for 10 to 15 minutes. Add the spinach and tortellini and cook until the tortellini are cooked through, 6 minutes. This soup will keep for up to 3 days in the refrigerator in an airtight container. Serve topped with Parmesan cheese.

For a lunch to go, put the warm soup into a wide-mouth thermal container designed to hold food. Pack the Parmesan cheese in a separate small bag. And don't forget a spoon!

ESSENTIAL OILS

Store shelves are stocked with fabulous healthy oils from avocado to organic grapeseed. Spring for them if you want to experiment, but to simplify your life these four will cover you in just about any dish.

AN INEXPENSIVE OLIVE OIL

Olive oil is versatile and loaded with heart-healthy monounsaturated fat. Get an inexpensive one as a staple for everyday cooking. Pure, virgin, or extra-virgin grades will all work, but extra-virgin is the least processed of the three so it has the most antioxidants and best taste, and you can easily find one at a low price.

UNFILTERED, COLD-PRESSED EXTRA-VIRGIN OLIVE OIL

This oil is really worth the splurge for dressing, drizzling, or dipping. It transforms the flavor of a dish with its fruity richness and gives you maximum health benefits because it is minimally processed.

CANOLA OIL

This is perfect for baking and other dishes where you want a neutral-tasting oil. Plus it has a high smoking point so it's great for high-heat cooking like stir-fries. It contains monounsaturated and omega-3 fat—both healthy fats.

TOASTED SESAME OIL

This oil has a distinctive rich, nutty taste and aroma that is essential in Asian cooking. It doesn't take the heat very well, though, so use it for low- to medium-heat sautéing, in dressings, or as a finishing drizzle.

lunch—
at home

* **MELTED CHEESE IS THE FIRST THING THAT COMES TO MIND** when I am home for lunch. It is one of those luxurious, **FRESH-OUT-OF-THE-OVEN** elements you just have to be home to do. And this chapter has its tantalizing share—from quick grilled sandwiches to easy pizzas and frittatas. But lunch at home also means **FOODS THAT ARE BEST ENJOYED JUST CUT,** like avocado, or just cooked, like crunchy potato chips. And it means you might have company you want to wow with a beautiful presentation, without having to work too hard, of course. Whether it's a day off and you have a little extra time or you just have a quick break between errands or home office work, there is a **PERFECT LUNCH** here to eat right at home.

ham & cheese panini

Grilled ham and cheese is an everyday, easy lunch fallback taken to a new level here with tender prosciutto, intensely flavorful provolone cheese, and peppery radicchio toasted to melty perfection on crusty bread.

MAKES 4 SERVINGS

SERVING SIZE
1 SANDWICH

PER SERVING
CALORIES 280
TOTAL FAT 15 G
   SAT FAT 6 G
   MONO FAT 4 G
   POLY FAT 0.5 G
PROTEIN 22 G
CARB 21 G
FIBER 4 G
CHOLESTEROL 40 MG
SODIUM 1200 MG

EXCELLENT SOURCE OF
CALCIUM, PROTEIN,
VITAMIN K

GOOD SOURCE OF
FIBER, FOLATE,
NIACIN, PHOSPHORUS,
RIBOFLAVIN, THIAMIN

1	8-ounce loaf whole-grain Italian bread
2	tablespoons balsamic vinegar
12	radicchio leaves
16	large basil leaves
4	ounces thinly sliced prosciutto
4	slices provolone cheese (4 ounces)
¼	teaspoon freshly ground black pepper
2	teaspoons olive oil
	Cooking spray

Slice the bread loaf in half lengthwise. Scoop out the bread to remove the soft inner portion and discard. Slice the loaf crosswise into 4 equal-size pieces. Drizzle the inside of each roll with 1½ teaspoons of the vinegar. Layer 3 radicchio leaves, 4 basil leaves, 1 ounce of prosciutto, and 1 ounce of provolone in each roll. Sprinkle with the pepper. Close the rolls and brush each panini with ½ teaspoon of the olive oil.

Heat a heavy cast-iron skillet or other skillet over medium-high heat and spray with cooking spray. Place 2 sandwiches in the skillet and weigh them down with another skillet or a panini weight. Toast until the cheese begins to melt and the bread is browned and toasted on the edges, 3 to 4 minutes. Flip the sandwiches and toast for an additional 2 to 3 minutes. Remove from the pan and slice in half; repeat with the remaining 2 sandwiches.

✷ EATING WELL TIP
Scooping out the inside of your crusty bread leaves you more room for the goodies inside your sandwich, and has 25 percent fewer calories than unscooped bread.

lamb and feta pita pizzas
with fennel-arugula salad

Just about every group of people around the world eats some kind of pizza. This version hails from the Middle East, with rich ground lamb fragrant with cinnamon, topped with crunchy pine nuts and salty feta cheese, and baked atop crisp pita bread, the ultimate no-fuss crust.

MAKES 4 SERVINGS

SERVING SIZE
1 PITA PIZZA
AND 1½ CUPS SALAD

PER SERVING
CALORIES 510
TOTAL FAT 29 G
  SAT FAT 9 G
  MONO FAT 13 G
  POLY FAT 4 G
PROTEIN 20 G
CARB 47 G
FIBER 8 G
CHOLESTEROL 55 MG
SODIUM 1140 MG

EXCELLENT SOURCE OF
FIBER, FOLATE, IRON,
MAGNESIUM,
MANGANESE, NIACIN,
PHOSPHORUS, POTASSIUM,
PROTEIN, RIBOFLAVIN,
SELENIUM, THIAMIN,
VITAMIN A, VITAMIN B6,
VITAMIN B12, VITAMIN C,
VITAMIN K, ZINC

GOOD SOURCE OF
COPPER, PANTOTHENIC ACID

1	small onion, chopped (about 1 cup)
8	ounces lean ground lamb
4	medium plum tomatoes, chopped
2	tablespoons chopped fresh parsley
¾	teaspoon ground cinnamon
¾	teaspoon salt
½	teaspoon freshly ground black pepper
4	whole-wheat pita breads
2	teaspoons olive oil
⅓	cup crumbled feta cheese
1	tablespoon pine nuts
1	recipe Fennel-Arugula Salad (recipe follows)

Preheat the oven to 400°F.

Put the onion and ground lamb into a large skillet over medium-high heat and cook, breaking the meat up with a spoon and stirring occasionally, until the onion is softened and the meat is no longer pink, about 5 minutes. Transfer the meat and onion to a plate lined with paper towels to drain the fat. Blot with an additional paper towel.

Wipe out the pan and return the meat and onion to the pan. Stir in the tomatoes, and cook over medium-high heat until the tomatoes soften slightly, about 2 minutes. Remove from the heat. Stir in the parsley, cinnamon, salt, and pepper. The lamb mixture may be made up to 2 days ahead and stored in an airtight container in the refrigerator.

Place the pita breads on a baking sheet. Brush the top of each pita with oil. Spread ⅓ cup of the lamb mixture onto each pita. Sprinkle with the feta and pine nuts. Cook until the cheese is warmed and softened and the pita is toasted, 10 to 12 minutes. Serve alongside the Fennel-Arugula Salad.

* fennel-arugula salad

This refreshing salad is the perfect complement to the deep flavors of the lamb pizza.

MAKES 4 SERVINGS

SERVING SIZE
1½ CUPS

1   medium bulb fennel, thinly sliced into half-moons
5   cups arugula (5 ounces)
2   tablespoons extra-virgin olive oil
2   tablespoons orange juice
2   tablespoons red wine vinegar
1   tablespoon finely chopped shallot
½   teaspoon finely grated orange zest
¼   teaspoon salt
¼   teaspoon freshly ground black pepper

Toss the fennel and arugula together in a large salad bowl. In a small bowl, whisk together the oil, orange juice, vinegar, shallot, orange zest, salt, and pepper. Add to the fennel and arugula and toss to coat.

egg, ham, and spinach pizza

I was in Italy the first time I had egg on a pizza. The idea seemed odd, but when I tried it, it was a revelation. When you cut into the egg, the yolk oozes out over the tender greens and crisp crust. With prosciutto and Parmesan packing a serious flavor punch, this is real Italian pizza like you never knew before. Store-bought crust and pre-washed spinach make this recipe practically effortless.

MAKES 4 SERVINGS

SERVING SIZE
1 SLICE

PER SERVING
CALORIES 390
TOTAL FAT 17 G
  SAT FAT 5 G
  MONO FAT 1.5 G
  POLY FAT 0.5 G
PROTEIN 28 G
CARB 37 G
FIBER 6 G
CHOLESTEROL 240 MG
SODIUM 1280 MG

EXCELLENT SOURCE OF
CALCIUM, FIBER, PROTEIN,
VITAMIN A, VITAMIN K

GOOD SOURCE OF
FOLATE, IRON,
MANGANESE, VITAMIN C

1	store-bought baked thin-crust pizza crust (preferably whole-wheat; such as Boboli)
4	cups baby spinach leaves, thinly sliced, (about 4 ounces)
2	teaspoons olive oil
3	ounces thinly sliced prosciutto, cut into thin strips
½	cup grated Parmesan cheese (1½ ounces)
3	cloves garlic, thinly sliced
4	large eggs

Preheat the oven to 450°F.

Place the pizza crust on a baking sheet. Scatter the spinach all over the crust and drizzle with the oil. Evenly distribute the prosciutto, Parmesan, and garlic on top of the spinach. Make 4 wells in the spinach topping, spacing them so there is 1 well on each quarter of the pizza. Crack 1 egg into each of the wells.

Bake for 12 to 15 minutes, until the spinach is wilted and the egg whites are fully cooked. Cut into 4 large slices.

★ EATING WELL TIP

For an ever-ready pizza crust, think out of the pizza box. Besides the pre-baked crusts in the store (get thin-crust so you don't overdo the bread), pita bread, tortillas, and English muffins all work great as pizza bases and all are now easy to find in whole-wheat versions.

spaghetti frittata with salad presto

A frittata is basically a crustless quiche—all the custard-y vegetable-studded egg filling without the fuss or fat of a pastry. In this recipe, marinara-laced spaghetti adds an extra layer of flavor and satisfaction. What a great way to use leftover pasta and sauce!

MAKES 4 SERVINGS

SERVING SIZE
2 WEDGES AND 1 CUP SALAD

PER SERVING
CALORIES 390
TOTAL FAT 20 G
  SAT FAT 5 G
  MONO FAT 8 G
  POLY FAT 2 G
PROTEIN 22 G
CARB 33 G
FIBER 7 G
CHOLESTEROL 275 MG
SODIUM 810 MG

EXCELLENT SOURCE OF
CALCIUM, FIBER, IRON, MANGANESE, PROTEIN, SELENIUM, VITAMIN A, VITAMIN C

GOOD SOURCE OF
IODINE, RIBOFLAVIN

5	large eggs
5	large egg whites
1	tablespoon olive oil
1	small onion, sliced thinly into half moons
5	cups baby spinach leaves
¼	cup sun-dried tomatoes (not oil-packed), reconstituted in boiling water for 10 minutes, chopped
1	large clove garlic, minced
½	teaspoon salt
¼	teaspoon freshly ground black pepper
2	cups cooked whole-wheat spaghetti (4 ounces dry spaghetti), tossed with ½ cup marinara sauce
⅓	cup grated Parmesan cheese
1	recipe Salad Presto (recipe follows)

In a medium bowl, whisk together the eggs and egg whites.

Heat the oil in a large ovenproof, nonstick skillet over medium-high heat. Add the onion and cook, stirring occasionally, until softened, 3 to 5 minutes. Add the spinach, sun-dried tomatoes, garlic, salt, and pepper and cook, stirring, until the spinach is wilted, about 1 minute. Add the spaghetti to the pan and stir to combine. Pour the eggs evenly over the spaghetti and vegetables. Lower the heat to medium-low and cook until the eggs are set on the edges but not in the middle, 6 to 8 minutes.

Preheat the broiler. Sprinkle the top of the frittata with cheese and place under the broiler. Cook until the top is set and golden brown, 2 to 3 minutes; be careful not to overcook or the eggs will become tough. Cut into 8 wedges and serve with the Salad Presto.

* salad presto

Just open a bag of greens, whisk up some oil and vinegar, and there you have it. Salad, presto!
You don't even need to take out a knife. Its crisp bright flavor goes perfectly with the frittata.

MAKES 4 SERVINGS

SERVING SIZE
1 CUP

1   5-ounce bag mixed greens
      (5 cups lightly packed)
2   tablespoons extra-virgin olive oil
1   tablespoon red wine vinegar
    Pinch of dried basil
    Salt and freshly ground black pepper to taste

Put the greens in a medium salad bowl. In a separate
bowl, whisk together the oil and vinegar. Drizzle the
dressing over the greens and sprinkle the dried basil
on top. Season with salt and pepper. Serve.

chicken paillard with watercress & tomato salad

Thin-cut chicken breast is a great shortcut here. It eliminates the need to pound the chicken out and it cooks up in minutes. Topped with a beautiful lemony watercress salad, this dish has real flair, and you barely have to lift a finger.

MAKES 4 SERVINGS

SERVING SIZE
4 OUNCES COOKED CHICKEN BREAST, 1½ CUPS SALAD, AND 2 PIECES BREAD

PER SERVING
CALORIES 260
TOTAL FAT 14 G
  SAT FAT 2.5 G
  MONO FAT 8.5 G
  POLY FAT 2 G
PROTEIN 30 G
CARB 4 G
FIBER 1 G
CHOLESTEROL 80 MG
SODIUM 520 MG

EXCELLENT SOURCE OF
NIACIN, PHOSPHORUS, PROTEIN, SELENIUM, VITAMIN A, VITAMIN B6, VITAMIN C, VITAMIN K

GOOD SOURCE OF
MAGNESIUM, PANTOTHENIC ACID, POTASSIUM

1¼	pounds thin-cut skinless boneless chicken breasts
3	tablespoons extra-virgin olive oil
1	clove garlic, minced
¾	teaspoon salt
¾	teaspoon freshly ground black pepper
3	tablespoons fresh lemon juice
1	large bunch watercress, tough stems removed, coarsely chopped (about 4 cups)
2	medium tomatoes, chopped
8	slices whole-grain baguette

Combine the chicken, 1 tablespoon of the olive oil, the garlic, and ½ teaspoon each of the salt and pepper in a bowl and toss to coat. Preheat a grill or nonstick grill pan over medium-high heat. Grill the chicken until grill marks form and the meat is just cooked through, 2 to 3 minutes per side. Remove from the grill and sprinkle with 1 tablespoon of the lemon juice.

In a large bowl, toss the watercress and tomatoes, with their seeds, with the remaining 2 tablespoons of each olive oil and lemon juice, and the remaining ¼ teaspoon of each salt and pepper. Distribute the chicken among 4 serving plates and top each with 1½ cups of the salad and 1 to 2 tablespoons of accumulated liquid from the salad. Serve with the baguette slices.

grilled beef, jícama, and apple salad

This Thai-inspired salad has that classic tart-sweet-spicy flavor balance that really gets your taste buds dancing. The cool, crunchy herb-laced salad is the yin to the yang of the rich tender beef. What's more, the food processor does most of the work.

MAKES 4 SERVINGS

SERVING SIZE
1½ CUPS SALAD,
ABOUT 7 SLICES BEEF,
AND 2 TEASPOONS PEANUTS

PER SERVING
CALORIES 370
TOTAL FAT 11 G
  SAT FAT 3.5 G
  MONO FAT 4.5 G
  POLY FAT 1.5 G
PROTEIN 34 G
CARB 37 G
FIBER 11 G
CHOLESTEROL 50 MG
SODIUM 670 MG

EXCELLENT SOURCE OF
FIBER, IRON, NIACIN,
PHOSPHORUS, POTASSIUM,
PROTEIN, SELENIUM,
VITAMIN B6, VITAMIN B12,
VITAMIN C, ZINC

GOOD SOURCE OF
COPPER, FOLATE,
MAGNESIUM, MANGANESE,
PANTOTHENIC ACID,
RIBOFLAVIN, THIAMIN,
VITAMIN K

1¼	pounds shoulder center steak (ranch steak) or top sirloin steak, boneless
1	teaspoon salt
¼	teaspoon freshly ground black pepper
¼	cup fresh lime juice
¼	cup rice vinegar
2	tablespoons sugar
1	large jícama (about 1½ pounds), peeled
2	green apples (about 1 pound), cored
½	cup fresh cilantro leaves, plus more for garnish
2	teaspoons finely grated lime zest
1	medium jalapeño pepper, seeded and diced (about 2 teaspoons)
3	tablespoons chopped roasted peanuts

Heat a grill pan over medium-high heat. Season the steak with the salt and pepper and grill until medium-rare, 3 to 4 minutes per side. Let the meat rest for 5 minutes, then cut across the grain into ¼-inch-thick slices.

In a small bowl, combine the lime juice, vinegar, and sugar and whisk until the sugar is partially dissolved. Using the shredder attachment of a food processor, shred the jícama and apples; transfer to a bowl. Add the cilantro, lime zest, jalapeño, and dressing, and toss to combine.

To serve, mound 1½ cups of the salad into each serving bowl and top with about 7 slices of beef. Garnish each bowl with additional cilantro leaves and about 2 teaspoons of toasted peanuts. Serve immediately.

strawberry and mozzarella salad

I get a kick out of using everyday ingredients in unexpected ways. The result is something exciting and different but not too far out of the comfort zone. This dish is a fresh take on the traditional Italian tomato and mozzarella salad. The juicy berries are a fragrant complement to the creamy, soft cheese, and the balsamic vinegar adds just the right touch of sweetness.

MAKES 4 SERVINGS

SERVING SIZE
3 CUPS SALAD AND
2 PIECES BREAD

PER SERVING:
CALORIES 400
TOTAL FAT 25 G
  SAT FAT 8 G
  MONO FAT 10 G
  POLY FAT 3 G
PROTEIN 16 G
CARB 34 G
FIBER 4 G
CHOLESTEROL 30 MG
SODIUM 720 MG

EXCELLENT SOURCE OF
CALCIUM, FOLATE,
MANGANESE, PROTEIN,
VITAMIN A, VITAMIN C,
VITAMIN K

GOOD SOURCE OF
FIBER, IRON, NIACIN,
SELENIUM, THIAMIN

¼ cup extra-virgin olive oil
2 tablespoons balsamic vinegar
¼ teaspoon salt
¼ teaspoon freshly ground pepper
2 hearts of romaine lettuce, torn or cut into bite-size pieces (5 lightly packed cups)
1 16-ounce container fresh strawberries, hulled and sliced
6 ounces part-skim mozzarella cheese, diced (about 1½ cups)
½ cup lightly packed fresh basil leaves, cut into ribbons
8 slices whole-grain Italian bread

In a small bowl, whisk together the oil, vinegar, salt, and pepper. Place the lettuce in a large bowl and toss with half of the dressing. Place the lettuce on 4 salad plates. Toss the strawberries with the remaining dressing and place ¼ of the berries on top of each mound of lettuce. Top each with cheese, then sprinkle with the basil. Serve the bread alongside.

cobb salad

This salad definitely has the wow factor with colorful rows of scrumptious goodies adorning a bed of crisp lettuce. It seems too decadent to be healthful, but a few simple tricks, like crisping the smoked ham in a skillet to give a bacon-like effect, make it as good for you as it tastes.

MAKES 4 SERVINGS

SERVING SIZE
3 CUPS

PER SERVING
CALORIES 350
TOTAL FAT 24 G
  SAT FAT 6 G
  MONO FAT 13 G
  POLY FAT 3 G
PROTEIN 25 G
CARB 10 G
FIBER 4 G
CHOLESTEROL 110 MG
SODIUM 760 MG

EXCELLENT SOURCE OF
FOLATE, NIACIN,
PHOSPHORUS, PROTEIN,
RIBOFLAVIN, SELENIUM,
THIAMIN, VITAMIN A,
VITAMIN B6, VITAMIN C,
VITAMIN K

GOOD SOURCE OF
CALCIUM, FIBER, IODINE,
IRON, MAGNESIUM,
MANGANESE, PANTOTHENIC
ACID, POTASSIUM,
VITAMIN B12, ZINC

FOR THE DRESSING

3 tablespoons extra-virgin olive oil
2 tablespoons red wine vinegar
1 tablespoon fresh lemon juice
1 teaspoon Dijon mustard
1 teaspoon Worcestershire sauce
1 small clove garlic, minced
¼ teaspoon salt
¼ teaspoon freshly ground black pepper

FOR THE SALAD

¼ pound sliced Black Forest ham
  Cooking spray
2 hard-boiled eggs
6 cups coarsely chopped romaine lettuce
    (about 6 ounces)
2 cups watercress, thick stems removed
2 medium tomatoes, seeded and diced (about 2 cups)
½ avocado, pitted, peeled and diced (about ¾ cup)
1 cup cooked diced chicken breast
½ cup crumbled Roquefort or blue cheese
  (about 2 ounces)

In a small bowl, whisk together all of the dressing ingredients.

Slice the ham into ½-inch strips. Spray a nonstick skillet with cooking spray and preheat it over medium-high heat. Cook the ham in the skillet, stirring frequently, until crisped, 3 to 5 minutes. Remove from the heat.

Remove and discard the yolk from one of the hard-boiled eggs. Chop the remaining egg white and whole egg and set aside.

In a large bowl, toss the romaine and watercress with two-thirds of the dressing. Put the dressed greens on a large serving dish. Place the tomatoes, avocado, chicken, cheese, diced egg, and the crisped ham on top of the greens. Drizzle with the remaining dressing.

crab and avocado duet
with cool cucumber soup

This stack of rich, succulent crab and creamy avocado is impressive and rich tasting yet barely counts as cooking. It is really just pulling together the best of nature and presenting it in an artful, inspired way. The funny thing is, you achieve such elegance with a very unfancy tool—an empty can. I like to serve this as part of a light summer luncheon after the Cool Cucumber Soup.

MAKES 4 SERVINGS

SERVING SIZE
1 "DUET," 1 CUP SOUP,
AND 2 SLICES OF BREAD

PER SERVING:
CALORIES 390
TOTAL FAT 12 G
  SAT FAT 2 G
  MONO FAT 7 G
  POLY FAT 2 G
PROTEIN 28 G
CARB 42 G
FIBER 6 G
CHOLESTEROL 70 MG
SODIUM 760 MG

EXCELLENT SOURCE OF
CALCIUM, FIBER, FOLATE,
POTASSIUM, PROTEIN,
VITAMIN C, VITAMIN K

GOOD SOURCE OF
COPPER, IRON, MAGNESIUM,
MANGANESE, NIACIN,
PANTOTHENIC ACID,
PHOSPHORUS, RIBOFLAVIN,
SELENIUM, THIAMIN,
VITAMIN A, VITAMIN B6

1	ripe avocado
3	tablespoons fresh lemon juice
¼	teaspoon salt, plus more to taste
1	teaspoon Dijon mustard
	Pinch of ground white pepper
½	pound lump crabmeat
2	tablespoons chopped chives
1	recipe Cool Cucumber Soup (recipe follows)
8	slices whole-grain baguette

Pit and peel the avocado and cut it into ½-inch chunks. In a small bowl, toss the avocado chunks gently with 1 tablespoon of the lemon juice and season with salt to taste. In a medium bowl, whisk together the remaining 2 tablespoons of lemon juice, the Dijon mustard, white pepper, and the ¼ teaspoon of salt. Add the crabmeat and toss.

For a decorative presentation, stand an empty 15-ounce can (with both the top and bottom removed) on a serving plate. Scoop a quarter of the avocado into the can, being careful to avoid any sharp edge on the rim. Place a quarter of the crabmeat on top and press down gently into the can. Gently pull the can off the avocado and crab mixture. Garnish with ½ tablespoon of the chives. Repeat with the remaining three servings and serve with the bread alongside or following the Cool Cucumber Soup.

* cool cucumber soup

If you could sip a refreshing summer breeze, this is what it would taste like. You'll stay cool making it because all you have to do is put the ingredients in a blender and whir.

MAKES 4 SERVINGS

SERVING SIZE
1 CUP SOUP WITH
2 SLICES BREAD

3 cups plain nonfat yogurt
1 English cucumber (about 1 pound), cut into chunks
1 scallion (white and green parts), coarsely chopped (about ¼ cup)
3 tablespoons chopped fresh dill, plus more for garnish
   Salt and freshly ground black pepper to taste
1 medium tomato (about 5 ounces), seeded and diced
2 teaspoons extra-virgin olive oil

In a blender, combine the yogurt, cucumber, scallion, and dill. Pulse until pureed. Season to taste with salt and pepper. Ladle into individual bowls. Top each serving with 2 tablespoons of diced tomato, drizzle with ½ teaspoon of olive oil, and garnish with a dill sprig.

PUNCH UP YOUR LUNCH—TEN EASY, EXCITING SANDWICH IDEAS

1) Try crisp Napa cabbage leaves and a drizzle of sweet, tangy hoisin sauce on your grilled chicken sandwich in place of the usual lettuce and mustard.

2) Layer thinly sliced pickle, radish, carrot, and cucumber on your ham sandwich for a flavorful rainbow of crunch.

3) Mix peanut butter with a dash of chili-garlic sauce and soy sauce and spread generously on a grilled chicken or sliced tofu sandwich.

4) For an antipasto platter you can eat with one hand, layer sundried tomatoes, marinated artichokes, grilled zucchini, arugula, and prosciutto on crusty whole-grain Italian bread.

5) Hummus is a great sandwich spread. Try it in a pita with sliced egg, cucumber, tomato, and hot sauce.

6) Boost your roast beef sandwich by brushing the bread with oil and toasting until golden brown. Halve a garlic clove and firmly rub the cut side of the garlic on the bread.

7) For a fresh take on tuna salad try it with diced green apple, celery, and chopped dried tart cherries tossed with a dressing of Greek-style yogurt, a touch of mayo, a little lemon juice, and Dijon mustard.

8) Caramelized onions add a healthy, decadent touch to just about any sandwich. Cook thinly sliced onion in a little olive oil over low heat, stirring occasionally, until deep golden brown, about 20 minutes.

9) Trade up the usual mayo for a more flavorful and healthier spread. Basil pesto adds a burst of excitement to a turkey, ham, or tomato-mozzarella sandwich. Chimichurri is a natural on roast beef and grilled chicken. (See Chimichurri recipe on page 125.)

10) Fresh herbs instantly awaken a ho-hum lunch. Try a few fresh mint leaves on your regular turkey-on-wheat, or a pile of fresh parsley on a ham sandwich for an effortless refresher.

shrimp roll with cracked pepper potato chips

This classic shrimp salad heaped onto a toasted hot dog bun served alongside warm, homemade potato chips is fun food that tastes seriously good.

MAKES 4 SERVINGS

SERVING SIZE
1 SHRIMP ROLL AND
ABOUT 15 POTATO CHIPS

PER SERVING
CALORIES 520
TOTAL FAT 19 G
  SAT FAT 3 G
  MONO FAT 8.5 G
  POLY FAT 7 G
 PROTEIN 33 G
CARB 56 G
FIBER 7 G
CHOLESTEROL 225 MG
SODIUM 560 MG

EXCELLENT SOURCE OF
COPPER, FIBER, IRON,
MAGNESIUM, MANGANESE,
NIACIN, PHOSPHORUS,
POTASSIUM, PROTEIN,
SELENIUM, VITAMIN B6,
VITAMIN B12, VITAMIN C,
VITAMIN D, ZINC

GOOD SOURCE OF
CALCIUM, FOLATE,
PANTOTHENIC ACID,
RIBOFLAVIN, THIAMIN,
VITAMIN K

⅓   cup plain Greek-style nonfat yogurt
3   tablespoons mayonnaise
1   stalk celery, finely chopped
1   tablespoon chopped scallion greens
    (from about 1 scallion)
1   tablespoon fresh lemon juice
1   pound cooked shelled medium shrimp
    Salt and freshly ground black pepper to taste
4   whole-wheat hot dog buns
1   tablespoon extra-virgin olive oil
1   recipe Cracked Pepper Potato Chips
    (recipe follows)

In a bowl, stir together the yogurt, mayonnaise, celery, scallions, and lemon juice. Fold in the shrimp and season to taste with salt and pepper. Chill until ready to use. Just before serving, open the hot dog buns and brush the inside with olive oil. Heat a grill pan over medium-high heat and grill the bread, cut side down, until toasted, about 3 minutes. Fill each with ¾ cup of the shrimp mixture and serve immediately with Cracked Pepper Potato Chips.

✳ EATING WELL TIP
Keep frozen cleaned shrimp on hand, both cooked and uncooked, for a quick, easy, and upscale protein, there when you need it.

* cracked pepper potato chips

Imagine, chips that are good for you! Just a touch of oil and some oven time make these potato rounds crispy and even more addictive than the packaged kind. A devilish sprinkle of pepper deters my daughter so there are more for me.

MAKES 4 SERVINGS

SERVING SIZE
ABOUT 15 CHIPS

2   large russet potatoes (1¾ pounds total), sliced into ⅛-inch-thick rounds
1   tablespoon plus 1 teaspoon olive oil
1   teaspoon coarsely ground black pepper
Salt to taste

Preheat the oven to 450°F. Toss the potatoes in a large bowl with the oil and pepper until well coated. Arrange the potato slices in 1 layer on a baking sheet; use 2 baking sheets if necessary. Bake for 20 to 25 minutes, until chips are crisped and lightly browned. Remove from the oven, season with salt, and cool.

open-face chicken parmesan sandwich

What sounds more appealing than a chicken Parm sandwich, drowning in melted cheese and zesty marinara sauce atop toasted Italian bread? How about knowing that with the right ingredients on hand you can have it on the table in less than 10 minutes, and it's good for you, too!

MAKES 4 SERVINGS

SERVING SIZE
1 PIECE

PER SERVING
CALORIES 420
TOTAL FAT 12 G
  SAT FAT 5 G
  MONO FAT 3 G
  POLY FAT 1.5 G
PROTEIN 44 G
CARB 34 G
FIBER 4 G
CHOLESTEROL 100 MG
SODIUM 1090 MG

EXCELLENT SOURCE OF
CALCIUM, FOLATE,
IRON, NIACIN,
PHOSPHORUS, PROTEIN,
SELENIUM, VITAMIN A,
VITAMIN B6, VITAMIN C,

GOOD SOURCE OF
FIBER, MAGNESIUM,
MANGANESE, PANTOTHENIC
ACID, RIBOFLAVIN, THIAMIN,
VITAMIN B12, ZINC

1	loaf whole-grain Italian bread (about 8 ounces)
2	cups jarred marinara sauce
4	5-ounce cooked skinless boneless chicken breasts
4	cups baby spinach leaves
1	cup shredded part-skim mozzarella cheese (4 ounces)
¼	cup grated Parmesan cheese (¾ ounce)

Preheat the broiler.

   Slice the bread in half lengthwise, then in half again crosswise so you wind up with 4 pieces. Scoop out the bread to remove the soft inner portion and discard. Place the bread scooped side up on a baking tray. Spoon ¼ cup of sauce into each piece of bread. Lay a piece of chicken on top and cover with 1 cup of spinach leaves. Pour another ¼ cup of sauce on top of the spinach, then sprinkle each sandwich with ¼ cup of mozzarella and 1 tablespoon of Parmesan.

   Broil until the spinach is wilted and the cheese is bubbly and browned, 4 to 5 minutes.

✴ EATING WELL TIP

Sure, it is easy to make a basic tomato sauce from scratch, but sometimes you need a shortcut, and jarred sauce can be your ticket to a fantastic meal in no time. The trick is to buy a good one. Here are some things to look for:

- olive oil instead of other oils (that's what you'd use, after all)
- no preservatives, stabilizers, or artificial ingredients
- less than 500 mg of sodium, 6 grams of sugar, and 4 grams of fat per ½ cup

dinner— rush hour

* If most days are so busy you are lucky to get a home-heated meal on the table, much less a home-cooked one, here comes the cavalry: **25 COMPLETE DINNERS YOU CAN WHIP UP IN ABOUT 30 MINUTES OR LESS.** Each is inspired, absolutely delicious, family friendly, and good for you—**ALL IN LESS TIME THAN IT TAKES TO ORDER A PIZZA.** They are the kind of dinners that magnetically **DRAW PEOPLE TOGETHER** around the table and leave everyone marveling about how you manage to do it all so well. **IT'S MAXIMUM REWARD FOR MINIMUM EFFORT.**

tri-color pepper steak

Sweet, savory sautéed onions and peppers with strips of steak in a mouthwatering sauce, all ready in 20 minutes using just one pan. This is destined to become one of your go-to dinners.

MAKES 4 SERVINGS

SERVING SIZE
2 CUPS PEPPER STEAK
PLUS ¼ CUP SAUCE,
¾ CUP BROWN RICE

PER SERVING
CALORIES 540
TOTAL FAT 14 G
　SAT FAT 4 G
　MONO FAT 6.5 G
　POLY FAT 2 G
PROTEIN 39 G
CARB 55 G
FIBER 7 G
CHOLESTEROL 50 MG
SODIUM 410 MG

EXCELLENT SOURCE OF
COPPER, FIBER,
FOLATE, IRON,
MAGNESIUM, MANGANESE,
NIACIN, PANTOTHENIC ACID,
PHOSPHORUS,
POTASSIUM, PROTEIN,
RIBOFLAVIN, SELENIUM,
THIAMIN, VITAMIN A,
VITAMIN B6, VITAMIN B12,
VITAMIN C, ZINC

GOOD SOURCE OF
VITAMIN K

4	teaspoons canola oil
1¼	pounds top round, London broil, or flank steak, thinly sliced
5	large assorted bell peppers (such as a mixture of red, yellow, and green; about 2 pounds total)
1	large onion, sliced into half moons (about 3 cups)
4	cloves garlic, sliced
1½	cups low-sodium beef broth
¾	cup dry red wine
3	tablespoons low-sodium soy sauce
½	teaspoon freshly ground black pepper
1½	teaspoons cornstarch, dissolved in ¼ cup cold water
3	cups cooked brown rice

Heat 2 teaspoons of the oil in a large skillet over medium-high heat. Add the beef and cook until browned on all sides, about 5 minutes. Transfer the meat with its juices to a plate.

Heat the remaining 2 teaspoons of oil in the same skillet over medium-high heat. Add the peppers and onion and cook, stirring occasionally, for 5 minutes. Add the garlic and continue cooking until the peppers are softened and onions are translucent, about 5 minutes more.

Return the beef and juices to the skillet and add the broth, wine, soy sauce, and pepper. Bring to a boil. Reduce the heat and simmer until the liquid has reduced by half, about 5 minutes. Stir in the dissolved cornstarch and cook until the mixture thickens, about 2 minutes. Serve over the rice.

⋆ DID YOU KNOW?
Red, yellow, and orange bell peppers are more than just brilliant, sweet, and crunchy; they are outstanding sources of vitamin C, with three to five times that of a medium orange.

beef stroganoff with green beans and grainy mustard

This dish is old-fashioned goodness for the modern-day dinner rush. Tender beef with mushrooms in creamy sauce over noodles—it's just like grandma's only better for you and a cinch to make.

MAKES 4 SERVINGS

SERVING SIZE
1 CUP NOODLES,
1½ CUPS BEEF-MUSHROOM MIXTURE,
1 TEASPOON PARSLEY,
AND ABOUT 16 GREEN BEANS

PER SERVING
CALORIES 560
TOTAL FAT 15 G
    SAT FAT 3.5 G
    MONO FAT 6.5 G
    POLY FAT 2.5 G
PROTEIN 42 G
CARB 60 G
FIBER 6 G
CHOLESTEROL 85 MG
SODIUM 590 MG

EXCELLENT SOURCE OF
COPPER, FIBER, FOLATE,
IRON, MAGNESIUM,
MANGANESE, NIACIN,
PANTOTHENIC ACID,
PHOSPHORUS,
POTASSIUM, PROTEIN,
RIBOFLAVIN, SELENIUM,
THIAMIN, VITAMIN B6,
VITAMIN B12, VITAMIN C,
VITAMIN K, ZINC

GOOD SOURCE OF
CALCIUM, VITAMIN A

4	teaspoons canola oil
1	pound top round, London broil, or flank steak, thinly sliced
1	small onion, thinly sliced
2	8-ounce packages white button mushrooms, cleaned, stemmed, and sliced (about 5 cups)
2	cloves garlic, minced
1	tablespoon all-purpose flour
2	cups low-sodium beef broth
½	cup dry red wine
¾	teaspoon salt
½	teaspoon freshly ground black pepper
⅔	cup plain Greek-style nonfat yogurt

FOR SERVING

4	cups cooked whole-wheat egg noodles
4	teaspoons minced fresh parsley
1	recipe Green Beans and Grainy Mustard (recipe follows)

Heat 2 teaspoons of the oil in a large skillet over medium-high heat. Add the beef and cook until browned on all sides, about 5 minutes. Transfer the meat with its juices to a plate.

Heat the remaining 2 teaspoons of oil in the skillet over medium-high heat. Add the onions and cook, stirring, until soft and translucent, about 3 minutes. Add the mushrooms and garlic and cook, stirring occasionally, until the mushrooms are soft and have released most of their water, about 5 minutes.

Return the beef and juices to the pan and stir to incorporate. Sprinkle with the flour and stir until well combined. Add the beef broth, wine, salt, and pepper and bring to a boil. Reduce the heat and simmer until the mixture thickens and reduces slightly, 5 minutes. Stir in the yogurt and cook for 1 minute more.

Spoon the mixture over the noodles and garnish with parsley. Serve alongside Green Beans and Grainy Mustard.

* green beans **and grainy mustard**

Crisp green beans are just the right counterpoint to the rich stroganoff.
Beads of tangy mustard dress them up deliciously with no effort at all.

MAKES 4 SERVINGS

SERVING SIZE
ABOUT 16 GREEN BEANS

1   pound fresh green beans, trimmed
2   teaspoons whole-grain mustard
    Salt and freshly ground black pepper to taste

Place the green beans in a steamer basket over a pot
of boiling water. Cover and cook until crisp and tender,
about 4 minutes. Drain the beans and transfer to a
large serving bowl. Add the mustard and toss to coat.
Season with salt and pepper and serve.

* DID YOU KNOW?
London broil is not technically a cut of beef. It is a way
of cooking meat that involves marinating, broiling, or
grilling, then slicing on the bias. What is labeled London
broil in the store is usually flank steak or top round—
lean beef choices that are best served thinly sliced.

emerald stir-fry with beef

Whenever I stir-fry I crank up the dance tunes because the beat of making one is so fast and fun. The key is to get all your ingredients ready before you heat the pan so you can get into a groove. With this recipe the prep is a breeze thanks to vegetables, like snow peas, that require little or no chopping.

MAKES 4 SERVINGS

SERVING SIZE
2 CUPS STIR-FRY,
3 TABLESPOONS SAUCE,
¾ CUP COOKED BROWN RICE

PER SERVING
CALORIES 530
TOTAL FAT 15 G
    SAT FAT 1.5 G
    MONO FAT 6 G
    POLY FAT 3 G
PROTEIN 32 G
CARB 61 G
FIBER 12 G
CHOLESTEROL 30 MG
SODIUM 450 MG

EXCELLENT SOURCE OF
FIBER, IRON, MAGNESIUM, MANGANESE, NIACIN, PHOSPHORUS, PROTEIN, SELENIUM, THIAMIN, VITAMIN A, VITAMIN B6, VITAMIN C, ZINC

GOOD SOURCE OF
CALCIUM, COPPER, FOLATE, PANTOTHENIC ACID, POTASSIUM, RIBOFLAVIN, VITAMIN B12

¼	cup low-sodium soy sauce
¼	cup mirin (Japanese rice wine), or semisweet white wine (such as Riesling)
¼	cup orange juice
¼	cup water
2	tablespoons rice vinegar
¼	teaspoon crushed red pepper flakes
2	tablespoons canola oil
8	ounces top round, London broil, or flank steak, thinly sliced
3	cloves garlic, minced
1	large bunch broccoli (1¼ pounds), trimmed and cut into small florets
1	bunch asparagus (1 pound), trimmed and sliced on diagonal into 2-inch pieces
2	cups (8 ounces) frozen shelled edamame
2	cups fresh snow peas (6 ounces)
1½	teaspoons cornstarch, dissolved in ¼ cup cold water
1	teaspoon toasted sesame oil
3	cups cooked brown rice

Combine the soy sauce, mirin or white wine, orange juice, water, rice vinegar, and red pepper flakes in a small bowl.

In a large wok or very large deep skillet, heat 1 tablespoon of the canola oil over medium-high heat. Add the beef and cook, stirring, until just browned, about 2 minutes. Transfer the beef to a plate. Heat the remaining tablespoon of canola oil in the same wok or skillet over medium heat. Add the garlic and cook, stirring, until fragrant, about 30 seconds. Add the broccoli, asparagus, edamame, and snow peas. Raise the heat to medium-high, and cook, stirring occasionally, until the vegetables are slightly softened, about 3 minutes.

Add the mirin-soy mixture and cook, stirring, until the vegetables are crisp-tender, about 4 minutes. Add the beef and dissolved cornstarch and stir to incorporate. Cook until the mixture thickens slightly and the beef is heated through, an additional 2 minutes. Drizzle with the sesame oil and serve over rice.

★ EATING WELL TIP

Brown rice is a whole grain that's loaded with antioxidants and fiber, and has a wonderful nutty taste. But with 45 minutes cooking time, it's not exactly rush-hour material. To the rescue, one of my favorite new convenience foods: ready brown rice pouches. Just 90 seconds in the microwave and voilà! Brown rice. Stick to the unseasoned variety rather than the flavored kind, which can be high in sodium and artificial flavors.

steak chimichurri with grilled garlic bread and grilled tomatoes

Chimichurri is a garlicky herb sauce, like pesto. It has been dubbed the ketchup of Argentina because they douse everything with it there—vegetables, bread, eggs, chicken, fish—you name it. But it is an absolute must-have on grilled meat. After you try this you'll see why. The sauce takes minutes to make and you can prep it ahead so it's there when you need it.

MAKES 4 SERVINGS

SERVING SIZE
ABOUT 7 SLICES MEAT,
2 TABLESPOONS SAUCE,
1 PIECE BREAD,
AND 2 TOMATO HALVES

PER SERVING
CALORIES 480
TOTAL FAT 25 G
  SAT FAT 5 G
  MONO FAT 15 G
  POLY FAT 3.5 G
PROTEIN 39 G
CARB 27 G
FIBER 6 G
CHOLESTEROL 50 MG
SODIUM 850 MG

EXCELLENT SOURCE OF
FIBER, FOLATE, IRON,
MAGNESIUM, MANGANESE,
NIACIN, PHOSPHORUS,
POTASSIUM, PROTEIN,
SELENIUM, THIAMIN,
VITAMIN A, VITAMIN B6,
VITAMIN B12, VITAMIN C,
VITAMIN K, ZINC

GOOD SOURCE OF
CALCIUM, COPPER,
PANTOTHENIC ACID,
RIBOFLAVIN

FOR THE CHIMICHURRI SAUCE

⅓	cup packed fresh cilantro
⅓	cup packed fresh Italian parsley
3	tablespoons olive oil
1	large clove garlic
1	tablespoon red wine vinegar
1	tablespoon water
¼	teaspoon crushed red pepper flakes
¼	teaspoon salt

TO CONTINUE

	Cooking spray
1¼	pounds shoulder center steak (ranch steak) or top sirloin steak, about 1¼ inches thick
¼	teaspoon salt
¼	teaspoon freshly ground black pepper
1	recipe Grilled Garlic Bread (recipe follows)
1	recipe Grilled Tomatoes (recipe follows)

Puree all the ingredients for the chimichurri sauce in the small bowl of a food processor until it reaches the consistency of a sauce. Transfer to a bowl. Chimichurri will keep in an airtight container in the refrigerator for up to 3 days.

To continue, spray a grill or grill pan with cooking spray and preheat over medium-high heat. Season the steak with the salt and pepper. Cook the steak, turning once, for 5 minutes per side for medium rare, or to your desired degree of doneness. Allow the steak to sit for 5 minutes before slicing thinly.

Serve the steak with the chimichurri sauce, Grilled Garlic Bread, and Grilled Tomatoes.

* grilled garlic bread

Since you are firing up the grill for the steak, why not toast your bread too?
The crisped bread acts as a gentle grater for fresh garlic, which takes it to the next level.

MAKES 4 SERVINGS

SERVING SIZE
1 PIECE

4	large slices crusty whole-grain country bread
1	tablespoon olive oil
1	clove garlic, cut in half
¼	teaspoon salt

Preheat a grill or grill pan over medium-high heat.
Brush both sides of each slice of bread with oil.
Grill until toasted and grill marks are formed, 2 to
3 minutes per side.
   Rub both sides of the toasted bread vigorously
with the garlic. Sprinkle with the salt and serve.

* grilled tomatoes

Grilling tomatoes transforms them by intensifying their flavor and bringing out their juiciness.

MAKES 4 SERVINGS

SERVING SIZE
2 TOMATO HALVES

4	large ripe but firm tomatoes
1	tablespoon olive oil
¼	teaspoon salt

Cut the tomatoes in half crosswise and squeeze them
gently to remove the seeds. Brush the cut side of each
tomato with oil and season with salt. Preheat a grill
or grill pan over medium-high heat. Place the tomatoes
into the pan cut side down and grill until warm,
softened, and browned on the cut side, but still
retaining their shape, about 10 minutes.

better burger with green olives and creamy broccoli slaw

This burger is big, bold, and bursting at the seams with flavor. The combination of mouthwatering green olives, cumin, and parsley is just exotic enough to make it intriguing while still satisfying that all-American burger craving.

MAKES 4 SERVINGS

SERVING SIZE
1 BURGER WITH ¾ CUP SLAW

PER SERVING
CALORIES 450
TOTAL FAT 21 G
  SAT FAT 3.5 G
  MONO FAT 8 G
  POLY FAT 9 G
PROTEIN 33 G
CARB 37 G
FIBER 7 G
CHOLESTEROL 65 MG
SODIUM 920 MG

EXCELLENT SOURCE OF
FIBER, FOLATE, IRON, MAGNESIUM, MANGANESE, NIACIN, PHOSPHORUS, PROTEIN, SELENIUM, THIAMIN, VITAMIN A, VITAMIN B12, VITAMIN C, VITAMIN K, ZINC

GOOD SOURCE OF
CALCIUM, COPPER, POTASSIUM, RIBOFLAVIN, VITAMIN B6

1	pound lean ground beef (at least 90% lean)
½	cup coarsely chopped pitted green olives (2 ounces)
2	tablespoons finely chopped fresh Italian parsley
½	teaspoon ground cumin
¼	teaspoon freshly ground black pepper
	Cooking spray
4	whole-wheat burger buns
4	slices beefsteak tomato
4	green lettuce leaves
¼	red onion, sliced
	Ketchup, to taste
1	recipe Creamy Broccoli Slaw (recipe follows)

Combine the beef, olives, parsley, cumin, and pepper in a mixing bowl and mix until well incorporated. Shape into 4 burgers.

Spray a nonstick grill pan with cooking spray and preheat over medium-high heat or prepare an outdoor grill. Cook the burgers for about 4 minutes per side for medium, turning once. Place the burgers on the buns piled with tomato, lettuce, and onion slices. Serve the ketchup and Creamy Broccoli Slaw alongside.

★ EATING WELL TIP
When buying ground beef, don't be misled by labels boasting "80% lean." With more than 13 grams of fat in just 3 ounces it is really not very lean at all. Instead go for ground beef that's 90% lean or higher and get all of beef's great taste, protein, and minerals with a fraction of the fat and calories.

3 OUNCES COOKED GROUND BEEF	CALORIES	FAT (GRAMS)
95% lean	139	5
90% lean	173	9.1
85% lean	197	11.9
80% lean	206	13.6

* creamy broccoli slaw

Like the burger, this slaw is comfort food with flair. Here the twist is using crisp-tender, shredded broccoli stalks and a nutty crunch of sunflower seeds. You can maximize the easy factor by using a package of pre-shredded broccoli slaw mix, or shred your own to put the often wasted part of the broccoli to good use.

MAKES 4 SERVINGS

SERVING SIZE
¾ CUP

½ cup plain Greek-style nonfat yogurt
3 tablespoons mayonnaise
2 tablespoons fresh lemon juice
2 teaspoons honey
½ teaspoon salt
¼ teaspoon freshly ground black pepper
1 12-ounce package broccoli slaw mix, or the stalks from 1 large head of broccoli and 1 large carrot
¼ cup shelled roasted sunflower seeds

In a large bowl, whisk together the yogurt, mayonnaise, lemon juice, honey, salt, and pepper. If using whole broccoli stalks and carrot, peel off the tough outer layer of the broccoli stalks and trim off ¼ inch from the bottom. Peel the carrot, then shred the broccoli stalks and carrot in a food processor with the shredder attachment. Add the shredded broccoli and carrots or broccoli slaw mix to the dressing and toss to combine. Stir in the sunflower seeds and serve.

pork & mango stir-fry

This dish is inspired by one of my favorite Chinese take-out orders. The pairing of succulent pork and sweet mango in a classic Asian sauce that balances savory-sweet-spicy and salty is absolutely mouthwatering.

MAKES 4 SERVINGS

SERVING SIZE
2 CUPS STIR-FRY PLUS
¾ CUP COOKED BROWN RICE

PER SERVING
CALORIES 460
TOTAL FAT 9 G
   SAT FAT 1.5 G
   MONO FAT 4.5 G
   POLY FAT 2.5 G
PROTEIN 32 G
CARB 58 G
FIBER 7 G
CHOLESTEROL 75 MG
SODIUM 470 MG

EXCELLENT SOURCE OF
FIBER, IRON, MAGNESIUM,
MANGANESE, NIACIN,
PANTOTHENIC ACID,
PHOSPHORUS,
POTASSIUM, PROTEIN,
RIBOFLAVIN, SELENIUM,
THIAMIN, VITAMIN A,
VITAMIN B6,
VITAMIN C, ZINC

GOOD SOURCE OF
COPPER, FOLATE,
VITAMIN B12

¾	cup low-sodium chicken broth
2	teaspoons cornstarch
4	teaspoons canola oil
1	pound lean pork tenderloin, thinly sliced
1	medium red onion, sliced
1	large red bell pepper, seeded and chopped
2	tablespoons minced peeled fresh ginger
2	cloves garlic, sliced
¾	pound snow peas
¼	cup Chinese cooking wine or dry sherry
3	tablespoons low-sodium soy sauce
1¼	teaspoons Chinese five-spice powder
½	teaspoon crushed red pepper flakes
1	large firm but ripe mango, peeled, pitted, and cut into chunks
3	cups cooked brown rice

In a small bowl, whisk together the chicken broth and cornstarch until the cornstarch is dissolved.

Heat 2 teaspoons of the oil in a wok or very large skillet over medium-high heat. Add the pork and cook, stirring occasionally, until just cooked through, about 4 minutes. Transfer the meat to a plate.

Heat the remaining 2 teaspoons of oil in the same wok or skillet. Add the onions, peppers, ginger, and garlic and cook, stirring, until the vegetables are softened, about 3 minutes. Add the snow peas, cornstarch-broth mixture, wine or sherry, soy sauce, Chinese five-spice powder, and red pepper flakes and toss to combine. Cook until the peas are crisp-tender and the sauce thickens slightly, about 3 minutes. Return the pork to the wok. Add the mango and heat through, about 2 minutes more. Serve over the rice.

pork piccata with spinach and garlic mashed potatoes

This dish showcases one of my everyday favorite ways to cook—browning meat in a skillet, then creating a sauce using the pan scrapings for maximum flavor. It is quick and simple, and you get your protein and sauce in one pan. Here the meat is meltingly tender pork tenderloin and the sauce is a delectable lemony wine reduction enhanced with briny capers.

MAKES 4 SERVINGS

SERVING SIZE
5 TO 6 MEDALLIONS,
2 TABLESPOONS SAUCE,
¼ CUP SPINACH, AND
¾ CUP MASHED POTATOES

PER SERVING
CALORIES 460
TOTAL FAT 15 G
   SAT FAT 2.5 G
   MONO FAT 9.5 G
   POLY FAT 2 G
PROTEIN 36 G
CARB 35 G
FIBER 5G
CHOLESTEROL 90 MG
SODIUM 880 MG

EXCELLENT SOURCE OF
COPPER, FOLATE, IRON,
MAGNESIUM, MANGANESE,
NIACIN, PHOSPHORUS,
POTASSIUM, PROTEIN,
RIBOFLAVIN, SELENIUM,
THIAMIN, VITAMIN A,
VITAMIN B6, VITAMIN C,
VITAMIN K, ZINC

GOOD SOURCE OF
FIBER, PANTOTHENIC ACID,
VITAMIN B12

¼	cup all-purpose flour
¾	teaspoon salt
¾	teaspoon freshly ground black pepper
1¼	pounds pork tenderloin, sliced crosswise into ¼-inch-thick medallions
2	tablespoons olive oil
3	cloves garlic, minced
1	cup dry white wine
1	cup low-sodium chicken broth
3	tablespoons fresh lemon juice
2	tablespoons drained capers
1	recipe Express "Steamed" Spinach (recipe follows)
1	recipe Garlic Mashed Potatoes (recipe follows)
2	tablespoons chopped parsley

Combine the flour and ¼ teaspoon each of salt and pepper in a sealable plastic bag. Place the pork medallions in the bag and shake until well-coated.

Heat 1 tablespoon of the oil in a large skillet (not nonstick) over medium-high heat. Working in 2 batches, cook the pork until it is browned on both sides, 1 to 2 minutes per side. Transfer the meat to a plate.

Add the garlic to the same skillet, then immediately add the wine and cook over medium-high heat. As the wine reduces, stir to dissolve the small bits and juices remaining in the pan from the meat. Cook until the wine is reduced by about half, 4 to 5 minutes.

Add the chicken broth, lemon juice, capers, and remaining salt and pepper and cook until the mixture has reduced slightly, an additional 3 to 4 minutes. Return the medallions to the skillet along with the remaining tablespoon of oil and heat until the sauce thickens and the meat is cooked to medium doneness, about 3 minutes.

Serve over the Express "Steamed" Spinach and Garlic Mashed Potatoes, and top with the parsley.

* express "steamed" spinach

Steamed spinach is a fresh, colorful, subtly flavored side that is heavenly with the lemony Pork Piccata sauce. When you make the spinach this way, you barely have to lift a finger.

MAKES 4 SERVINGS

SERVING SIZE
¼ CUP

5 ounces pre-washed baby spinach leaves

Place the spinach in a large microwave-safe bowl and cover tightly. Microwave on high for 90 seconds.

* garlic mashed potatoes

What better bed for pork with lemon and wine sauce than garlicky mashed potatoes? This mash owes its luxurious texture to the natural creaminess of Yukon Gold potatoes and a touch of olive oil. At first glance 4 cloves of garlic may seem like a lot, but the garlic mellows as it steams with the potatoes, so when they are mashed together you get just the right garlic infusion.

MAKES 4 SERVINGS

SERVING SIZE
¾ CUP

1¼	pounds Yukon Gold potatoes, left unpeeled and cut into 1-inch pieces
4	large cloves garlic, peeled and quartered
½	cup low-sodium chicken broth
1	tablespoon olive oil
½	teaspoon salt

Place the potatoes and garlic in a steamer basket fitted over a large pot of boiling water. Cover and steam until the potatoes are knife-tender, 12 to 15 minutes. Warm the chicken broth in a small saucepan on the stove or in a glass container in the microwave. Remove the steamer basket and drain the water from the large pot. Transfer the potatoes and garlic to the pot, add the oil, salt, and broth, and mash until smooth.

chipotle orange glazed pork chops with maple squash puree and spinach-green apple salad

The simplicity of this recipe belies its complex flavors—spicy, sweet, smoky, and citrus—all lighting up succulent grilled pork chops.

MAKES 4 SERVINGS

SERVING SIZE
1 PORK CHOP,
⅔ CUP SQUASH PUREE,
AND 2 CUPS SALAD

PER SERVING
CALORIES 550
TOTAL FAT 24 G
    SAT FAT 6 G
    MONO FAT 10 G
    POLY FAT 6 G
PROTEIN 36 G
CARB 51 G
FIBER 5 G
CHOLESTEROL 100 MG
SODIUM 550 MG

EXCELLENT SOURCE OF
COPPER, FOLATE,
IRON, MAGNESIUM,
MANGANESE, NIACIN,
PHOSPHORUS, POTASSIUM,
PROTEIN, RIBOFLAVIN,
SELENIUM, THIAMIN,
VITAMIN A, VITAMIN B6,
VITAMIN C, ZINC

GOOD SOURCE OF
CALCIUM, FIBER,
PANTOTHENIC ACID,
VITAMIN B12

2	tablespoons pure maple syrup
2	tablespoons thawed frozen orange juice concentrate
1	teaspoon finely chopped, seeded, canned chipotle chile plus ½ teaspoon adobo sauce it comes in
	Cooking spray
4	¾-inch-thick center cut, bone-in pork loin chops (about 8 ounces each)
½	teaspoon salt
1	recipe Maple Squash Puree (recipe follows)
1	recipe Spinach-Green Apple Salad (recipe follows)

In a small bowl, combine the maple syrup, orange juice concentrate, and chipotle.

Spray a nonstick grill pan or grill with cooking spray and preheat over medium-high heat.

Sprinkle both sides of the chops with the salt. Brush one side of the chops generously with the maple-orange glaze. Place the chops on the grill pan, glazed-side down. Brush the other side with glaze. Cook over medium-high heat until cooked through but with a slight blush in the center, 3 to 4 minutes per side.

Serve with the Maple Squash Puree and Spinach-Green Apple Salad.

* EATING WELL TIP
Chop the leftover chipotle peppers and divide them, along with the adobo sauce, among three or four small sealable plastic bags, then store them in the freezer.

* maple squash puree

Brilliant orange squash is a vegetable everyone in the family loves, especially when you sweeten the deal with maple syrup. A dab of butter works wonders to make it ultra rich and creamy. You can also make this slow-food style with fresh roasted squash, but frozen works perfectly when time is tight.

MAKES 4 SERVINGS

SERVING SIZE
⅔ CUP

2 12-ounce packages frozen cooked butternut squash or winter squash
⅓ cup water
2 tablespoons pure maple syrup
1 tablespoon butter
   Salt to taste

Put the frozen squash and water into a large saucepan. Cover and cook over medium heat, stirring frequently, until the squash is thawed, about 10 minutes. Whisk in the maple syrup and butter and season with salt.

* DID YOU KNOW?
Mangos, squash, and carrots get their bright orange hue from beta-carotene, a powerful antioxidant which actually imparts a yellow-orange color to food.

✳ spinach-green apple salad

This salad is just as easy as your run-of-the-mill lettuce, tomato, and cucumber salad, but oh, so much more interesting. It is a gorgeous balance of texture, color, and taste and has a real autumnal feel.

MAKES 4 SERVINGS

SERVING SIZE
2 CUPS

2	tablespoons extra-virgin olive oil
1	tablespoon cider vinegar
1	teaspoon Dijon mustard
	Salt and freshly ground black pepper to taste
5	ounces baby spinach leaves (about 5 cups lightly packed)
1	Granny Smith apple
⅓	cup walnut pieces, toasted in a dry skillet over medium-high heat until fragrant, about 2 minutes

In a small bowl, whisk together the oil, vinegar, and mustard. Season with salt and pepper. In a large bowl, toss the spinach with the dressing until evenly coated, then divide the spinach among 4 serving plates.

Core the apple and slice it into matchsticks. Sprinkle a quarter of the apple pieces on top of each salad. Follow with the walnut pieces. Serve immediately.

chicken-mushroom quesadillas

This recipe upgrades quesadillas from the appetizer menu to a first-class dinner entrée. It has everything you need—protein, vegetables, and whole grain, all brought together quick as can be with oozy melted cheddar.

MAKES 4 SERVINGS

SERVING SIZE
2 QUESADILLA PIECES,
2 TABLESPOONS SALSA,
AND 1 TABLESPOON
SOUR CREAM

PER SERVING
CALORIES 430
TOTAL FAT 19 G
  SAT FAT 8 G
  MONO FAT 5 G
  POLY FAT 1.5 G
PROTEIN 22 G
CARB 43 G
FIBER 8 G
CHOLESTEROL 55 MG
SODIUM 1000 MG

EXCELLENT SOURCE OF
CALCIUM, FIBER,
MANGANESE, NIACIN,
PHOSPHORUS, PROTEIN,
RIBOFLAVIN, SELENIUM

GOOD SOURCE OF
COPPER, PANTOTHENIC ACID,
POTASSIUM, VITAMIN A,
VITAMIN B6, VITAMIN C,
VITAMIN K, ZINC

1	tablespoon canola oil
1	large onion, chopped
8	ounces white button mushrooms, coarsely chopped (about 3 cups)
3	cloves garlic, minced
2	cups cooked diced skinless boneless chicken breast (1 breast half)
1	teaspoon ground cumin
1	teaspoon chili powder
1	teaspoon dried oregano
2	cups baby spinach leaves, coarsely chopped
½	teaspoon salt
¼	teaspoon freshly ground black pepper
4	10-inch whole-wheat-flour tortillas
1	cup shredded sharp cheddar cheese (4 ounces)
½	cup salsa
¼	cup reduced-fat sour cream

Heat the oil in a large skillet over medium heat. Add the onions and mushrooms and cook, stirring occasionally, until the mushroom water has evaporated and they begin to brown, 5 to 7 minutes. Add the garlic and cook, stirring, for 1 minute more. Add the chicken, cumin, chili powder, and oregano and stir until all the spices are incorporated. Stir in the spinach, salt, and pepper and cook until the spinach is wilted, about 2 minutes.

Lay the tortillas on a flat surface. Sprinkle half of each tortilla with 2 tablespoons of shredded cheese. Spoon ¼ of the chicken mixture on top of the cheese on each tortilla, then top each with 2 more tablespoons of cheese and fold the tortillas over into half-moons, pressing down lightly to seal them closed.

Spray a large nonstick skillet with cooking spray and preheat over medium heat. Place 2 quesadillas in the pan and cook, turning once, until lightly browned and the cheese is melted, about 3 minutes per side. Repeat with the remaining quesadillas. Slice each quesadilla in half. Serve with the salsa and sour cream.

pulled bbq chicken sandwiches with classic coleslaw

Rotisserie chicken is a reliable fallback, but as is, it can be just plain boring. In less than 30 minutes, this recipe turns that chicken into a fabulous sandwich with a tangy barbecue sauce that tastes like you have been cooking all day.

MAKES 6 SERVINGS

SERVING SIZE
1 SANDWICH AND
⅔ CUP COLESLAW

PER SERVING
CALORIES 550
TOTAL FAT 19 G
  SAT FAT 3.5 G
  MONO FAT 6.5 G
  POLY FAT 7.5 G
PROTEIN 39 G
CARB 57 G
FIBER 7 G
CHOLESTEROL 95 MG
SODIUM 680 MG

EXCELLENT SOURCE OF
COPPER, FIBER,
IRON, MAGNESIUM,
MANGANESE, NIACIN,
PHOSPHORUS, POTASSIUM,
PROTEIN, SELENIUM,
VITAMIN A, VITAMIN B6,
VITAMIN C, ZINC

GOOD SOURCE OF
CALCIUM, PANTOTHENIC ACID,
RIBOFLAVIN, THIAMIN,
VITAMIN K

1	tablespoon canola oil
1	large onion, chopped
3	cloves garlic, minced
1	14-ounce can low-sodium tomato sauce
½	cup water
⅓	cup cider vinegar
5	tablespoons unsulfured molasses
¼	cup tomato paste
½	teaspoon liquid smoke
¼	teaspoon freshly ground black pepper
1	whole rotisserie chicken
6	whole-wheat hamburger buns
6	large green lettuce leaves
1	recipe Classic Coleslaw (recipe follows)

Heat the oil in a large skillet over medium heat. Add the onions and cook, stirring, until soft and translucent, about 5 minutes. Add the garlic and cook, stirring, for 1 minute more. Add the tomato sauce, water, vinegar, molasses, tomato paste, liquid smoke, and pepper and bring to a boil. Reduce the heat to medium-low and simmer for 15 minutes.

Meanwhile, take the meat off the chicken, discarding the skin and bones, and shred the meat into thin strips. Add the chicken to the sauce in the pan, return to a simmer, and cook for an additional 10 minutes.

Split the buns. Place a leaf of lettuce on each, then pile ¾ cup of the chicken mixture onto the buns. Serve with the Classic Coleslaw.

✳ DID YOU KNOW?
Molasses is the only sweetener that can boast a significant amount of nutrients, including calcium, magnesium, potassium, and iron. It has a distinctive, deep flavor that is perfect in American classics like barbecue sauce, baked beans, and pumpkin bread. It's also delicious on oatmeal.

* classic coleslaw

What goes better with BBQ than classic creamy coleslaw? Well, here you have it. Lickety split.

MAKES 6 SERVINGS

SERVING SIZE
⅔ CUP

½ cup plain Greek-style nonfat yogurt
¼ cup mayonnaise
¼ cup cider vinegar
1 tablespoon honey
½ teaspoon salt
¼ teaspoon freshly ground black pepper
1 16-ounce bag shredded coleslaw mix or
½ head of green cabbage and 3 large
carrots, peeled and shredded
2 teaspoons caraway seeds (optional)

In a large bowl, whisk together the yogurt, mayonnaise, vinegar, honey, salt, and pepper. Add the coleslaw mix or the shredded cabbage and carrots, and the caraway seeds, if using, and toss to coat.

savory peach chicken

This dish transforms basic chicken breast into a fantastic meal with a teriyaki-like sauce chock-full of peaches that give it an absolutely delightful fruity infusion.

MAKES 4 SERVINGS

SERVING SIZE
1 PIECE CHICKEN,
⅔ CUP SAUCE,
½ TABLESPOON ALMONDS,
¾ CUP BROCCOLI, AND
¾ CUP COOKED BROWN RICE

PER SERVING
CALORIES 520
TOTAL FAT 14 G
    SAT FAT 2 G
    MONO FAT 7 G
    POLY FAT 4 G
PROTEIN 37 G
CARB 62 G
FIBER 7 G
CHOLESTEROL 80 MG
SODIUM 580 MG

EXCELLENT SOURCE OF
FIBER, MAGNESIUM,
MANGANESE, NIACIN,
PANTOTHENIC ACID,
PHOSPHORUS, POTASSIUM,
PROTEIN, SELENIUM,
VITAMIN A, VITAMIN B6,
VITAMIN C

GOOD SOURCE OF
COPPER, FOLATE, IRON,
RIBOFLAVIN, THIAMIN,
VITAMIN K, ZINC

¼	cup orange juice
2	tablespoons brown sugar
2	tablespoons low-sodium soy sauce
2	tablespoons rice vinegar
2	tablespoon canola oil
4	skinless boneless chicken breasts (about 1¼ pounds total)
½	teaspoon salt
¼	teaspoon freshly ground black pepper
1	teaspoon grated peeled fresh ginger
2	cloves garlic, minced
½	cup low-sodium chicken broth
4	large firm but ripe peaches, sliced into ¼-inch slices, or two 10-ounce packages frozen peaches (about 4½ cups)
3	cups cooked brown rice
2	tablespoons sliced almonds, toasted in a dry skillet over medium-high heat for 2 minutes
3	cups steamed broccoli spears

In a small bowl, whisk together the orange juice, brown sugar, soy sauce, and rice vinegar until the sugar is dissolved.

Heat 1 tablespoon of the oil in a large skillet over medium-high heat. Season the chicken on both sides with the salt and pepper. Add to the skillet and cook until browned, about 2 minutes per side. Transfer the chicken to a plate.

Heat the remaining tablespoon of oil in the same skillet, then add the ginger and garlic and cook, stirring, for 30 seconds. Add the chicken broth, soy sauce mixture, and peaches; turn the heat up to high and cook, uncovered, stirring occasionally, until the sauce is slightly thickened and the peaches soften, about 6 minutes. Add the chicken back to the pan, reduce the heat to medium-low, cover, and cook until the chicken is cooked through, about 5 minutes.

Serve the chicken over the rice, topped with the sauce and sprinkled with the toasted almonds. Place a few broccoli spears alongside.

chicken with warm tomato-corn salad

This recipe evokes a summer day. It's packed with seasonal bounty—tomatoes, corn, scallions, and fresh herbs—enlivened with a splash of lime, and enriched with buttery avocado slices. Whip it up in the summer (without breaking a sweat!) after a trip to the farm stand, or anytime you just need a taste of a sun-soaked season.

MAKES 4 SERVINGS

SERVING SIZE
1 CUP VEGETABLES,
1 PIECE CHICKEN BREAST,
AND ¼ AVOCADO

PER SERVING
CALORIES 390
TOTAL FAT 16 G
   SAT FAT 3 G
   MONO FAT 10 G
   POLY FAT 3 G
PROTEIN 34 G
CARB 31 G
FIBER 8 G
CHOLESTEROL 80 MG
SODIUM 230 MG

EXCELLENT SOURCE OF
FIBER, FOLATE,
MAGNESIUM, MANGANESE,
NIACIN, PHOSPHORUS,
POTASSIUM, PROTEIN,
SELENIUM, THIAMIN,
VITAMIN A, VITAMIN B6,
VITAMIN C, VITAMIN K

GOOD SOURCE OF
COPPER, IRON,
PANTOTHENIC ACID,
RIBOFLAVIN, ZINC

1¼	pounds thin-cut skinless boneless chicken breasts
¼	teaspoon salt, plus more to taste
¼	teaspoon freshly ground black pepper, plus more to taste
4	teaspoons olive oil
4	scallions, white and green separated
2	cloves garlic, minced
2	pints grape tomatoes, halved
2	cups corn kernels (from 4 ears fresh uncooked corn or frozen)
1	ripe avocado, pitted, peeled, sliced
3	tablespoons fresh lime juice
3	tablespoons chopped fresh cilantro

Season the chicken with ¼ teaspoon each of salt and pepper. Heat 2 teaspoons of the oil in a large nonstick skillet over medium-high heat. Add the chicken to the pan and cook until the chicken is browned and cooked through, about 3 minutes per side. Transfer the chicken to a plate.

Add the remaining 2 teaspoons of oil to the pan and heat over medium-high heat. Add the scallion whites and cook, stirring, for 1 minute. Add the garlic and cook, stirring, for 30 seconds more. Add the tomatoes and corn to the pan and cook until they are softened but still retain their shape, about 3 minutes. Stir in the scallion greens and season with salt and pepper to taste.

Place about a cup of the vegetable mixture on each plate. Top with a piece of chicken breast and slices of avocado. Sprinkle with lime juice and cilantro and serve.

SHORT CUTS IN THE PRODUCE AISLE

While it's ideal to buy vegetables and fruit from the farmer's market, just picked with dirt still clinging to them, sometimes you just need a shortcut. The produce aisle of the supermarket is awash in products to save you time and effort in the kitchen. They can often mean the difference between a home-cooked meal and take-out, or having a vegetable or not. So why not take advantage?

PRE-WASHED GREENS

Mixed lettuces make for effortless salads, and spinach and arugula are perfect for tossing into pasta and other sauces. Hearty greens like kale are ready to sauté.

PREPPED PRODUCE

Pre-cut broccoli and cauliflower florets, peeled and cubed butternut squash, shredded cabbage and slaw mixes, cored and peeled pineapple, and mango chunks—these products let you walk into the kitchen as if a prep chef has done knife work for you.

FINGER FOOD

Baby carrots, cut peppers, celery sticks, apple slices, fruit salads—all ready to be eaten. They are perfect in a sandwich, as a side, or part of a healthy snack.

But, you ask, don't pre-cut veggies lose their nutritional value? Yes and no. It is true that as soon as you cut a fruit or vegetable you begin to lose vitamins and jump-start spoilage. But the bags that these products are packed in are specially designed to breathe so that nutrients are retained and spoilage is slowed. So while it's best to buy whole fresh produce and cut it yourself right before eating, buying pre-cut is still a good option. Just make sure to keep it refrigerated and abide by the sell-by date.

panzanella with chicken sausage

The first time I ever had panzanella (tomato and bread salad) I was sitting in the garden of an Italian restaurant on a warm, crystal clear day in New York. The dish was a revelation—so simple yet so satisfying. One bite of this dish brings me right back there, and it is practically as relaxing to make.

MAKES 4 SERVINGS

SERVING SIZE
2½ CUPS PANZANELLA
AND 1 SAUSAGE

PER SERVING:
CALORIES 520
TOTAL FAT 25 G
  SAT FAT 5 G
  MONO FAT 8 G
  POLY FAT 3 G
PROTEIN 36 G
CARB 39 G
FIBER 10 G
CHOLESTEROL 110 MG
SODIUM 540 MG

EXCELLENT SOURCE OF
FIBER, FOLATE, MANGANESE,
POTASSIUM, PROTEIN,
SELENIUM, VITAMIN A,
VITAMIN C, VITAMIN K

GOOD SOURCE OF
COPPER, IRON, MAGNESIUM,
NIACIN, PHOSPHORUS,
THIAMIN, VITAMIN B6

8	medium ripe tomatoes, cut into wedges (about 1½ pounds)
1	small English cucumber, cut into half moons
½	medium red onion, thinly sliced into half moons
3	tablespoons olive oil
1	tablespoon red wine vinegar
½	teaspoon salt
¼	teaspoon freshly ground black pepper
1	small whole-grain baguette or other crusty bread (preferably day-old; about 8 ounces), cut into ¾-inch chunks
⅓	cup basil leaves, coarsely chopped
1	12-ounce package Italian-style pre-cooked chicken sausage

In a large bowl, toss together the tomatoes, cucumber, onion, oil, vinegar, salt, and pepper. Add the bread chunks and basil and toss well so all the bread is well moistened.

Preheat a grill or grill pan over medium-high heat. Add the sausage and cook, turning once or twice, until warmed through and grill marks are formed, about 8 minutes. Serve the sausage, whole, alongside the panzanella.

* DID YOU KNOW?
Chicken and turkey sausage contain ⅓ the calories and ⅓ the fat of regular pork sausage.

flounder with almond topping, saffron rice, and lemon broccolini

The almonds toast and become golden brown as the fish cooks, crowning the mild, flaky flounder with delightful richness and crunch. It's amazing how much taste and appeal you get from such a simple topping.

MAKES 4 SERVINGS

SERVING SIZE
1 FISH FILLET, ¾ CUP RICE, AND 1 CUP BROCCOLINI

PER SERVING
CALORIES 490
TOTAL FAT 12 G
  SAT FAT 1.5 G
  MONO FAT 7 G
  POLY FAT 3 G
PROTEIN 44 G
CARB 51 G
FIBER 4 G
CHOLESTEROL 80 MG
SODIUM 940 MG

EXCELLENT SOURCE OF
FOLATE, IRON, MAGNESIUM, MANGANESE, NIACIN, PHOSPHORUS, POTASSIUM, PROTEIN, SELENIUM, THIAMIN, VITAMIN A, VITAMIN B6, VITAMIN B12, VITAMIN C, VITAMIN D

GOOD SOURCE OF
CALCIUM, COPPER, FIBER, PANTOTHENIC ACID, RIBOFLAVIN, ZINC

Cooking spray
4   6-ounce flounder fillets
½   cup sliced almonds, finely chopped
1   tablespoon plus 1 teaspoon fresh thyme, chopped, or 1½ teaspoons dried
½   teaspoon finely grated lemon zest
½   teaspoon salt
½   teaspoon freshly ground black pepper
⅛   teaspoon cayenne pepper
3   tablespoons fresh lemon juice
1   recipe Lemon Broccolini (recipe follows)
1   recipe Saffron Rice (recipe follows)

Preheat the oven to 400°F. Spray a baking sheet with cooking spray. Rinse and pat dry the fish fillets and lay them on the baking sheet.

In a small bowl, combine the almonds, thyme, lemon zest, salt, black pepper, and cayenne pepper. Sprinkle ¼ of the nut mixture onto each fillet and gently press into the surface. Bake for 10 minutes, then broil on high until the fish flakes easily and the nuts are golden brown, about 2 minutes. Drizzle with the lemon juice and serve with the Lemon Broccolini and Saffron Rice.

* saffron rice

This is one place I prefer to use white rice because it really lets the brilliant orange-yellow color and distinctive taste of the saffron come through. Cooking the rice in chicken broth makes it extra-rich and flavorful. It makes a tasty and gorgeous background for the nutty fish and lemony broccolini.

MAKES 4 SERVINGS

SERVING SIZE
¾ CUP

2 cups low-sodium chicken broth
Generous pinch of saffron threads
1 cup long-grain white rice
½ teaspoon salt

Put the broth and saffron into a medium pot and bring to a boil. Stir in the rice and salt, then cover and simmer over low heat until all the water is absorbed, about 20 minutes.

* lemon broccolini

Broccolini is a cross between regular broccoli and Chinese broccoli and has longer, more tender stems and a slightly sweeter taste than regular broccoli. Here it gets the lemon-olive oil treatment, which makes it lip-smackingly delicious.

MAKES 4 SERVINGS

SERVING SIZE
1 CUP

1 pound broccolini
1 tablespoon fresh lemon juice
1 tablespoon olive oil
1 teaspoon finely grated lemon zest
¼ teaspoon salt
Pinch of freshly ground black pepper

Wash and trim the broccolini. Place it in a steamer basket fitted over a pot of boiling water. Cover and steam until it is crisp yet tender, about 5 minutes. Drain. In a large bowl, whisk together the lemon juice, oil, zest, salt, and pepper. Add the broccolini to the bowl and toss to coat.

garlic-basil shrimp

This recipe wins hands down in the easy, fast, and delicious category. It takes just 6 minutes to cook, you hardly have to chop a thing, and you get a plateful of garlicky shrimp and warm plump tomatoes in a lovely light sauce.

MAKES 4 SERVINGS

SERVING SIZE
1 CUP SHRIMP MIXTURE AND
¾ CUP ORZO

PER SERVING
CALORIES 380
TOTAL FAT 10 G
   SAT FAT 1.5 G
   MONO FAT 5.5 G
   POLY FAT 2 G
PROTEIN 35 G
CARB 35 G
FIBER 4 G
CHOLESTEROL 215 MG
SODIUM 490 MG

EXCELLENT SOURCE OF
COPPER, IRON, MAGNESIUM,
MANGANESE, NIACIN,
PHOSPHORUS, PROTEIN,
SELENIUM, VITAMIN B12,
VITAMIN D, VITAMIN K

GOOD SOURCE OF
CALCIUM, FIBER,
POTASSIUM, THIAMIN,
VITAMIN A, VITAMIN B6,
VITAMIN C, ZINC

2	tablespoons olive oil
1¼	pounds large shrimp (20 to 25 per pound), peeled and deveined
3	garlic cloves, minced
⅛	teaspoon crushed red pepper flakes, or more to taste
¾	cup dry white wine
1½	cups grape tomatoes, halved
¼	cup finely chopped fresh basil
	Salt and freshly ground black pepper, to taste
3	cups cooked orzo pasta, preferably whole wheat

Heat the oil in a large heavy skillet over medium-high heat until hot but not smoking, then add the shrimp and cook, turning over once, until just cooked through, about 2 minutes. Transfer with a slotted spoon to a large bowl.

Add the garlic and red pepper flakes to the oil remaining in the skillet and cook until fragrant, about 30 seconds. Add the wine and cook over high heat, stirring occasionally, for 3 minutes. Stir in the tomatoes and basil and season the sauce with salt and pepper. Return the shrimp to the pan and cook just until heated through. Serve with the orzo.

salmon with chickpea ragu

Hooray for the versatile chickpea! It is happily eaten mashed or whole, hot or cold, and it is at home around the world, in the Americas, the Mediterranean, or the Middle East. Here it finds itself in a flavorful herbed vegetable stew as a satisfying bed for buttery salmon.

MAKES 4 SERVINGS

SERVING SIZE
1½ CUPS CHICKPEA RAGU
AND 1 SALMON FILLET

PER SERVING
CALORIES 460
TOTAL FAT 17 G
   SAT FAT 2.5 G
   MONO FAT 7
   POLY FAT 5 G
PROTEIN 46 G
CARB 30 G
FIBER 6 G
CHOLESTEROL 95 MG
SODIUM 550 MG

EXCELLENT SOURCE OF
COPPER, FIBER, IRON,
MAGNESIUM, NIACIN,
PANTOTHENIC ACID,
PHOSPHORUS, POTASSIUM,
PROTEIN, RIBOFLAVIN,
SELENIUM, THIAMIN,
VITAMIN A, VITAMIN B6,
VITAMIN B12, VITAMIN C,
VITAMIN D, VITAMIN K

GOOD SOURCE OF
CALCIUM, FOLATE,
MANGANESE, ZINC

1	tablespoon olive oil
1	small onion, chopped
1	large carrot, peeled and diced
1	large zucchini, diced
2	cloves garlic, minced
2	tablespoons tomato paste
4	cups low-sodium chicken broth
1	15.5-ounce can chickpeas (preferably low-sodium), drained and rinsed
1	cup basil leaves, sliced into ribbons, plus more for garnish
½	teaspoon salt
½	teaspoon freshly ground black pepper
4	6-ounce skinless salmon fillets

Heat the oil in a large skillet over medium-high heat, add the onion, and cook until soft and translucent, about 3 minutes. Add the carrot, zucchini, and garlic and cook, stirring, until the carrots are firm-tender, 4 to 5 minutes. Add the tomato paste, stirring to incorporate completely. Add the chicken broth and chickpeas and bring to a boil. Reduce the heat to low and cook, covered, until the liquid thickens slightly, 8 to 10 minutes.

Remove the skillet from the heat, add 1 cup of the basil and ¼ teaspoon each of salt and pepper, and stir to incorporate. Cover to keep warm while you cook the salmon.

Preheat the broiler. Season the salmon with the remaining ¼ teaspoon each of salt and pepper. Broil the salmon for 8 to 10 minutes per inch thickness, turning once.

To serve, spoon 1½ cups of the chickpea ragu into a shallow bowl or rimmed plate. Top with a fillet of salmon and garnish with ribbons of basil.

prosciutto-wrapped cod with pesto potatoes and green beans

Talk about fast! You barely need twenty minutes to make this unbelievably delicious and impressive-looking dish. The decadent pairing of flaky rich cod and cured Italian ham give new meaning to surf-and-turf.

MAKES 4 SERVINGS

SERVING SIZE
1 PROSCIUTTO-WRAPPED
FILLET AND 1¾ CUPS
POTATOES AND GREEN
BEANS

PER SERVING
CALORIES 410
TOTAL FAT 8 G
  SAT FAT 1.5 G
  MONO FAT 0 G
  POLY FAT 0.5 G
PROTEIN 42G
CARB 43 G
FIBER 7 G
CHOLESTEROL 90 MG
SODIUM 750 MG

EXCELLENT SOURCE OF
COPPER, FIBER,
FOLATE, MAGNESIUM,
MANGANESE, NIACIN,
PHOSPHORUS, POTASSIUM,
PROTEIN, SELENIUM,
THIAMIN, VITAMIN A,
VITAMIN B6, VITAMIN B12,
VITAMIN C, VITAMIN K

GOOD SOURCE OF
CALCIUM, IRON,
RIBOFLAVIN,
VITAMIN D, ZINC

4	6-ounce cod fillets
¼	teaspoon salt
¼	teaspoon freshly ground black pepper
2	ounces thinly sliced prosciutto
	Cooking spray
1	recipe Pesto Potatoes and Green Beans (recipe follows)

Season the fish on both sides with the salt and pepper. Wrap one wide or two thin slices of prosciutto around each piece of cod. Spray a large nonstick skillet with cooking spray and preheat it over medium-high heat. Add the fish fillets and cook until the prosciutto is crisp and the fish is cooked through, 3 to 4 minutes per side. Serve with the Pesto Potatoes and Green Beans.

✻ DID YOU KNOW?
The fat found in fish—called omega-3—can help protect your heart, alleviate symptoms of arthritis, keep your brain healthy, and improve your mood. It's also a beauty must—key for maintaining healthy, dewy skin.

* pesto potatoes **and green beans**

This dish is a real two-for-one deal where you get both sides in one super-simple dish. It's a warm potato and green bean salad dressed in aromatic basil pesto that's a great match for the Prosciutto-Wrapped Cod. It is also excellent at room temperature the next day if you are lucky enough to have leftovers.

MAKES 4 SERVINGS

SERVING SIZE
1¾ CUPS

1½ pounds red new potatoes, cut into
        1-inch chunks
1   pound green beans, trimmed and cut
        into 1-inch pieces
3   tablespoons store-bought basil pesto
        Salt and freshly ground black pepper to taste

Place the potatoes in a large steamer basket fitted over a pot of boiling water. Cover and steam for 6 minutes. Add the green beans to the potatoes in the steamer and continue to cook, covered, for another 4 minutes. Transfer the vegetables to a large serving bowl. Add the pesto and stir to coat evenly. Season with salt and pepper and serve.

mussels provençal with blt frisée salad

Mussels are an everyday food in France and Belgium, and when you try this recipe you'll see why. They are fast and effortless to make, fun to eat, and utterly delicious. They are an upscale treat for grown-ups, but kids love them too because they get to eat out of a shell. This recipe makes two servings because that's all that fits in a typical pot. If you want to serve four, just double the recipe and use two pots or a jumbo stock pot.

MAKES 2 SERVINGS

SERVING SIZE
ABOUT 20 MUSSELS,
2 BREAD SLICES,
AND 1½ CUPS SALAD

PER SERVING
CALORIES 570
TOTAL FAT 24 G
    SAT FAT 4 G
    MONO FAT 14 G
    POLY FAT 3 G
PROTEIN 33 G
CARB 54 G
FIBER 10 G
CHOLESTEROL 50 MG
SODIUM 1410 MG

EXCELLENT SOURCE OF
CALCIUM, COPPER,
FIBER, FOLATE, IRON,
MAGNESIUM, MANGANESE,
NIACIN, PANTOTHENIC ACID,
PHOSPHORUS, POTASSIUM,
PROTEIN, RIBOFLAVIN,
SELENIUM, THIAMIN,
VITAMIN A, VITAMIN B6,
VITAMIN B12, VITAMIN C,
VITAMIN K, ZINC

2	teaspoons olive oil
2	shallots, finely chopped (about ½ cup)
2	cloves garlic, very thinly sliced
1	teaspoon chopped fresh thyme, or ½ teaspoon dried
1	15-ounce can whole tomatoes, drained and chopped
1	tablespoon tomato paste
⅓	cup dry white wine
2	pounds cultivated mussels, rinsed and debearded
4	slices whole-wheat baguette
1	recipe BLT Frisée Salad (recipe follows)

In a large pot, heat the oil over medium heat. Add the shallots and cook, stirring occasionally, until softened, 3 to 5 minutes. Add the garlic and thyme and cook, stirring, until fragrant, 1 to 2 minutes longer. Stir in the canned tomatoes and tomato paste and simmer, partially covered, for 10 minutes.

Add the wine and bring to a boil over high heat. Add the mussels, cover, and cook just until the mussels have opened, about 3 minutes; discard any mussels that have not opened. Transfer the mussels and sauce to individual serving bowls and serve with the bread and the salad on the side.

* blt frisée salad

The tried and true trio of bacon, lettuce, and tomato make a scrumptious side for the mussels. Something magical happens when you serve shellfish with pork, especially when the pork has a deep smokiness, like the lean Canadian bacon used here.

MAKES 2 SERVINGS

SERVING SIZE
1½ CUPS

Cooking spray
3   slices Canadian bacon (3 ounces), diced
1   tablespoon plus 2 teaspoons olive oil
2   teaspoons red wine vinegar
⅛   teaspoon salt
      Pinch of freshly ground black pepper
1   medium head frisée lettuce (about 3 cups
          lightly packed), torn
2   medium tomatoes, seeded and diced

Spray a nonstick skillet with cooking spray and heat over medium-high heat. Add the Canadian bacon and cook, stirring occasionally, until the bacon is crisp, about 5 minutes. Remove from the heat.

In a large bowl, whisk together the oil, vinegar, salt, and pepper. Add the frisée and toss until well coated. Divide the frisée between 2 serving plates. Top with the diced tomatoes and crisped bacon and serve.

★ DID YOU KNOW?
Pork doesn't always deserve its fatty reputation. Canadian bacon gives you that smoky flavor with just 2 grams of fat per slice. And pork tenderloin is nearly as lean as skinless chicken breast, weighing in at just 4 grams of fat in 3 ounces. Lean ham and pork loin are also good skinny pig choices. Just watch out for the ribs and shoulder cuts, where 3 ounces can have up to 20 (yes, two-zero!) grams of fat.

sesame shrimp fried rice with cabbage

This dish is a ten-minute meal in a bowl that gives you all the full-flavor satisfaction of fried rice without loads of grease and salt. Make sure you use very cold cooked rice (hello leftover Chinese food), or you will wind up with a sticky mess.

MAKES 4 SERVINGS

SERVING SIZE
2 CUPS

PER SERVING
CALORIES 460
TOTAL FAT 12 G
　SAT FAT 1.5 G
　MONO FAT 4.5 G
　POLY FAT 3.5 G
PROTEIN 32 G
CARB 55 G
FIBER 7 G
CHOLESTEROL 220 MG
SODIUM 580 MG

EXCELLENT SOURCE OF
COPPER, FIBER, IRON, MAGNESIUM, MANGANESE, NIACIN, PHOSPHORUS, PROTEIN, SELENIUM, THIAMIN, VITAMIN B6, VITAMIN B12 VITAMIN C, VITAMIN D, VITAMIN K, ZINC

GOOD SOURCE OF
CALCIUM, FOLATE, PANTOTHENIC ACID, POTASSIUM, VITAMIN A

1　tablespoon canola oil
1　pound peeled cleaned small shrimp
4　scallions (white and green parts), thinly sliced
1　tablespoon grated peeled fresh ginger
5　cups thinly sliced green cabbage, cut crosswise into 3-inch pieces
1　tablespoon toasted sesame oil
4　cups very cold cooked brown rice
3　tablespoons low-sodium soy sauce
2　tablespoons sesame seeds, toasted in a dry skillet over medium-high heat for about 1 minute, until golden

Heat the oil in a very large nonstick skillet or wok over high heat. Add the shrimp, scallions, and ginger and cook, stirring frequently, until the shrimp turn pink, about 1½ minutes. Add the cabbage and continue cooking, stirring occasionally, until it begins to soften but is still somewhat crisp, about 2 minutes more. Transfer the shrimp-cabbage mixture to a bowl.

　Heat the sesame oil in the same skillet or wok over medium-high heat. Add the rice and cook, stirring frequently, until heated through, about 3 minutes. Add the shrimp-cabbage mixture back to the skillet, stir in the soy sauce and sesame seeds, and serve.

pasta primavera

Brilliantly colored garden vegetables and herbs tossed with linguini
and covered in a light creamy sauce—this dish is freshness by the forkful.

MAKES 4 SERVINGS

SERVING SIZE
2 CUPS PASTA PLUS
2 TABLESPOON CHEESE
AND 1 TABLESPOON BASIL

PER SERVING
CALORIES 480
TOTAL FAT 11 G
    SAT FAT 3 G
    MONO FAT 3 G
    POLY FAT 0.5 G
PROTEIN 22 G
CARB 76 G
FIBER 10 G
CHOLESTEROL 10 MG
SODIUM 610 MG

EXCELLENT SOURCE OF
CALCIUM, FIBER, POTASSIUM,
PROTEIN, VITAMIN A,
VITAMIN C, VITAMIN K

GOOD SOURCE OF
IRON, MANGANESE,
NIACIN, PHOSPHORUS,
RIBOFLAVIN, SELENIUM,
VITAMIN B6

¾   pound whole-wheat linguine
1   tablespoon olive oil
3   cloves garlic, minced
1   red bell pepper, seeded and cut into strips
½   pound thin asparagus, trimmed and cut
        into 2-inch pieces
1   cup grape or cherry tomatoes, sliced in half
1   cup sliced button mushrooms
1   tablespoon all-purpose flour
1   cup low-sodium chicken broth
½   cup low-fat (1%) milk
½   teaspoon salt
½   teaspoon freshly ground black pepper
1   large carrot, peeled and sliced into strips
        with a peeler (about 2 cups carrot ribbons)
½   cup (1½ ounces) grated Parmesan cheese
½   cup shredded basil

Bring a large pot of water to a boil. Add the pasta and
cook until al dente according to the directions on the
package. Before draining, reserve ½ cup of the pasta
cooking water.

Heat the oil in a large skillet over medium-high heat.
Cook the garlic, stirring, until softened, about 1 minute.
Add the bell peppers and cook, stirring, until they begin
to soften, about 3 minutes. Add the asparagus, tomatoes, and mushrooms. Cook, stirring, until softened,
an additional 5 minutes. Stir in the flour and cook for
1 minute more. Add the chicken broth, milk, salt, and
pepper and bring to a boil; reduce the heat to a simmer
and cook until the liquid has thickened slightly, about
5 minutes. Stir in the carrot strips.

Toss the pasta with the vegetables and sauce, adding
the pasta water, if necessary, to loosen the mixture.
Serve garnished with the Parmesan and basil.

asian noodle bowl

You can substitute whatever vegetables you have on hand to create this fabulous chicken, veggie, and noodle dish that is heady with Asian flavor and aroma.

MAKES 4 SERVINGS

SERVING SIZE
2½ CUPS NOODLE MIXTURE

PER SERVING
CALORIES 530
TOTAL FAT 8 G
   SAT FAT 1 G
   MONO FAT 3.5 G
   POLY FAT 2.5 G
PROTEIN 38 G
CARB 77 G
FIBER 11 G
CHOLESTEROL 65 MG
SODIUM 800 MG

EXCELLENT SOURCE OF
FIBER, FOLATE, IRON,
NIACIN, PHOSPHORUS,
POTASSIUM, PROTEIN,
RIBOFLAVIN, SELENIUM,
VITAMIN A, VITAMIN B6,
VITAMIN C, VITAMIN K

GOOD SOURCE OF
COPPER, MAGNESIUM,
MANGANESE, PANTOTHENIC
ACID, THIAMIN, ZINC

8	ounces soba noodles or whole-wheat spaghetti
2	teaspoons canola oil
1	bunch scallions (white and green parts), sliced (¼ cup reserved for garnish)
1	tablespoon minced peeled fresh ginger
1	pound skinless boneless chicken breasts, thinly sliced
1	15-ounce can baby corn, drained
½	pound broccoli florets (about 3 cups)
½	pound fresh shiitake mushrooms, stemmed and sliced
1	red bell pepper, seeded and thinly sliced
⅓	cup low-sodium chicken broth
¼	cup low-sodium soy sauce
1	teaspoon toasted sesame oil

Bring a large pot of water to a boil. Add the noodles or pasta and cook according to the directions on the package.

Heat the canola oil in a wok or very large skillet over medium heat. Add the scallions and ginger and cook, stirring, until fragrant but not browned, about 30 seconds. Add the chicken and cook, stirring occasionally, until just cooked through, 4 to 5 minutes. Add the baby corn, broccoli, mushrooms, pepper slices, broth, and soy sauce and cook, stirring occasionally, until the broccoli is bright green and crisp-tender and the peppers are crisp-tender, 5 to 6 minutes. Add the noodles and sesame oil and toss to combine. Divide among 4 bowls and garnish with the reserved ¼ cup of scallions.

shrimp fra diavlo **with spinach**

This recipe is your cheat sheet for whipping up an incredible meal even when your fridge is empty, a tasty accomplishment you're sure to earn extra credit for with your family and friends. Just make sure you keep shrimp in the freezer—it thaws in five minutes—and although I call for fresh, you can substitute 1½ cups of frozen chopped spinach.

MAKES 4 SERVINGS

SERVING SIZE
2 CUPS

PER SERVING
CALORIES 570
TOTAL FAT 10 G
    SAT FAT 1.5 G
    MONO FAT 5.5 G
    POLY FAT 2 G
PROTEIN 38 G
CARB 76 G
FIBER 13 G
CHOLESTEROL 170 MG
SODIUM 560 MG

EXCELLENT SOURCE OF
COPPER, FIBER,
FOLATE, IRON,
MAGNESIUM, MANGANESE,
NIACIN, PHOSPHORUS,
PROTEIN, SELENIUM,
THIAMIN, VITAMIN A,
VITAMIN B6,VITAMIN B12,
VITAMIN C,VITAMIN D,
VITAMIN K, ZINC

GOOD SOURCE OF
PANTOTHENIC ACID,
POTASSIUM, RIBOFLAVIN

¾ pound whole-wheat thin spaghetti
2   tablespoons olive oil
1   medium red onion, thinly sliced
5   cloves garlic, minced
1   14.5-ounce no-salt-added diced tomatoes
1   cup dry white wine
1   tablespoon tomato paste
1   teaspoon dried oregano
½   teaspoon crushed red pepper flakes
½   teaspoon salt
½   teaspoon freshly ground black pepper
1   pound large shrimp, peeled and deveined
3   cups lightly packed baby spinach leaves
        (3 ounces), coarsely chopped

Bring a large pot of water to a boil. Add the spaghetti and cook until al dente and according to the directions on the package.

While the pasta is cooking, heat 1 tablespoon of the oil in a large pot over medium-high heat. Add the onion and cook, stirring, until softened, about 3 minutes. Add the garlic and cook, stirring, for 1 additional minute. Add the tomatoes, wine, tomato paste, the remaining 1 tablespoon of olive oil, the oregano, red pepper flakes, salt, and pepper, and simmer until the sauce thickens slightly, 8 to 10 minutes. Add the shrimp and spinach and cook, stirring, until the shrimp is just cooked through, about 5 minutes. Remove from the heat. Add the drained cooked pasta to the sauce and toss until well combined.

penne with zucchini and mint

The bright, clean flavors and simplicity of this dish make it destined for regular rotation at your home as it is in mine. Toasting the garlic in the oil first infuses the dish with deep flavor and the fresh mint adds an unexpected wow factor.

MAKES 4 SERVINGS

SERVING SIZE
2 CUPS

PER SERVING
CALORIES 530
TOTAL FAT 21 G
  SAT FAT 4 G
  MONO FAT 10 G
  POLY FAT 2 G
PROTEIN 18 G
CARB 70 G
FIBER 9 G
CHOLESTEROL 10 MG
SODIUM 710 MG

EXCELLENT SOURCE OF
CALCIUM, FIBER,
PROTEIN, VITAMIN C

GOOD SOURCE OF
IRON, MANGANESE,
POTASSIUM, VITAMIN B6

¾ box (12 ounces) whole-wheat penne pasta
¼ cup olive oil
4 large cloves garlic, thinly sliced
2 medium zucchini (8 ounces each), sliced into
    ¼-inch-thick half moons
2 tablespoons fresh lemon juice
1 teaspoon finely grated lemon zest
¾ teaspoon salt
½ teaspoon freshly ground black pepper
½ cup freshly grated Parmesan cheese
    (1½ ounces)
¼ cup chopped fresh mint leaves

Bring a large pot of water to a boil. Add the penne and cook until al dente and according to the directions on the package.

Meanwhile, add the oil and garlic to a large deep skillet and cook over a medium-low heat, stirring frequently, until the garlic is lightly golden, about 6 minutes; be careful not to let the garlic burn. Add the zucchini. Cover and cook, stirring occasionally, until the zucchini is tender, 6 to 8 minutes. Remove from the heat. Stir in the lemon juice, zest, salt, and pepper.

Drain the pasta, then return it to the pasta pot. Add the zucchini mixture, Parmesan cheese, and mint, and toss to combine.

✳ EATING WELL TIP

Fresh herbs not only light up a dish with flavor, aroma, and color, they also provide nutrients like vitamin A and antioxidants. To store them, wrap the bunch in a slightly moist paper towel, place in a plastic bag, and put them in the crisper in the refrigerator, where they should keep for 5 to 10 days, depending on the tenderness of the leaf.

fettuccine with crab & asparagus

Succulent crab mingled with fresh, fragrant herbs and crisp tender asparagus in a wine-infused lemon garlic sauce. It's a simple pasta dish, effortlessly elevated to fabulous.

MAKES 4 SERVINGS

SERVING SIZE
3 CUPS PASTA MIXTURE,
¼ CUP SAUCE, AND 1
TABLESPOON EACH PARSLEY
AND TARRAGON GARNISH

PER SERVING
CALORIES 560
TOTAL FAT 11 G
  SAT FAT 1.5 G
  MONO FAT 5.5 G
  POLY FAT 2.5 G
PROTEIN 39 G
CARB 72 G
FIBER 13 G
CHOLESTEROL 115 MG
SODIUM 820 MG

EXCELLENT SOURCE OF
CALCIUM, COPPER, FIBER,
FOLATE, IRON,
MAGNESIUM, MANGANESE,
NIACIN, PHOSPHORUS,
POTASSIUM, PROTEIN,
SELENIUM, THIAMIN,
VITAMIN A, VITAMIN B6,
VITAMIN B12, VITAMIN C,
VITAMIN K, ZINC

GOOD SOURCE OF
PANTOTHENIC ACID,
RIBOFLAVIN

12	ounces whole-wheat fettuccine
2	tablespoons olive oil
4	cloves garlic, thinly sliced
1	cup dry white wine
1	cup fish stock or water
1	bunch (¾ pound) asparagus, trimmed and cut into 1-inch pieces
3	tablespoons fresh lemon juice
2	teaspoons finely grated lemon zest
½	teaspoon salt
¼	teaspoon freshly ground black pepper
1	pound cooked lump crabmeat, drained
¼	cup chopped fresh parsley, plus more for garnish
¼	cup chopped fresh tarragon, plus more for garnish

Bring a large pot of water to a boil. Add the fettuccine and cook until al dente and according to the directions on the package.

Meanwhile, add the oil and garlic to a large deep skillet and cook over low heat, stirring, until the garlic is lightly golden, about 5 minutes; be careful not to let the garlic burn. Add the wine and stock and bring to a boil; reduce the heat to a vigorous simmer and cook until the liquid has reduced slightly, about 5 minutes. Add the asparagus, lemon juice, lemon zest, salt, and pepper and cook until the asparagus is just cooked, about 3 minutes. Add the crabmeat and ¼ cup each of parsley and tarragon, and stir to combine until the crabmeat is heated through, 1 to 2 minutes.

Drain the pasta and return it to the pasta pot. Add the crabmeat mixture and stir to combine. Serve garnished with the additional herbs.

ravioli toss

This recipe barely counts as cooking, yet you can take full credit as everyone devours it. It is one of those "saves the day" dishes you will make over and over again.

MAKES 4 SERVINGS

SERVING SIZE
2 CUPS

PER SERVING
CALORIES 450
TOTAL FAT 20 G
  SAT FAT 8 G
  MONO FAT 5 G
  POLY FAT 1.5 G
PROTEIN 18 G
CARB 51 G
FIBER 7 G
CHOLESTEROL 75 MG
SODIUM 1000 MG

EXCELLENT SOURCE OF
CALCIUM, FIBER,
PROTEIN, VITAMIN A,
VITAMIN C, VITAMIN K

GOOD SOURCE OF
IRON

4	plum tomatoes (about ¾ pound), chopped (about 2 cups)
1	12-ounce jar roasted red peppers, drained, rinsed, and chopped
2	tablespoons olive oil
1½	tablespoons red wine vinegar
1	clove garlic, minced
	Salt and freshly ground black pepper to taste
1	pound store-bought fresh or frozen cheese ravioli, preferably whole-wheat
5	cups arugula leaves, coarsely chopped (about 5 ounces)

In a large bowl, combine the tomatoes, roasted peppers, olive oil, vinegar, and garlic. Season to taste with salt and black pepper. Let the vegetable mixture sit at room temperature while you are cooking the ravioli.

Cook the ravioli according the directions on the package. Drain and add to the vegetables along with the arugula. Toss and serve at once.

✳ EATING WELL TIP
Yes, you can have that big bowlful of pasta you crave without overdoing carbs or calories. The secret is keeping servings to a generous, but not excessive, 3 ounces of uncooked pasta per person (1½ cups cooked), and amping it up with lots of vegetables and chunks of lean protein. Also, go for whole-wheat pasta, which is no longer the cardboard of yore. Now they make it tender and mild and even have whole-wheat blends for the best of both worlds.

dinner—
kickin' back

* Kickin' back dinners have a **RELAXED, EASYGOING PACE** for days when you have a little more time and **YOU MAY BE UP FOR SOME CASUAL ENTERTAINING OR COOKING TO GET AHEAD FOR THE WEEK,** but you just don't want to work too hard. These meals are supremely satisfying—soups, stews, chili, marinated meats, roasted vegetables, steak house–inspired dinners, and comfort casseroles that will feed a crowd. Each is designed so you can **PUT EXTRAORDINARY FOOD ON THE TABLE** without putting a kink in that laid-back feeling.

sirloin steak with grainy mustard sauce and parmesan steak "fries"

This flavor-packed sauce is a breeze to whip up and brings out the most in the juicy beef. Served with ripe beefsteak tomato slices and steak "fries," this meal really satisfies that steak house craving.

MAKES 4 SERVINGS

SERVING SIZE
5 TO 7 SLICES STEAK,
ABOUT 2 TABLESPOONS
SAUCE, 3 TOMATO SLICES,
AND 4 WEDGES OF "FRIES"

PER SERVING
CALORIES 420
TOTAL FAT 15 G
  SAT FAT 3 G
  MONO FAT 7 G
  POLY FAT 3 G
PROTEIN 32 G
CARB 41 G
FIBER 3 G
CHOLESTEROL 40 MG
SODIUM 640 MG

EXCELLENT SOURCE OF
IRON, MANGANESE, NIACIN,
PHOSPHORUS, POTASSIUM,
PROTEIN, SELENIUM,
VITAMIN B6, VITAMIN C,
VITAMIN K, ZINC

GOOD SOURCE OF
CALCIUM, COPPER, FIBER,
FOLATE, MAGNESIUM,
PANTOTHENIC ACID,
RIBOFLAVIN, THIAMIN,
VITAMIN A, VITAMIN B12

4	teaspoons canola oil
1	small shallot, finely chopped (about ¼ cup)
1	tablespoon all-purpose flour
2	cups low-sodium chicken broth
1	boneless sirloin steak, about 1¼ pounds
¼	teaspoon salt, plus more to taste
⅛	teaspoon freshly ground black pepper, plus more to taste
3	tablespoons whole-grain mustard
2	large ripe beefsteak tomatoes, thickly sliced
1	recipe Parmesan Steak "Fries" (recipe follows)

In a medium saucepan, heat 2 teaspoons of the oil over medium heat. Add the shallot and cook, stirring, until softened, about 2 minutes. Stir in the flour and cook for 30 seconds. Stir in the broth, bring to a boil, and cook until reduced to 1 cup, about 10 minutes.

Meanwhile, cook the steak. Pat the steak dry and sprinkle both sides with ¼ teaspoon of salt and ⅛ teaspoon of pepper. Heat the remaining 2 teaspoons of oil in a heavy skillet over medium-high heat. Cook the steak, turning once, for 6 to 8 minutes total for medium rare, or to desired doneness. Transfer to a cutting board and cover with foil to keep warm.

Discard the fat from the pan. Add the reduced stock mixture and bring to a simmer, being sure to scrape up any brown bits from the bottom of the pan. Stir in the mustard and season to taste with salt and pepper. Pour any juices that have accumulated on the board into the sauce. Thinly slice the steak and divide among 4 plates. Spoon the sauce over the steak and serve the sliced tomatoes and the "fries" alongside.

* EATING WELL TIP
Thinly slicing steak is a great way to make an appropriate serving look more plentiful and be more satisfying.

* parmesan steak "fries"

If you know anything about me, you know that French fries are my weakness. I love them every which way—thick, thin, fast-food, or fancy restaurant style. I've been on a mission to get my fry fix in a healthier way. With these thick, tender-on-the-inside, crisp-on-the-outside, Parmesan-crusted wedges I am happy to say: mission accomplished.

MAKES 4 SERVINGS

SERVING SIZE
4 WEDGES

Cooking spray
2   large russet potatoes (about 1½ pounds total), unpeeled
1   tablespoon canola oil
¼   cup grated Parmesan cheese (¾ ounce)
Salt to taste

Preheat the oven to 450°F. Spray a baking sheet with cooking spray.

Cut each of the potatoes in half lengthwise. Rest each half on its flat side and cut each half lengthwise, straight down into 4 even slices. You will have 16 slices altogether. Cut the rounded edge off of the outermost slices so each slice can lie completely flat on either side. Put the potatoes into a medium-size bowl and toss with the oil.

Place the potatoes on the prepared baking sheet and bake for 20 minutes. Sprinkle the potatoes with cheese and continue to bake for another 15 to 20 minutes, until they are crisp and golden brown; there is no need to turn them. Season with salt and serve immediately.

THE DISH ON SALT

Salt unlocks the flavor and aroma in food and is an essential element in most recipes. But most Americans get way too much sodium—up to double the recommended daily cap of 2300 mg. Here are a few ideas for using salt wisely.

GET FRESH

Three-quarters of the salt in our diets comes from processed foods like prepared meals, cured meats, and canned foods. Simply cooking at home with fresh ingredients is one of the best ways to keep sodium intake down without even thinking about it. So focus on what's fresh and seasonal.

TAKE CHARGE

When buying canned and packaged ingredients opt for reduced-sodium varieties. You may need to add salt in cooking or at the table to get the taste you want, but chances are you'll add less than the food company does, and this way you are in the driver's seat.

SPICE IT UP

Use flavorful and aromatic ingredients like herbs, spices, chili peppers, garlic, citrus peel, juices, and vinegars liberally to punch up taste healthfully.

KOSHER, SEA, OR IODIZED?

Kosher and sea salts are less dense than standard table salt, so they have less sodium per teaspoon. The catch is you need more to get the same amount of saltiness, so it could just even out in the end. Also, kosher and sea salts are not fortified with iodine, a mineral essential for thyroid health, as table salt usually is. Unrefined sea salt contains scant amounts of minerals, like magnesium and calcium and has more nuanced flavor than regular salt, but when used in cooking the flavor difference is basically undetectable. I usually choose iodized salt for cooking and sea salt at the table and for finishing a dish.

porcini crusted filet mignon with creamed spinach and herbed mashed potatoes

A crust of ground porcini mushrooms that crisps as the steak cooks gives the tender meat an incredible flavor and texture you can't quite put your finger on if you are not in the know. It's a huge reward for a little extra effort. Served with the mashed potatoes and creamed spinach, it is the centerpiece of the ultimate inspired comfort food dinner.

MAKES 4 SERVINGS

SERVING SIZE
1 STEAK, ¾ CUP MASHED POTATOES, AND ¾ CUP CREAMED SPINACH

PER SERVING:
CALORIES 450
TOTAL FAT 14 G
    SAT FAT 6 G
    MONO FAT 5 G
    POLY FAT 1 G
PROTEIN 41 G
CARB 44 G
FIBER 8 G
CHOLESTEROL 95 MG
SODIUM 550 MG

EXCELLENT SOURCE OF
CALCIUM, FIBER, FOLATE, IODINE, IRON, MAGNESIUM, MANGANESE, NIACIN, PHOSPHORUS, POTASSIUM, PROTEIN, RIBOFLAVIN, SELENIUM, THIAMIN, VITAMIN A, VITAMIN B6, VITAMIN B12, VITAMIN C, VITAMIN K, ZINC

GOOD SOURCE OF
COPPER, PANTOTHENIC ACID, VITAMIN D

⅓   cup (⅓ ounce) dried porcini mushrooms
4   1-inch-thick filet mignon steaks (about 1¼ pounds total)
¼   teaspoon salt
⅛   teaspoon freshly ground black pepper
     Cooking spray
1   recipe Herbed Mashed Potatoes (recipe follows)
1   recipe Creamed Spinach (recipe follows)

Process the dried porcini mushrooms in a spice mill or the small bowl of a food processor until they are a fine powder; it's okay if the powder isn't uniform and there are some larger pieces. Transfer the ground mushrooms to a plate. Season the steaks with the salt and pepper on both sides, then press the steaks into the mushroom powder until well coated on both sides.

Spray a large nonstick skillet with cooking spray and preheat over medium heat. Cook the steaks for about 6 minutes per side for medium rare, or to desired doneness. Serve with the Herbed Mashed Potatoes and Creamed Spinach.

* DID YOU KNOW?
Sweet, sour, salty, and bitter are the four tastes we learned about in grade school. But we now know there is a fifth taste, called umami, which is often described as "deliciousness." It's the mouthwatering savory flavor found in aged cheese, meat, mushrooms, and soy and Worcestershire sauces. Umami ingredients amplify each other, so when they are used together you get a major burst of deliciousness.

* herbed mashed potatoes

The heady herbal aroma tells you half the story of how good these potatoes are before you even try them. The pool of melted butter tells you more. Then the picture is complete with the first creamy, luxurious bite. Feel free to use whatever herb combination you have around the house; just about any tender herb—parsley, chervil, or dill—works here.

MAKES 4 SERVINGS

SERVING SIZE
¾ CUP

1¼	pounds Yukon Gold potatoes (about 4 medium), peeled and cut into 1-inch pieces
½	cup low-fat (1%) milk
2	teaspoons finely chopped fresh chives
2	teaspoons finely chopped fresh tarragon leaves
¼	teaspoon salt, plus more to taste
4	teaspoons butter

Place the potatoes in a steamer basket fitted over a large pot of boiling water. Cover and steam until the potatoes are knife-tender, 12 to 15 minutes. Meanwhile, heat the milk in a saucepan over low heat until hot. When the potatoes are done, drain the water and transfer the potatoes to the pot. Add the hot milk and mash to the desired consistency. Stir in the chives, tarragon, and salt. Serve with a teaspoon of butter on top of each serving.

* DID YOU KNOW?
One medium potato has nearly double the potassium of a banana! Potatoes also have vitamin C and essential minerals, and they are a great source of fiber. Keep the skins on for maximum benefits—you'll get about twice the fiber and minerals compared to peeled.

* creamed spinach

I love creamed spinach so much I decided to make it easy enough and healthy enough to enjoy every day. The easy factor comes from using frozen spinach, which is not noticeably different from fresh-cooked in this dish, and the healthy factor comes from a revamped cream sauce made with thickened low-fat milk. A finishing touch of all-natural evaporated milk gives another hit of creaminess without the downsides. If you are skeptical, try it. I have won over the most ardent purists.

MAKES 4 SERVINGS

SERVING SIZE
¾ CUP

2	10-ounce packages frozen chopped spinach, thawed
2	teaspoons olive oil
2	small shallots, finely chopped (about ½ cup)
4	teaspoons all-purpose flour
1½	cups low-fat (1%) milk
½	cup low-sodium chicken broth
2	tablespoons evaporated milk
	Pinch of ground nutmeg
	Salt and freshly ground black pepper to taste

Squeeze all of the water from the spinach. In a large saucepan, heat the oil over medium heat. Add the shallots and cook, stirring, until softened, about 2 minutes. Add the flour to the pan and cook, stirring, for 30 seconds. Add the low-fat milk and broth and cook, scraping up any bits from the bottom of the pan. Bring to a simmer and cook for 2 minutes. Add the spinach and simmer until tender, about 5 minutes. Stir in the evaporated milk and nutmeg, and season to taste with salt and pepper.

* EATING WELL TIP

Evaporated milk is one of my secret weapons in the quest for creamy. It is pure, real milk that has had most of its water evaporated off so it's extra thick and rich. In many recipes it is a great stand-in for cream but with half the calories and a quarter of the fat.
What to do with the leftovers? How about a fabulous chocolate fondue (see page 211)?

aromatic beef stew with butternut squash

Far from your run-of-the-mill beef stew, this one transports you to another land with a unique combination of everyday ingredients. In it tender beef is nestled with chunks of sweet butternut squash in a rich Moroccan spiced tomato sauce. That exotic inspiration continues as it is served over fluffy couscous and topped with crunchy almonds. It's just as easy as, if not easier than, the same-old stew, but so much more rewarding.

MAKES 4 SERVINGS

SERVING SIZE
1¾ CUPS STEW,
¾ CUPS COUSCOUS, AND
1 TABLESPOON ALMONDS

PER SERVING
CALORIES 480
TOTAL FAT 13 G
　SAT FAT 3 G
　MONO FAT 6 G
　POLY FAT 2 G
PROTEIN 34 G
CARB 56 G
FIBER 8 G
CHOLESTEROL 65 MG
SODIUM 150 MG

EXCELLENT SOURCE OF
COPPER, FIBER,
IRON, MAGNESIUM,
MANGANESE, NIACIN,
PHOSPHORUS, POTASSIUM,
PROTEIN, RIBOFLAVIN,
SELENIUM, THIAMIN,
VITAMIN A, VITAMIN B6,
VITAMIN B12, VITAMIN C,
VITAMIN K, ZINC

GOOD SOURCE OF
CALCIUM, FOLATE,
PANTOTHENIC ACID

2	teaspoons olive oil
1	pound stew beef (round or chuck), cut into chunks
1	large onion, chopped
1	tablespoon minced peeled fresh ginger
2	cloves garlic, minced
1	pound peeled cubed butternut squash, cut into 1½-inch cubes (about 2½ cups)
1	14.5-ounce can no-salt-added diced tomatoes
1	8-ounce can no-salt-added tomato sauce
1½	cups low-sodium beef broth
1½	teaspoons ground cumin
1	teaspoon ground cinnamon
½	teaspoon crushed red pepper flakes
3	cups cooked whole-wheat couscous
¼	cup sliced almonds, toasted in a dry skillet over medium-high heat, stirring frequently, until golden brown and fragrant, about 2 minutes
4	teaspoons minced fresh parsley

Heat the oil in a 4-quart saucepan over medium-high heat. Add the beef and cook until browned on all sides, about 5 minutes. Transfer the meat to a plate, leaving the juices in the saucepan. Add the onion and cook, stirring, until softened and translucent, about 6 minutes. Add the ginger and garlic and cook, stirring, for 1 additional minute. Return the beef to the pot and stir in the squash, diced tomatoes, tomato sauce, beef broth, cumin, cinnamon, and red pepper flakes. Bring to a boil, then reduce the heat to a simmer. Cover and cook until the beef is tender, 30 to 35 minutes.

　Spoon the stew over the couscous, and sprinkle each serving with almonds and parsley.

marinated flank steak
with blue cheese sauce

This recipe is a collision of intense umami flavors—steak, balsamic vinegar, aged cheese, grilled onion, and a spike of Worcestershire. Eaten together over peppery radicchio with a side of Grilled Garlic Bread (see page 126), they make a big bang of deliciousness.

MAKES 4 SERVINGS

SERVING SIZE
5 TO 7 SLICES STEAK,
1½ TABLESPOONS BLUE
CHEESE SAUCE,
ABOUT 6 ONION RINGS

PER SERVING
CALORIES 320
TOTAL FAT 18 G
  SAT FAT 5 G
  MONO FAT 9 G
  POLY FAT 1.5 G
PROTEIN 33 G
CARB 7 G
FIBER 1 G
CHOLESTEROL 50 MG
SODIUM 480 MG

EXCELLENT SOURCE OF
NIACIN, PHOSPHORUS,
PROTEIN, SELENIUM,
VITAMIN B6, VITAMIN B12,
VITAMIN K, ZINC

GOOD SOURCE OF
COPPER, FOLATE,
IRON, MAGNESIUM,
PANTOTHENIC ACID,
POTASSIUM, RIBOFLAVIN,
VITAMIN C

3	tablespoons olive oil
1	tablespoon balsamic vinegar
1	teaspoon brown sugar
2	cloves garlic, minced
1¼	pounds flank steak
	Cooking spray
1	medium red onion, cut into ¼-inch-thick rounds
½	teaspoon salt
¼	teaspoon freshly ground black pepper
3	tablespoons crumbled blue cheese
3	tablespoons low-fat buttermilk
	Dash of Worcestershire sauce
12	radicchio leaves
2	tablespoon chopped fresh parsley

In a small bowl, whisk together 2 tablespoons of the olive oil, the balsamic vinegar, brown sugar, and garlic. Put the steak into a sealable plastic bag with the marinade and put in the refrigerator for at least 1 hour and up to 8 hours. Allow the meat to come to room temperature before cooking.

Spray a large grill pan with cooking spray and preheat it over medium-high heat, or prepare an outdoor grill. Brush both sides of the onion slices with the remaining tablespoon of oil and grill until they are softened, about 6 minutes per side. Separate into rings and set aside.

Remove the meat from the marinade and season both sides with salt and pepper. Discard the marinade. Grill the meat over medium-high heat for about 5 minutes per side for medium rare. Let rest for 5 to 10 minutes before slicing thinly on a bias.

In a small bowl, combine the blue cheese and buttermilk with a fork, mashing until creamy. Stir in the Worcestershire sauce.

Arrange 3 radicchio leaves and a pile of onions on each serving plate. Top with the slices of steak. Drizzle with the blue cheese sauce and top with a sprinkle of parsley.

baked beans with ham
and green apple and cabbage salad

These tangy sweet baked beans have big chunks of smoky ham—and lots of them—making it a main course that even satisfies the likes of my devotedly carnivorous husband.

MAKES 4 SERVINGS

SERVING SIZE
1¼ CUPS BAKED BEANS
AND 1¾ CUPS SALAD

PER SERVING
CALORIES 570
TOTAL FAT 13 G
   SAT FAT 2 G
   MONO FAT 6.5 G
   POLY FAT 2.5 G
PROTEIN 33 G
CARB 81 G
FIBER 18 G
CHOLESTEROL 45 MG
SODIUM 1260 MG

EXCELLENT SOURCE OF
CALCIUM, FIBER,
IRON, MAGNESIUM,
MANGANESE, NIACIN,
PHOSPHORUS, POTASSIUM,
PROTEIN, SELENIUM,
THIAMIN, VITAMIN A,
VITAMIN B6, VITAMIN C,
VITAMIN K, ZINC

GOOD SOURCE OF
COPPER, IODINE,
RIBOFLAVIN

2	teaspoons canola oil
1	medium onion, diced
12	ounces smoked Virginia ham, cut into ¼-inch cubes
2	cloves garlic, minced
2	15-ounce cans navy beans (preferably low-sodium), drained and rinsed
1	15-ounce can crushed tomatoes (preferably no salt added)
½	cup water
¼	cup unsulfured molasses
1	tablespoon Dijon mustard
1	tablespoon cider vinegar
½	teaspoon freshly ground black pepper
1	recipe Green Apple and Cabbage Salad (recipe follows)

Heat the oil in a large skillet over medium-high heat. Add the onion and cook until softened and translucent, about 5 minutes. Add the ham and garlic and cook for an additional 3 minutes. Stir in the beans, crushed tomatoes, water, molasses, mustard, vinegar, and pepper. Bring to a boil, then reduce the heat to a simmer. Cover and cook until about half of the liquid is absorbed, 15 minutes. Serve alongside the Green Apple and Cabbage Salad.

* DID YOU KNOW?

Don't let their small size fool you—beans pack a mighty nutritional punch. They are loaded with protein, iron, folic acid, magnesium, iron, and fiber. They are a rich source of antioxidants and they have been shown to help with weight management. All that and you can't beat their price or versatility. Canned beans are a super convenience food. Just buy the low-sodium variety (organic and natural brands tend to have less sodium to begin with) and give them a good rinse to remove sodium further before using.

* green apple and cabbage salad

This crisp bright salad is like a rough-cut, chunky slaw with a tangy vinaigrette dressing. It is refreshing and hearty all at once.

MAKES 4 SERVINGS

SERVING SIZE
1¾ CUPS SALAD

5	tablespoons red wine vinegar
¼	cup water
2	tablespoons sugar
4	teaspoons canola oil
1½	teaspoons Dijon mustard
½	teaspoon salt
¼	teaspoon freshly ground black pepper
1	small head red cabbage (1 pound), leaves cut into 1-inch squares
1	large green apple (about 8 ounces), skin on, cored and sliced into thin half-moons
3	scallions (white and green parts), chopped (about ½ cup)

In a large bowl, whisk together the vinegar, water, sugar, oil, mustard, salt, and pepper. Add the cabbage, apple, and scallions and toss to combine.

* green salad with shallot vinaigrette

One bite and you'll know why this simple dressing is such a classic. You'll also wonder why you ever bothered to buy the bottled stuff.

MAKES 4 SERVINGS

SERVING SIZE
2 CUPS

2	tablespoons olive oil
1	tablespoon finely chopped shallot
1	tablespoon white wine vinegar
2	teaspoons Dijon mustard
¼	teaspoon salt
	Pinch of freshly ground black pepper
8	cups mixed salad greens (about 8 ounces)

In a large bowl, whisk together the oil, shallot, vinegar, mustard, salt, and pepper until well combined. Add the salad greens to the bowl and toss until well coated.

ham-wrapped endive au gratin and green salad with shallot vinaigrette

I first had this gratin at a neighbor's Belgian food and beer tasting, which was part of a fund-raiser for our children's school. Days later I couldn't get this rich cheesy bake out of my mind. I've lightened it without losing the sumptuous flavor by making the sauce with low-fat milk and holding the butter, and I made it easier by "blanching" the endive in the same pan as you bake it in. It is just as heavenly as I remember it.

MAKES 4 SERVINGS

SERVING SIZE
2 PIECES ENDIVE,
1 THICK SLICE BREAD,
AND 2 CUPS SALAD

PER SERVING
CALORIES 420
TOTAL FAT 18 G
  SAT FAT 6 G
  MONO FAT 8 G
  POLY FAT 2 G
PROTEIN 27 G
CARB 39 G
FIBER 9 G
CHOLESTEROL 60 MG
SODIUM 1070 MG

EXCELLENT SOURCE OF
CALCIUM, FIBER, FOLATE,
MANGANESE, PHOSPHORUS,
PROTEIN, RIBOFLAVIN,
SELENIUM, THIAMIN,
VITAMIN A, VITAMIN C

GOOD SOURCE OF
COPPER, IODINE, IRON,
MAGNESIUM, NIACIN,
PANTOTHENIC ACID,
POTASSIUM,
VITAMIN B6, VITAMIN B12,
VITAMIN D, ZINC

8   small heads Belgian endive (about 1½ pounds)
8   medium-thick slices Black Forest ham
        (about ½ pound)
1½   cups cold low-fat (1%) milk
3   tablespoons all-purpose flour
     Pinch of ground nutmeg
¼   teaspoon salt
¼   teaspoon freshly ground black pepper
½   cup packed grated Gruyère cheese (3 ounces)
4   thick slices crusty dark brown bread
1   recipe Green Salad with Shallot Vinaigrette
        (recipe on page 180)

Preheat the oven to 350°F.

Cut the bottom off of each endive, removing just enough so they remain intact. Rinse clean and, without drying, place in a 9 x13-inch microwave-safe baking dish. Cover tightly with plastic wrap and microwave for 8 minutes. Transfer the endive to paper towels until cool enough to handle, about 5 minutes. Wipe out the baking dish. Wrap each endive with a slice of ham and place in the baking dish.

In a medium saucepan, whisk together the cold milk and flour until the flour is dissolved. Heat over high heat, whisking constantly, until the mixture thickens and comes to a boil, about 5 minutes. Remove from the heat. Add the nutmeg, salt, and pepper. Spoon the sauce over the endive rolls, spreading it out evenly. Sprinkle with the cheese and bake until bubbling and golden brown, 30 to 40 minutes. Serve with the bread and Green Salad with Shallot Dressing.

chicken paella with sausage and olives

This luscious dish of moist golden rice studded with juicy chicken, smoky sausage, and mouthwatering olives is a heartwarming meal that has both down-home and upscale appeal. It is deceptively easy to make and it reheats well, in case you're lucky enough to have leftovers.

MAKES 4 SERVINGS

SERVING SIZE
2 CUPS

PER SERVING
CALORIES 600
TOTAL FAT 25 G
   SAT FAT 7 G
   MONO FAT 12.5 G
   POLY FAT 4.5 G
PROTEIN 36 G
CARB 55 G
FIBER 5 G
CHOLESTEROL 95 MG
SODIUM 910 MG

EXCELLENT SOURCE OF
FOLATE, IRON, MANGANESE, NIACIN, PHOSPHORUS, POTASSIUM, PROTEIN, RIBOFLAVIN, SELENIUM, THIAMIN, VITAMIN A, VITAMIN B6, VITAMIN C, VITAMIN K, ZINC

GOOD SOURCE OF
COPPER, FIBER, MAGNESIUM, PANTOTHENIC ACID, VITAMIN B12

1	tablespoon plus 2 teaspoons olive oil
3	ounces chorizo sausage, casing removed, sliced into ¼-inch rounds
1	pound skinless boneless chicken thighs, cut into 1-inch pieces
1	medium onion, chopped
2	cloves garlic, minced
2½	cups low-sodium chicken broth
1	10-ounce package frozen peas
1	cup uncooked white rice
1	large ripe tomato, chopped
¼	cup sliced green Spanish pimento-stuffed olives
½	teaspoon salt
¼	teaspoon freshly ground black pepper
⅛	teaspoon ground turmeric
	Small pinch of saffron threads

Preheat the oven to 375°F. Heat 1 tablespoon of the oil in a large, heavy skillet over medium-high heat (use a skillet that has a cover). Add the chorizo and cook, stirring occasionally, until browned, about 3 minutes. Add the chicken and cook, stirring occasionally, until browned, about 5 minutes. Transfer the chicken and chorizo to a plate.

Heat the remaining 2 teaspoons of oil in the skillet. Add the onions and cook, stirring, until softened and translucent, 3 to 5 minutes. Add the garlic and cook, stirring, for 1 additional minute. Return the chicken and chorizo to the skillet and add the chicken broth, peas, rice, tomato, olives, salt, pepper, turmeric, and saffron. Bring to a boil, cover, and transfer to oven. Cook until the rice is tender and the liquid is absorbed, 25 to 30 minutes.

marinated chicken and grape skewers with garden lentil pilaf

Juicy green grapes give these chicken skewers a big wow factor. The fruit softens, sweetens, and plumps further on the grill, providing an unexpected counterpoint to the savory, citrus-laced poultry.

MAKES 4 SERVINGS

SERVING SIZE
2 SKEWERS (EACH SKEWER
HAS 4 PIECES OF CHICKEN
AND 4 GRAPES)
AND ¾ CUP PILAF

PER SERVING
CALORIES 440
TOTAL FAT 16 G
  SAT FAT 2.5 G
  MONO FAT 9 G
  POLY FAT 2 G
PROTEIN 35 G
CARB 45 G
FIBER 10 G
CHOLESTEROL 65 MG
SODIUM 680 MG

EXCELLENT SOURCE OF
FIBER, IRON, NIACIN,
PHOSPHORUS, POTASSIUM,
PROTEIN, SELENIUM,
VITAMIN A, VITAMIN B6,
VITAMIN C, VITAMIN K

GOOD SOURCE OF
MANGANESE, THIAMIN

2	tablespoons olive oil
1	tablespoon fresh lemon juice
½	teaspoon finely grated lemon zest
2	cloves garlic, minced
1	teaspoon ground cumin
½	teaspoon ground coriander
½	teaspoon salt
1	pound skinless boneless chicken breasts, cut into ¾-inch cubes
8	10-inch skewers
1½	cups seedless green grapes
	Cooking spray
2	tablespoons chopped fresh mint leaves
1	recipe Garden Lentil Pilaf (recipe follows)
1	lemon, cut into wedges

In a medium-size bowl, whisk together the oil, lemon juice, zest, garlic, cumin, coriander, and salt. Add the chicken to the marinade and toss to coat. Marinate the chicken in the refrigerator for at least 20 minutes and up to 4 hours. While the chicken is marinating, soak the skewers in water if wooden.

Thread the chicken cubes onto the skewers, alternating them with grapes. Spray a grill pan with cooking spray and preheat over medium-high heat, or prepare an outdoor grill. Grill the chicken until cooked through, 3 to 4 minutes per side. Sprinkle with the mint and serve with the pilaf and lemon wedges.

* garden lentil pilaf

This delightful dish is like a warm salad brimming with garden fresh flavor, color, and aroma. It is delicious and satisfying on its own as a light meal or vegetarian entrée, but it is a wonderful accompaniment to the chicken and grape skewers. It is important to use green or French lentils here because, unlike other varieties, they hold their shape when cooked.

MAKES 4 SERVINGS

SERVING SIZE
¾ CUP

1	cup green lentils
2	cups water
2	tablespoons olive oil
2	tablespoons diced shallots
3	cups baby spinach leaves (about 3 ounces)
1	cup halved grape tomatoes (about ½ pint)
¼	cup chopped fresh basil leaves
¼	cup chopped fresh mint leaves
¼	cup chopped fresh parsley
2	tablespoons fresh lemon juice
½	teaspoon salt
¼	teaspoon freshly ground black pepper

Place the lentils in a pot with the water and bring to a boil. Reduce the heat, cover, and simmer until the lentils are tender but still retain their shape, 30 to 35 minutes. Drain any excess water from the lentils and set them aside.

Heat the olive oil in a large skillet over medium-high heat. Add the shallots and cook, stirring, until softened, about 3 minutes. Add the spinach and cook until just wilted, about 2 minutes. Add the tomatoes, cooked lentils, basil, mint, and parsley to the pan and stir to combine. Cook until warmed through, about 1 minute. Stir in the lemon juice, salt, and pepper, and serve.

lemon-garlic turkey breast with roasted rosemary potatoes and brussels sprouts

Fresh roasted turkey breast isn't something you think of making regularly, but it should be! It couldn't be simpler to cook and it gives enough juicy lean meat to feed a crowd or have fabulous leftovers for sandwiches and other dishes the next few days. This lemon, garlic, and rosemary version with its quick pan sauce alongside crisp-tender roasted vegetables means you can have a Thanksgiving-worthy turkey dinner in less than 90 minutes any week of the year.

MAKES 8 SERVINGS

SERVING SIZE
4 ¼-INCH SLICES TURKEY,
2 TABLESPOONS SAUCE,
¾ CUP POTATOES, AND
¾ CUP BRUSSELS SPROUTS

PER SERVING
CALORIES 590
TOTAL FAT 11 G
  SAT FAT 2 G
  MONO FAT 7 G
  POLY FAT 2 G
PROTEIN 80 G
CARB 40 G
FIBER 7 G
CHOLESTEROL 200 MG
SODIUM 770 MG

EXCELLENT SOURCE OF
COPPER, FIBER, FOLATE,
IRON, MAGNESIUM,
MANGANESE, NIACIN,
PANTOTHENIC ACID,
PHOSPHORUS, POTASSIUM,
PROTEIN, RIBOFLAVIN,
SELENIUM, THIAMIN,
VITAMIN B6, VITAMIN C,
VITAMIN K, ZINC

GOOD SOURCE OF
VITAMIN A, VITAMIN B12

1	tablespoon olive oil
2	teaspoons finely chopped fresh rosemary
2	teaspoons finely grated lemon zest
1	teaspoon salt
½	teaspoon freshly ground black pepper
1	whole bone-in turkey breast, skin removed (about 6 pounds)
2	cups low-sodium chicken broth
4	small cloves garlic, peeled
3	tablespoons fresh lemon juice
1	recipe Roasted Rosemary Potatoes (recipe follows)
1	recipe Roasted Brussels Sprouts (recipe follows)

Preheat the oven to 375°F.

In a small bowl, combine the oil, rosemary, lemon zest, ¾ teaspoon salt, and ¼ teaspoon pepper. Place the turkey in a medium-sized flame-proof roasting pan, breast side up, and rub the rosemary-lemon mixture onto the breast. Pour 1 cup of the broth into the dish and add the garlic and half of the lemon juice.

Roast, uncovered, until the juices run clear when pierced and a meat thermometer registers 165°F, 1 to 1¼ hours. Transfer the turkey breast to a carving board and allow it to rest for 10 minutes before carving.

Place the pan directly on top of the stove. Add the remaining 1 cup of broth and cook over high heat until it comes to a boil, scraping up any browned bits and allowing them to dissolve in the broth, and mashing the garlic cloves into the broth. Cook over high heat until the broth is reduced by roughly half, about 6 minutes. Stir in the remaining lemon juice and remaining ¼ teaspoon each of salt and pepper.

Carve the turkey and serve topped with the sauce. Serve alongside the mashed potatoes and Brussels sprouts.

* roasted rosemary potatoes

Crunchy and golden brown outside with a tender soft center, these rosemary-spiked potatoes are absolutely heavenly. And you hardly have to do a thing.

MAKES 8 SERVINGS

SERVING SIZE
¾ CUP

2½	pounds small red new potatoes, halved
2	tablespoons olive oil
2	teaspoons chopped fresh rosemary leaves, or ¾ teaspoon dried
½	teaspoons salt

Preheat the oven to 375°F.

Place the potatoes on a baking sheet and toss them with the oil, rosemary, and salt. Roast until they are golden brown and crisp on the outside and softened and tender on the inside, about 1¼ hours.

* roasted brussels sprouts

I have turned around countless Brussels sprout naysayers with this simple dish. In the oven the humble vegetable is transformed. Its outer leaves crisp and its natural sugars caramelize the outside, while the inside becomes yieldingly tender. Its flavor mellows to a delightfully nutty essence. I wish I could be there to see your face light up when you taste them.

MAKES 8 SERVINGS

SERVING SIZE
¾ CUP

2	pounds Brussels sprouts, halved
2	tablespoons olive oil
½	teaspoon salt

Preheat the oven to 375°F.

Place the Brussels sprouts on a baking sheet and toss them with the oil and salt. Roast until they are golden brown and crisp on the outside and softened and tender inside, about 1 hour.

white turkey chili

To me, chili is the ultimate one-pot meal. It's a breeze to make and satisfying to eat, and the variations are only limited by your imagination. This one is all white—with white beans, turkey, and white corn (hominy)—with hints of green from flavorful poblano peppers. Double the recipe and you have a party. Just put out the fixin's and let guests help themselves.

MAKES 4 SERVINGS

SERVING SIZE
2¼ CUPS,
1 TABLESPOON SOUR CREAM,
AND 1½ TEASPOONS CILANTRO

PER SERVING
CALORIES 490
TOTAL FAT 11 G
   SAT FAT 2 G
   MONO FAT 3 G
   POLY FAT 2 G
PROTEIN 47 G
CARB 55 G
FIBER 13 G
CHOLESTEROL 55 MG
SODIUM 900 MG

EXCELLENT SOURCE OF
FIBER, IRON, MAGNESIUM,
PHOSPHORUS, POTASSIUM,
PROTEIN, RIBOFLAVIN,
THIAMIN, VITAMIN C,
VITAMIN K, ZINC

GOOD SOURCE OF
CALCIUM, COPPER,
IODINE, MANGANESE,
NIACIN, VITAMIN A

1	tablespoon canola oil
1	medium onion, diced
2	stalks celery, diced
3	medium poblano peppers, seeded, white ribs removed, and finely diced
1	clove garlic, minced
1	teaspoon ground cumin
½	teaspoon ground coriander
¼	teaspoon cayenne pepper, plus more to taste
1	pound ground white-meat turkey
2	15.5-ounce cans white beans (such as cannelini; preferably low sodium), drained and rinsed
4	cups low-sodium chicken broth
¾	teaspoon dried oregano
1	15.5-ounce can hominy, drained and rinsed
¾	teaspoon salt, plus more to taste
¼	cup reduced-fat sour cream
2	tablespoons chopped fresh cilantro
	Lime wedges

Heat the oil in a large pot or Dutch oven over medium heat. Add the onion, celery, and poblano peppers and cook, stirring occasionally, until the vegetables are softened, about 8 minutes. Add the garlic, cumin, coriander, and ¼ teaspoon of cayenne and cook, stirring, until fragrant, about 30 seconds.

   Add the ground turkey and cook, breaking up the meat with a spoon, until the meat is no longer pink, about 2 minutes. Add the white beans, broth, and oregano. Cook, partially covered and stirring occasionally, for 25 minutes.

(CONTINUED)

*white turkey chili (cont.)

Add the hominy, ¾ teaspoon of salt, and more cayenne pepper to taste and continue cooking, partially covered, for 10 minutes longer. Ladle into individual bowls and top each serving with 1 tablespoon of sour cream and 1½ teaspoons of cilantro. Garnish with a lime wedge.

EATING WELL TIP

* When it comes to creamy foods and soft cheeses, like sour cream, ice cream, cream cheese, and ricotta and mozzarella cheeses, I prefer reduced fat (or part skim) over nonfat. Reduced fat still has enough fat to give you the taste you want without lots of artificial stabilizers and other additives, while I find nonfat creams and cheeses compromise taste and their ingredient lists are not as pure. One creamy treat with no equal is whipped cream. For that—as well as for deeply flavorful cheeses like blue, Gruyère and cheddar—I just go for a little of the real thing.

new tuna noodle casserole

Who doesn't have fond childhood memories of mom's tuna noodle casserole? This one brings you right back to that warm fuzzy place, but it tastes better than you remembered because it is better. With a simple from-scratch cream sauce and chunks of fresh mushrooms subbing for the condensed soup, plus lots of bright green vegetables and pasta that is tender but not mushy, it's a welcomed retro remake.

MAKES 6 SERVINGS

SERVING SIZE
2½ CUPS

PER SERVING
CALORIES 480
TOTAL FAT 8G
  SAT FAT 2 G
  MONO FAT 2 G
  POLY FAT 1 G
PROTEIN 49 G
CARB 51 G
FIBER 10 G
CHOLESTEROL 80 MG
SODIUM 990 MG

EXCELLENT SOURCE OF
CALCIUM, FIBER,
FOLATE, IODINE,
IRON, MANGANESE,
PROTEIN, RIBOFLAVIN,
VITAMIN A, VITAMIN C,
VITAMIN K

GOOD SOURCE OF
COPPER, NIACIN,
PANTOTHENIC ACID,
PHOSPHORUS, POTASSIUM,
SELENIUM, THIAMIN,
VITAMIN B6, VITAMIN D

¾ pound whole-wheat fettuccine
1 tablespoon canola oil
1 small onion, chopped
1 large stalk celery, finely diced
10 ounces white mushrooms, stemmed and chopped
¼ cup all-purpose flour
3 cups low-fat (1%) milk
1 cup low-sodium chicken broth or vegetable broth
¾ teaspoon salt
¼ teaspoon freshly ground black pepper
4 6-ounce cans chunk light tuna in water, drained
1 10-ounce box frozen chopped broccoli, thawed
1 10-ounce box frozen peas, thawed
⅓ cup plain bread crumbs
3 tablespoons freshly grated Parmesan cheese

Preheat the oven to 425°F.

Bring a large pot of water to a boil. Break the fettuccine into thirds, and cook until tender but firm, a minute or two less than the package directions call for. Drain.

Heat the oil in a large deep skillet over medium heat. Add the onion and cook, stirring, until softened, 5 minutes. Add the celery and cook, stirring occasionally, until just tender, 6 minutes. Add the mushrooms and cook until they release their water, about 5 minutes more.

Sprinkle the flour over the mushroom mixture and stir immediately to incorporate. Add the milk and broth and bring the mixture to a boil, stirring frequently. Reduce the heat to medium-low and cook, stirring occasionally, until the liquid has thickened, about 8 minutes. Add the salt and pepper, cooked fettuccine, tuna, broccoli, and peas, and toss to incorporate. Pour mixture into a 9x13-inch casserole dish.

In a small bowl, combine the bread crumbs and Parmesan cheese. Sprinkle them over the casserole and bake until bubbly, about 25 minutes.

ratatouille with red snapper and herbed goat cheese crostini

This dish is inspired by a dinner I had at a lovely little restaurant in Paris, where the food was just the opposite of what you might expect from French cuisine. It was uncomplicated, with clean, clear flavors and a modern lightness. In this take on the classic eggplant, zucchini, and tomato stew, each vegetable is finely diced and cooked just enough to be tender while retaining its fresh individuality. It makes a scrumptious, luxurious bed for the red snapper fillet.

MAKES 4 SERVINGS

SERVING SIZE
1 CUP RATATOUILLE,
1 FISH FILLET,
AND 2 PIECES CROSTINI

PER SERVING
CALORIES 420
TOTAL FAT 17 G
    SAT FAT 4.5 G
    MONO FAT 9 G
    POLY FAT 2.5 G
PROTEIN 39 G
CARB 29 G
FIBER 9 G
CHOLESTEROL 60 MG
SODIUM 770 MG

EXCELLENT SOURCE OF
COPPER, FIBER, FOLATE,
MAGNESIUM, MANGANESE,
PHOSPHORUS, POTASSIUM,
PROTEIN, SELENIUM,
VITAMIN A, VITAMIN B6,
VITAMIN B12, VITAMIN C,
VITAMIN K

GOOD SOURCE OF
CALCIUM, IRON, NIACIN,
PANTOTHENIC ACID,
RIBOFLAVIN,
THIAMIN, ZINC

3	tablespoons olive oil
1	large eggplant (about 1 pound), trimmed and cut into small dice
1	medium onion, cut into small dice
2	medium zucchini (1 pound total), trimmed and cut into small dice
2	cloves garlic, minced
1	14.5-ounce can no-salt-added diced tomatoes
1	teaspoon herbes de Provence, or ½ teaspoon dried thyme and ¼ teaspoon each of dried rosemary and dried marjoram
¾	teaspoon salt, plus more to taste
½	teaspoon freshly ground black pepper
¼	cup chopped fresh basil, plus more for garnish
4	5-ounce red snapper fillets, skin-on
2	teaspoons fresh lemon juice
1	recipe Herbed Goat Cheese Crostini (recipe follows)

In a large nonstick skillet, heat 1 tablespoon of olive oil over medium-high heat. Add the eggplant and cook, stirring, until softened, about 5 minutes. Remove the eggplant from the skillet. Heat another tablespoon of oil in the same skillet over medium-high heat. Add the onion and cook, stirring, until softened, about 5 minutes. Add the zucchini and garlic to the pan and cook, stirring occasionally, until the zucchini is softened, 6 minutes. Return the eggplant to the pan and add the tomatoes, herbes de Provence, ½ teaspoon of the salt, and ¼ teaspoon of the pepper. Simmer for 10 minutes. Season with more salt to taste. Stir in ¼ cup of the basil and remove from the heat.

Preheat the broiler. Sprinkle the fillets with the remaining ¼ teaspoon each of salt and pepper. Combine the remaining 1 tablespoon of olive oil with the lemon juice and brush on the fillets. Broil until the fish is cooked and firm, about 7 minutes.

Mound 1 cup of the ratatouille onto 4 plates and top each with 1 fish fillet. Garnish with basil. Serve with the crostini.

* herbed goat cheese crostini

Just about any toasted cheese and bread combination is a winner to me. But this one is a standout, with the aroma of herbs and garlic and warm creamy cheese atop the crunch of baguette. It is easy enough to make just for you but has an elegant flair that makes it worthy of company.

MAKES 4 SERVINGS

SERVING SIZE
2 PIECES

8   ½-inch-thick slices whole-wheat baguette
1   large clove garlic
2   ounces herbed goat cheese (chèvre)

Preheat the broiler.

Place the bread slices on a baking tray. Cut the garlic clove in half and rub the top of each slice of bread well with the cut side of the garlic clove. Spread ¼ ounce of the goat cheese on each slice of bread. Broil until the bread is toasted and the cheese is warmed and lightly browned.

* DID YOU KNOW?
Soft cheeses like chèvre and feta naturally have about a third less fat and fewer calories than hard cheeses like cheddar.

salmon in aromatic tomato sauce with swiss chard

What do you get when you top a pile of tender greens with a juicy fillet of fish, smother them with the most wonderfully fragrant and flavorful sauce, and let them simmer, soften, and meld together in the oven? A meal that lights up your taste buds and warms your belly, heart, and soul.

MAKES 4 SERVINGS

SERVING SIZE
1 SALMON FILLET,
¾ CUP CHARD AND SAUCE,
AND ¾ CUP COUSCOUS

PER SERVING
CALORIES 520
TOTAL FAT 16 G
  SAT FAT 2.5 G
  MONO FAT 6 G
  POLY FAT 5.5 G
PROTEIN 43 G
CARB 48 G
FIBER 7 G
CHOLESTEROL 95 MG
SODIUM 700 MG

EXCELLENT SOURCE OF
COPPER, FIBER, FOLATE,
IRON, MAGNESIUM,
MANGANESE, NIACIN,
PANTOTHENIC ACID,
PHOSPHORUS, POTASSIUM,
PROTEIN, RIBOFLAVIN,
SELENIUM, THIAMIN,
VITAMIN A, VITAMIN B6,
VITAMIN B12, VITAMIN C,
VITAMIN D, VITAMIN K

GOOD SOURCE OF
CALCIUM, ZINC

1	tablespoon olive oil
4	cloves garlic, minced
1	14.5-ounce can no-salt-added diced tomatoes
1	12-ounce can no-salt-added tomato sauce
1	7-ounce jar roasted red peppers, drained, rinsed, and thinly sliced
2	dried whole red chile peppers
1	teaspoon ground cumin
½	teaspoon ground coriander
½	teaspoon salt
½	teaspoon freshly ground black pepper
1	large bunch Swiss chard, washed well and dried, tough center stems removed, coarsely chopped (about 8 cups)
4	6-ounce skinless salmon fillets
¼	cup chopped cilantro
3	cups cooked whole-grain couscous

Preheat the oven to 350°F. Heat the oil in a large skillet over medium-low heat. Add the garlic and cook, stirring, until softened and golden, about 1 minute. Add the diced tomatoes with juice, tomato sauce, red peppers, chili peppers, cumin, coriander, and ¼ teaspoon each of salt and pepper. Bring to a boil, then reduce the heat to medium-low and simmer until the sauce thickens slightly, about 10 minutes. Remove from the heat and remove and discard the chile peppers.

Place the Swiss chard on the bottom of a 9x13-inch glass baking dish. Season the fish fillets with the remaining ¼ teaspoon each of salt and pepper and place on top of the chard. Top with the sauce and bake, covered, until the fish is just cooked and the chard is wilted, about 15 minutes. Remove the cover and bake for an additional 5 minutes. Sprinkle with cilantro and serve over couscous.

salmon florentine and quinoa pilaf with pine nuts

This dish is as impressive looking as it is delicious and nutrient packed. It is a two-tiered wonder with a buttery salmon base and flavorful spinach topping. It is a special preparation that takes no special skill or effort to make.

MAKES 4 SERVINGS

SERVING SIZE
1 PIECE SALMON
AND 1 CUP PILAF

PER SERVING
CALORIES 600
TOTAL FAT 25 G
  SAT FAT 4.5 G
  MONO FAT 10 G
  POLY FAT 8 G
PROTEIN 53 G
CARB 43 G
FIBER 8 G
CHOLESTEROL 100 MG
SODIUM 640 MG

EXCELLENT SOURCE OF
CALCIUM, COPPER, FIBER,
FOLATE, IRON, MAGNESIUM,
MANGANESE, NIACIN,
PHOSPHORUS,
POTASSIUM, PROTEIN,
RIBOFLAVIN, SELENIUM,
THIAMIN, VITAMIN A,
VITAMIN B6, VITAMIN C,
VITAMIN D, VITAMIN K, ZINC

GOOD SOURCE OF
PANTOTHENIC ACID

2	10-ounce packages frozen spinach, thawed
1	tablespoon olive oil
¼	cup minced shallots
2	teaspoons minced garlic
5	sun-dried tomatoes, chopped
¼	teaspoon crushed red pepper flakes
½	teaspoon salt, plus more to taste
¼	teaspoon freshly ground black pepper, plus more to taste
½	cup part-skim ricotta cheese
4	6-ounce skinless salmon fillets, rinsed and patted dry
1	recipe Quinoa Pilaf with Pine Nuts (recipe follows)

Preheat the oven to 350°F. Using your hands, squeeze all excess liquid from the spinach.

Heat the olive oil in a large skillet over medium heat. Add the shallots and cook, stirring, until they begin to soften, about 3 minutes. Add the garlic and cook for 1 minute more. Add the spinach, sun-dried tomatoes, red pepper flakes, salt, and pepper and cook, stirring, for an additional 2 minutes. Remove from the heat and let cool for approximately 15 minutes. Add the ricotta and stir to combine. Season with additional salt and pepper to taste.

Using your hands, pack approximately ½ cup of the spinach mixture on top of each salmon fillet, forming the mixture to the shape of the fillet. Place the fillets on a rimmed baking sheet or in a glass baking dish and bake for 15 minutes, until the salmon is cooked through. Serve alongside the pilaf.

* quinoa pilaf with pine nuts

This is a perfect example of how to keep things interesting without going out of your comfort zone or working too hard. A traditional pilaf flavor combo of parsley and pine nuts flavor an exciting, new (but ancient) grain—quinoa—that cooks up tender and mild, just like rice.

MAKES 4 SERVINGS

SERVING SIZE
1 CUP

2	cups low-sodium chicken broth
1	cup quinoa
¼	cup pine nuts
1	tablespoon olive oil
½	large onion, chopped
⅓	cup fresh parsley leaves, chopped
	Salt and freshly ground black pepper to taste

Put the broth and quinoa in a medium-size saucepan and bring to a boil. Reduce the heat to simmer, then cover and cook until the liquid is absorbed and the grain is tender, about 15 minutes.

Meanwhile, toast the pine nuts in a large dry skillet over medium-high heat, stirring frequently, until golden brown and fragrant, about 2 minutes. Remove the nuts from the pan and set aside. Heat the oil in the same skillet over medium-high heat. Add the onions and cook, stirring occasionally, until they are softened and beginning to brown, about 6 minutes.

When the quinoa is done, fluff with a fork and transfer to a large serving bowl. Stir in the pine nuts, onions, and parsley. Season with salt and pepper and serve.

cioppino

Cioppino (pronounced cho-pee-no) is an Italian fish stew with a savory tomato and wine broth chock-full of fish and shellfish. It is perfect for a relaxed dinner but you can easily turn it into a rush-hour meal by making the broth ahead and refrigerating or freezing it.

MAKES 4 SERVINGS

SERVING SIZE
1½ CUPS CIOPPINO
AND 2 SLICES BREAD

PER SERVING
CALORIES 440
TOTAL FAT 8G
  SAT FAT 1.5G
  MONO FAT 3.5G
  POLY FAT 2G
PROTEIN 40G
CARB 36G
FIBER 4G
CHOLESTEROL 125 MG
SODIUM 1100 MG

EXCELLENT SOURCE OF
FOLATE, IRON,
MAGNESIUM, MANGANESE,
NIACIN, PHOSPHORUS,
POTASSIUM, PROTEIN,
SELENIUM, THIAMIN,
VITAMIN A, VITAMIN B6,
VITAMIN B12, VITAMIN C,
VITAMIN D, VITAMIN K

GOOD SOURCE OF
CALCIUM, COPPER, FIBER,
RIBOFLAVIN, ZINC

1	tablespoon olive oil
1	large onion, chopped
2	stalks celery, chopped
4	cloves garlic, minced
1	tablespoon chopped fresh thyme leaves, or 1 teaspoon dried
1	bay leaf
¼	teaspoon crushed red pepper flakes
1	tablespoon tomato paste
1	cup dry white wine
2	14.5-ounce cans no-salt-added diced tomatoes
1	cup fish stock or water
1	tablespoon red wine vinegar
¾	teaspoon salt
¼	teaspoon freshly ground black pepper
½	pound medium shrimp, peeled and deveined
½	pound scallops
½	pound skinless halibut fillet, cut into 1-inch chunks
2	teaspoons chopped fresh parsley
1	loaf whole-wheat Italian bread

Heat the olive oil over medium-high heat in a large soup pot. Add the onion and celery and cook, stirring, until slightly softened, about 5 minutes. Add the garlic, thyme, bay leaf, and red pepper flakes and cook, stirring, an additional 1 minute. Stir in the tomato paste. Add the wine, bring to a boil, and cook over medium-high heat for 3 minutes.

Add the tomatoes with their juices and the fish stock or water and bring to a boil. Reduce the heat and simmer, for 10 minutes. Stir in the vinegar, salt, and pepper. This base may be made ahead of time and stored in the refrigerator for up to 3 days.

When ready to serve, reheat the soup base on the stovetop, if necessary, and bring to a boil. Add the shrimp, scallops, and halibut. Reduce the heat and simmer, until everything is just cooked, about 5 minutes. Divide among 4 bowls and garnish with the parsley. Serve with the bread.

four-cheese baked penne with romaine hearts mediterranean

Nothing makes a hungry crowd happier than a bubbling tray of saucy pasta covered with melted cheese. This one can even be made a day or two ahead—ready to pop in the oven when you need it.

MAKES 8 SERVINGS

SERVING SIZE
ABOUT 2 CUPS PASTA
AND 1 ROMAINE HEART

PER SERVING
CALORIES 500
TOTAL FAT 20 G
   SAT FAT 6 G
   MONO FAT 9.5 G
   POLY FAT 2 G
PROTEIN 24 G
CARB 58 G
FIBER 8 G
CHOLESTEROL 25 MG
SODIUM 900 MG

EXCELLENT SOURCE OF
CALCIUM, FIBER,
PHOSPHORUS,
PROTEIN, VITAMIN A,
VITAMIN C, VITAMIN K

GOOD SOURCE OF
COPPER, IODINE, IRON,
MANGANESE, POTASSIUM,
RIBOFLAVIN, SELENIUM,
VITAMIN B6, VITAMIN B12

1½	cups small-curd low-fat cottage cheese
1	cup part-skim ricotta cheese
1¼	cups shredded part-skim mozzarella cheese
3	tablespoons chopped fresh parsley
1	pound whole-wheat penne
2	teaspoons olive oil
1	medium onion, chopped
4	cloves garlic, finely chopped
1	15-ounce can crushed tomatoes (preferably no-salt-added)
1	8-ounce can no-salt-added tomato sauce
1	teaspoon dried oregano
1	teaspoon dried rosemary
½	teaspoon crushed red pepper flakes
¾	teaspoon salt
¼	teaspoon freshly ground black pepper Cooking spray
¼	cup shredded Parmesan cheese (¾ ounce)
1	recipe Romaine Hearts Mediterranean (recipe follows)

Preheat the oven to 400°F.

Combine the cottage cheese, ricotta cheese, ½ cup of the mozzarella, and the parsley in a bowl and stir to incorporate.

Cook the pasta in a large pot of boiling water until tender but still firm. Drain.

Heat the oil in the same pot over medium heat. Add the onion and cook, stirring occasionally, about 5 minutes. Add the garlic and cook, stirring, for 30 seconds more. Add the tomatoes, tomato sauce, oregano, rosemary, red pepper flakes, salt, and pepper. Bring to a boil, then reduce the heat and simmer until the sauce thickens slightly, about 10 minutes. Add the pasta to the pot and turn off the heat. Stir in the cottage cheese-parsley mixture.

Spray a 9x13-inch glass baking dish with cooking spray, then transfer the pasta mixture to the dish. Top with remaining ¾ cup of mozzarella and the Parmesan. Bake until heated through and the cheese is melted, 30 minutes. Serve with the romaine hearts.

* romaine hearts **mediterranean**

I think about the phrase "work smarter, not harder" whenever I make this salad, because you get so much in terms of taste and presentation, but there is so little to do to make it happen.

MAKES 8 SERVINGS

SERVING SIZE
1 HEART OF ROMAINE LETTUCE

8	small hearts of romaine lettuce
½	medium red onion, thinly sliced into rings
1¼	cups Calamata olives
¼	cup extra-virgin olive oil
3	tablespoons fresh lemon juice
1	teaspoon finely grated lemon zest
1	teaspoon dried oregano
¼	teaspoon salt
⅛	teaspoon freshly ground black pepper

Cut each of the romaine lettuce hearts in half, leaving the stem end intact so the leaves stay together. Top each with a few rings of onion and place 4 olives in a small pile on each plate. In a small bowl, whisk together the oil, lemon juice and zest, oregano, salt, and pepper. Drizzle some dressing over each lettuce half and serve.

* EATING WELL TIP

Canned tomato products are the best food source of lycopene, a powerful antioxidant that helps protect the skin from signs of aging and helps keep your heart healthy. I always cook with "no-salt-added" tomatoes so I have control of the salt in my dishes. You can always add more salt to your food, but with regular canned tomatoes you are starting off with up to twelve times the sodium.

lemony lentil soup **with greens**

This deeply satisfying, hearty soup gets a bright flavor lift from lemon juice and zest. It's just the right touch to keep this Old World classic fresh and modern. It is wonderful served with the Herbed Goat Cheese Crostini (see page 194).

MAKES 6 SERVINGS

SERVING SIZE
2 CUPS

PER SERVING
CALORIES 410
TOTAL FAT 7 G
   SAT FAT 1 G
   MONO FAT 2 G
   POLY FAT 1 G
PROTEIN 30 G
CARB 65 G
FIBER 15 G
CHOLESTEROL 0 MG
SODIUM 600 MG

EXCELLENT SOURCE OF
CALCIUM, COPPER, FIBER, IRON, MANGANESE, NIACIN, PHOSPHORUS, POTASSIUM, PROTEIN, VITAMIN A, VITAMIN C, VITAMIN K

GOOD SOURCE OF
MAGNESIUM, RIBOFLAVIN, THIAMIN, VITAMIN B6

2	teaspoons canola oil
1	small onion, chopped
1	large carrot, peeled and chopped
2	stalks celery, chopped
2	cloves garlic, minced
12	cups low-sodium chicken broth, plus more as needed
16	ounces green lentils
1	teaspoon dried basil
1	teaspoon dried thyme
1	teaspoon salt
6	cups chopped kale leaves (about 6 ounces)
3	tablespoons fresh lemon juice
1	teaspoon finely grated lemon zest

Heat the oil in a 6-quart soup pot over medium-high heat. Add the onion and cook, stirring, until softened and translucent, 3 to 5 minutes. Add the carrot, celery, and garlic and cook, covered, stirring occasionally, until the carrots are softened, about 5 minutes. Add 12 cups of the broth, the lentils, basil, thyme, and salt and bring to a boil. Reduce the heat to low, add the kale, and cook until the lentils are tender, 30 to 35 minutes, adding more broth if necessary. Stir in the lemon juice and zest, and serve.

* EATING WELL TIP
There are a number of soups and stews in this book that are thermos friendly for an on-the-go meal. Try the Roasted Tomato and Black Bean Soup (page 205), Tortellini-Spinach Soup (page 90), White Turkey Chili (page 189), Baked Beans with Ham (page 179), and Aromatic Beef Stew with Butternut Squash (page 176).

roasted tomato and black bean soup with avocado-mango salad

This robust, satisfying soup is a savory meal in a bowl layered with flavor from roasted tomatoes, onion, and garlic. A quick puree at the end takes it from rustic to refined.

MAKES 4 SERVINGS

SERVING SIZE
2 CUPS SOUP,
1 TABLESPOON EACH SOUR
CREAM AND CILANTRO,
AND 1 LETTUCE CUP FILLED
WITH 8 TO 10 AVOCADO
AND MANGO SLICES

PER SERVING
CALORIES 510
TOTAL FAT 19 G
 SAT FAT 4 G
 MONO FAT 11 G
 POLY FAT 2 G
PROTEIN 22G
CARB 66 G
FIBER 17 G
CHOLESTEROL 8 MG
SODIUM 877 MG

EXCELLENT SOURCE OF
CALCIUM, FIBER, IRON,
MAGNESIUM, PHOSPHORUS,
POTASSIUM, PROTEIN,
VITAMIN A, VITAMIN B6,
VITAMIN C, VITAMIN K

GOOD SOURCE OF
COPPER, FOLATE, IODINE,
MANGANESE, RIBOFLAVIN,
THIAMIN, VITAMIN B6, ZINC

7 medium tomatoes, quartered
1 large onion, cut into large pieces
  (about 1½ inches)
3 cloves garlic, peeled
2 tablespoons olive oil
1 teaspoon salt
½ teaspoon freshly ground black pepper
5 cups low-sodium chicken broth or
  vegetable broth
2 15.5-ounce cans black beans (preferably
  low-sodium), drained and rinsed
1½ teaspoons ground cumin
1 teaspoon chili powder
¼ teaspoon hot pepper sauce (like Tabasco)
¼ cup reduced-fat sour cream
¼ cup chopped cilantro
1 recipe Avocado-Mango Salad (recipe follows)

Preheat the oven to 375°F. Toss the tomatoes, onion, and garlic with the oil, ½ teaspoon of the salt, and ¼ teaspoon of the pepper in a large bowl, then transfer to a baking sheet. Roast until the garlic cloves have softened, the edges of the onions are browned, and the tomatoes have collapsed, 35 to 40 minutes, stirring once after the first 20 minutes.

Transfer the roasted vegetable mixture to a 4-quart saucepan. Add the broth, beans, cumin, chili powder, and the remaining ½ teaspoon of salt and ¼ teaspoon of pepper. Bring to a boil, reduce the heat, and simmer for 10 minutes. Remove from the heat and blend until smooth with an immersion blender or in batches in a regular blender. Stir in the hot pepper sauce. Divide among the 4 bowls and garnish with a dollop of sour cream and a sprinkle of cilantro. Serve with the Avocado-Mango Salad.

* avocado-mango salad

This tropical salad is the cool, creamy, fruity counterpoint to the warm, hearty, spicy soup. The contrast makes each dish taste even more delightful.

MAKES 4 SERVINGS

SERVING SIZE
1 LETTUCE CUP WITH 8 TO
10 AVOCADO AND MANGO
SLICES

4	large Bibb or Boston lettuce leaves
1	medium avocado, pitted, peeled, and sliced ¼ inch thick
1	medium mango, pitted, peeled, and sliced ¼ inch thick
¼	red onion, very thinly sliced into rounds
4	lime wedges
¼	teaspoon salt
	Pinch of freshly ground black pepper

Place a lettuce leaf on each serving plate. Arrange 4 to 5 slices each of avocado and mango, alternating them in a row, into each lettuce cup. Top each with a few onion rounds, and then squeeze a lime wedge over each salad. Season with salt and pepper and serve.

GET AHEAD: COOK AND FREEZE DINNERS

Whenever I make a soup, chili, or stew I make a double batch and freeze what's left in individual portions so there is always a great meal on hand when I need it. Knowing dinner is taken care of takes a load of stress out of the most hectic days. Even if the head chef (you!) isn't home, anyone in the family who can reheat something can get dinner on the table. Creamy soups and dishes containing potatoes don't freeze well because freezing compromises their texture. And pasta can get mushy with freezing and reheating, so when cooking a pasta dish with the intention of freezing it, do not cook the pasta completely. Follow this five-step plan for smart freezing and thawing.

COOL

Chill just-cooked soups, stews, and chili in the fridge for an hour or two before packing and freezing.

PACK

Portion the food into airtight, freezer-safe containers or plastic bags. To allow for expansion with freezing, leave at least ½ inch of space at the top of hard containers. Fill plastic bags halfway, press the air out, and lay them flat in the freezer—a great space saver!

LABEL

Be sure to label all the containers with the date and the kind of food in them, so you don't have any frozen mystery meals to worry about.

STORE

Freeze soups, stews, or chili no longer than three months for optimal quality.

THAW

Never thaw food at room temperature because of the potential for bacteria growth. Instead, thaw in the fridge or immerse the bag or container in hot water. Then transfer the food to a microwave-safe dish or pot on the stove where it can be thoroughly heated.

desserts—
in a flash

* These desserts are so **FABULOUS, YET SO QUICK AND SIMPLE,** making them is like making magic. They are sweet treats you can whip up fast but **YOU'LL WANT TO EAT NICE AND SLOW,** savoring every bite.

chocolate fondue

What better way to get your fruit than to dip it in warm chocolate! This dish is guaranteed to get the whole family around the table at the same time. If you prefer your chocolate on the sweeter side, you can substitute a lighter chocolate that is 40% to 50% cocoa solids.

MAKES 4 SERVINGS

SERVING SIZE
3 TABLESPOONS FONDUE
AND ¾ CUP FRUIT

PER SERVING
CALORIES 230
TOTAL FAT 9 G
  SAT FAT 5 G
  MONO FAT 1 G
  POLY FAT 0 G
PROTEIN 6 G
CARB 41 G
FIBER 7 G
CHOLESTEROL 10 MG
SODIUM 35 MG

EXCELLENT SOURCE OF
COPPER, FIBER,
MANGANESE, VITAMIN C

GOOD SOURCE OF
CALCIUM, IODINE,
IRON, MAGNESIUM,
PHOSPHORUS,
POTASSIUM, PROTEIN

1	banana
1	apple
1	8-ounce container fresh strawberries, stems removed
2	teaspoons orange juice
½	cup unsweetened natural cocoa powder
⅓	cup sugar
½	cup evaporated milk
2	ounces dark chocolate (60% to 70% cocoa solids), finely chopped
1	teaspoon vanilla extract

Peel and cut the banana and core and slice the apple. Place the banana slices, apple slices, and strawberries in separate piles on a serving plate. Sprinkle the banana and apple slices with the orange juice and toss gently. Cover the fruit with plastic wrap and refrigerate while you make the fondue.

In a medium saucepan, whisk together the cocoa powder and sugar. Gradually pour in the evaporated milk and whisk well to make a paste. Place the saucepan over low heat and cook, stirring constantly, until simmering. Remove from the heat, whisk in the chocolate and vanilla, and stir until the chocolate is melted. The mixture will thicken as it cools slightly. Transfer the chocolate to a fondue pot and keep warm. Serve with the fruit and skewers for dipping.

drowned ice cream (affogato)

This heavenly dish of ice cream "drowning" in espresso coffee is hot and cold, black and white, sweet and bitter—a delicious example of how opposites attract. If you don't have an espresso maker, don't worry. Instant espresso works just fine here—regular or decaf.

MAKES 4 SERVINGS

SERVING SIZE
½ CUP ICE CREAM AND
2 OUNCES ESPRESSO
COFFEE

PER SERVING
CALORIES 110
TOTAL FAT 3 G
　SAT FAT 2 G
　MONO FAT 1 G
　POLY FAT 0 G
PROTEIN 3 G
CARB 17 G
FIBER 0 G
CHOLESTEROL 20 MG
SODIUM 55 MG

GOOD SOURCE OF
CALCIUM, IODINE,
RIBOFLAVIN

1　pint light vanilla ice cream
4　shots hot espresso coffee

Put a ½-cup scoop of ice cream into each serving bowl. Pour 1 shot of espresso over the ice cream. Serve immediately.

* EAT WELL TIP

Light ice creams are richer and creamier than ever, thanks to a new churning technique that distributes the fat more evenly. For the best taste, go for "light" instead of nonfat, and look for those with all-natural ingredients.

chocolate haystacks

I always feel a little mischievous when I make these because I know I have a trick up my sleeve. These rich morsels look like they took a lot of effort to make, like something between a decadent drop cookie and chocolate candy. It's fun to see the shock on everyone's face when I reveal the dessert's two innocent ingredients and how easy they are to pull together.

MAKES 8 SERVINGS

SERVING SIZE
2 PIECES

PER SERVING
CALORIES 140
TOTAL FAT 7 G
   SAT FAT 4 G
   MONO FAT 0 G
   POLY FAT 0 G
PROTEIN 2 G
CARB 20 G
FIBER 3 G
CHOLESTEROL 0 MG
SODIUM 0 MG

GOOD SOURCE OF
FIBER, MANGANESE

3   large shredded-wheat biscuits
      (about 2½ ounces)
6   ounces dark chocolate (60% to 70%
      cocoa solids), chopped

Line a baking sheet with wax paper. With your hands, crush the shredded wheat into thread-like pieces in a small bowl.

Place the chocolate in the top of a double boiler set over barely simmering water. Make sure the bottom of the pan does not touch the water. Melt the chocolate, stirring frequently, for about 1 minute. Remove the pan from the heat. Add the crushed shredded wheat to the chocolate and stir until the cereal is well coated.

With your fingers, place tablespoon-size stacks of the cereal-chocolate mixture on the wax paper. Place in the refrigerator to cool and set, about 20 minutes. Store and serve at room temperature.

cherry-almond-chocolate clusters

The combination of crunchy toasted almonds and chewy sweet-tart cherries covered in rich dark chocolate is about as close to the definition of "pure pleasure" as you can possibly get. Close your eyes as you eat one for the maximum effect.

MAKES 12 SERVINGS

SERVING SIZE
1 CLUSTER

PER SERVING
CALORIES 150
TOTAL FAT 10 G
 SAT FAT 3 G
 MONO FAT 4 G
 POLY FAT 1.5 G
PROTEIN 4 G
CARB 15 G
FIBER 2 G
CHOLESTEROL 0 MG
SODIUM 5 MG

GOOD SOURCE OF
MANGANESE

1   cup whole roasted almonds, coarsely chopped
½   cup dried cherries, coarsely chopped
6   ounces dark or bittersweet chocolate (60% to 70% cocoa solids), finely chopped

In a medium bowl, toss together the almonds and cherries. Line a baking sheet with wax paper.

Melt half of the chocolate in the top of a double boiler over slightly simmering water, over the lowest possible heat, stirring frequently; make sure the water is not touching the top pan. Remove the double boiler from the heat, and stir in the rest of the chocolate until melted. Remove the top pan with the chocolate in it, gently wipe the bottom of it, and set it aside for a moment. Replace the simmering water in the bottom pan with warm tap water. Put the pan of melted chocolate on top of the warm water. This will keep the chocolate at the right temperature while you make the clusters.

Stir the fruit/nut mixture into the chocolate. Spoon out heaping tablespoon-size clusters of the chocolate mixture onto the baking sheet about 1 inch apart. Put them in the refrigerator to cool and set for about 20 minutes. Store and serve at room temperature.

CHOCOLATE RULES!

Chocolate is the ultimate feel-good food because it works its magic in both the short and long run. It makes you feel great immediately because it tastes intoxicatingly good and it contains substances that quickly impart a sense of well-being. No wonder so many people crave it! But chocolate may also help you feel and look better later in life. That's because the cocoa bean, from which chocolate is made, is rich in flavonols, protective compounds that could help improve your skin and circulation and help prevent heart disease.

But not all chocolate is created equal—and just because some may be good, that doesn't mean more is better. Here are three chocolate rules to live by.

GO DARK

The antioxidant power in chocolate is in its cocoa solids, which also determine the darkness of the chocolate. When it comes to health, remember: the darker (the higher the percentage of cocoa solids) the better. But 100 percent cocoa solids taste incredibly bitter. So for the ideal balance of taste and health, go for 60 percent (bittersweet) to 70 percent (extra bittersweet) dark chocolate. Cocoa powder and baking chocolate also have loads of antioxidant power. Milk chocolate has very little, and white chocolate has practically none.

GET THE GOOD STUFF

High-quality (usually more expensive) chocolate will have a simpler and more healthful ingredient list than the typical mass-produced candy bar, which is often loaded with high-fructose corn syrup, hydrogenated oils, and artificial flavors. Treat yourself to the really good stuff. It tastes better and it's better for you.

SAVOR SLOWLY

Instead of snarfing down a whole box of chocolate in one sitting, savor it slowly to make it last. You get the most flavor when you let it melt slowly in your mouth anyway.

chocolate-dipped dried fruit

Something magical happens when dried fruit meets dark chocolate. Each has its own concentrated and complex flavors that, taken together, amplify and balance one another— a real marriage made in heaven.

MAKES 6 SERVINGS

SERVING SIZE
3 PIECES

PER SERVING
CALORIES 160
TOTAL FAT 4 G
SAT FAT 2.5 G
MONO FAT 0 G
POLY FAT 0 G
PROTEIN 1 G
CARB 31 G
FIBER 2 G
CHOLESTEROL 0 MG
SODIUM 15 MG

GOOD SOURCE OF
VITAMIN A

2½ ounces dark or bittersweet chocolate (60% to 70% cocoa solids), chopped
8 ounces mixed dried fruit (such as pears, apricots, mango, and crystallized ginger)

Line a baking sheet with wax paper.

Place the chocolate in the top of a double boiler set over barely simmering water. Make sure the bottom of the pan does not touch the water. Melt the chocolate, stirring frequently, for about 1 minute. Remove the pan from the heat.

Dip each piece of fruit into the chocolate so that half of the piece is coated with chocolate. Place on the wax paper and place in the refrigerator to cool and set, about 20 minutes. Store and serve at room temperature.

powdered sugar crisps

If you are craving something crunchy and sweet, these treats are the perfect solution. They are fun to experiment with too. Try a sprinkle of cinnamon or cocoa or cut them into different shapes with a cookie cutter, an especially fun project with kids.

MAKES 4 SERVINGS

SERVING SIZE
5 CRISPS

PER SERVING
CALORIES 80
TOTAL FAT 2.5 G
  SAT FAT 0 G
  MONO FAT 1.5 G
  POLY FAT 0 G
PROTEIN 2 G
CARB 12 G
FIBER 0 G
CHOLESTEROL 0 MG
SODIUM 115 MG

Cooking Spray
10 wonton wrappers
2 teaspoons canola oil
1 teaspoon confectioners' sugar

Preheat the oven to 375°F. Spray a baking sheet with the cooking spray.

Cut the wonton wrappers in half on the diagonal so you wind up with 20 triangles. In a medium-size bowl, toss the triangles gently with the canola oil, separating the pieces gently so each piece is coated with oil.

Place the triangles on the baking sheet in a single layer. Bake for about 10 minutes, until they are golden brown and crisped.

Dust with confectioners' sugar and serve. Crisps will keep up to 4 days in an airtight container.

chocolate–cream cheese panini bites

Chocolate, cream cheese, and raspberry jam melted together on crusty bread—yum! It's not exactly health food but it's testament to my philosophy that no food is off limits. Sometimes a little of what you crave is exactly what you need to hit the spot and move on. These are mini bites of maximum satisfaction.

MAKES 4 SERVINGS

SERVING SIZE
2 PIECES

PER SERVING
CALORIES 250
TOTAL FAT 11 G
  SAT FAT 5 G
  MONO FAT 1 G
  POLY FAT 0.5 G
PROTEIN 6 G
CARB 35 G
FIBER 2 G
CHOLESTEROL 10 MG
SODIUM 300 MG

EXCELLENT SOURCE OF
FOLATE

GOOD SOURCE OF
PROTEIN, SELENIUM, THIAMIN

½ loaf ciabatta or other Italian bread (about 6 ounces, 8x4 inches)
¼ cup (2 ounces) Neufchâtel cheese (reduced-fat cream cheese), softened
2 ounces dark or bittersweet chocolate (60% to 70% cocoa solids), coarsely chopped
2 tablespoons raspberry jam
   Cooking spray

Slice the bread open and spread one side evenly with cream cheese. Distribute the chocolate evenly on top of the cream cheese. Spread the other side of the bread with jam and close the bread to make a sandwich.

Spray a large cast-iron or nonstick skillet with cooking spray and heat over medium-high heat. Place the bread in the pan. Cover it with another smaller, heavy skillet and weigh it down with a heavy can. Cook until the underside of the bread is well toasted, 3 to 4 minutes. Flip and cook until the chocolate is melted and the other side of the bread is browned, about 3 more minutes. Remove from the heat and slice into 8 equal-size pieces.

honeydew soup with raspberry sorbet

Fresh, cool, and colorful, this elegant dessert is special enough for company but quick and simple enough for every day.

MAKES 4 SERVINGS

SERVING SIZE
1 CUP OF SOUP AND
¼ CUP SCOOP OF SORBET

PER SERVING
CALORIES 170
TOTAL FAT 2 G
  SAT FAT 1.5 G
  MONO FAT 0 G
  POLY FAT 0 G
PROTEIN 2 G
CARB 40 G
FIBER 3 G
CHOLESTEROL 0 MG
SODIUM 45 MG

EXCELLENT SOURCE OF
VITAMIN C

GOOD SOURCE OF
FIBER, FOLATE,
POTASSIUM

5	cups tightly packed honeydew chunks (from half of a 6½-pound honeydew, peeled and seeded)
1	tablespoon honey
2	tablespoons fresh lime juice
½	cup unsweetened light coconut milk
1	cup raspberry sorbet
2	teaspoons finely chopped fresh mint

In a food processor, puree the honeydew, honey, and lime juice. Pour into a bowl and stir in the coconut milk. The soup will keep in the refrigerator in an airtight container for up to 4 days.

To serve, ladle the soup into 4 shallow soup plates. Place a scoop of raspberry sorbet in the center of each serving and top with the chopped mint.

oranges in rosemary honey with toasted hazelnuts

Gorgeous, juicy orange slices are given the royal treatment here, dressed in a golden, rosemary-infused, honey-lemon syrup and crowned with a sprinkle of rich hazelnuts. It is a perfect finish for a hearty autumn or winter dinner.

MAKES 4 SERVINGS

SERVING SIZE
5 ORANGE SLICES,
1½ TABLESPOONS
HONEY MIXTURE,
2 TEASPOONS HAZELNUTS

PER SERVING
CALORIES 180
TOTAL FAT 4 G
  SAT FAT 0 G
  MONO FAT 3 G
  POLY FAT 0.5 G
PROTEIN 2 G
CARB 36 G
FIBER 4 G
CHOLESTEROL 0 MG
SODIUM 0 MG

EXCELLENT SOURCE OF
MANGANESE, VITAMIN C

GOOD SOURCE OF
FIBER, FOLATE

3	tablespoons hazelnuts
¼	cup honey
4	teaspoons fresh lemon juice
1	sprig fresh rosemary, plus more sprigs for garnish
4	navel oranges

Place the hazelnuts in a dry skillet and toast over medium-high heat, stirring frequently, until fragrant and light brown, about 3 minutes. Allow to cool, then roughly chop.

Place the honey, lemon juice, and 1 rosemary sprig in a small saucepan and bring to a boil. Remove from the heat and let the rosemary steep for 10 minutes, or up to 1 hour, then remove the rosemary sprig.

Slice off the tops and bottoms of the oranges, then slice down the sides of the oranges, removing the skin and the white pith. Slice each orange into 4 or 5 rings and place in a bowl or on a serving plate. Stir the juice that accumulated from cutting the oranges into the honey-lemon mixture.

To serve, drizzle the orange slices with the honey-lemon mixture. Top with the hazelnuts and garnish with additional rosemary sprigs.

★ DID YOU KNOW?
Honey isn't just sweet, it is rich in antioxidants—the darker the honey, the more it has.

pineapple with spicy sugar dip

This fun-to-eat sugar dip brings out the best in the sweet, tangy pineapple and leaves you with an exciting, warm tingle on your tongue.

MAKES 6 SERVINGS

SERVING SIZE
3 PINEAPPLE CHUNKS AND
1 TABLESPOON SUGAR DIP

PER SERVING
CALORIES 70
TOTAL FAT 0 G
  SAT FAT 0 G
  MONO FAT 0 G
  POLY FAT 0 G
PROTEIN 0 G
CARB 19 G
FIBER 1 G
CHOLESTEROL 0 MG
SODIUM 390 MG

EXCELLENT SOURCE OF
MANGANESE, VITAMIN C

⅓   cup sugar
1½   teaspoons chili powder
1   teaspoon salt
1   pineapple, peeled, cored, and cut into
      1½-inch chunks (about 3 cups)
6   6-inch wooden skewers

Combine the sugar, chili powder, and salt in a dry, small bowl and stir to incorporate. Place in a shallow serving dish. Thread 3 pineapple chunks onto each skewer. Arrange the skewers on a serving dish and serve with the sugar dip.

pears with almond cream

This rich, subtly tangy cream spiked with almond essence gives ripe, sliced pears just the embellishment they need to go from fruit to fabulous.

MAKES 8 SERVINGS

SERVING SIZE
½ PEAR, 3 TABLESPOONS CREAM, AND
½ TABLESPOON ALMONDS

PER SERVING
CALORIES 140
TOTAL FAT 7 G
  SAT FAT 3.5 G
  MONO FAT 2.5 G
  POLY FAT 0.5 G
PROTEIN 3 G
CARB 17 G
FIBER 3 G
CHOLESTEROL 20 MG
SODIUM 10 MG

GOOD SOURCE OF
FIBER

¼ cup sliced almonds
½ cup heavy whipping cream
2 tablespoons confectioners' sugar
½ cup plain Greek-style nonfat yogurt
¾ teaspoon almond extract
4 firm ripe pears

Toast the almonds in a dry skillet over medium-high heat, stirring frequently, until golden brown and fragrant, about 2 minutes.

Whip the cream with an electric beater until it is thickened. Add the sugar and continue beating until soft peaks are formed. Gently fold in the yogurt and almond extract. The cream will keep in the refrigerator, covered, for 2 days.

Core and slice the pears and arrange slices of half a pear on each serving plate. Top each with 3 tablespoons of the cream and sprinkle with almonds.

fruit salad with honey-lime dressing

Honey, mint, and a hit of lime give this multicolored fruit salad a bold flavor punch.

MAKES 6 SERVINGS

SERVING SIZE
1 CUP

PER SERVING
CALORIES 110
TOTAL FAT 0.5 G
  SAT FAT 0 G
  MONO FAT 0 G
  POLY FAT 0 G
PROTEIN 2 G
CARB 27 G
FIBER 4 G
SODIUM 10 MG
CHOLESTEROL 0 MG

EXCELLENT SOURCE OF
VITAMIN A, VITAMIN C,
VITAMIN K

GOOD SOURCE OF
FIBER, FOLATE,
MANGANESE, POTASSIUM

⅓   cantaloupe, peeled, seeded, and cut into ¾-inch chunks (about 2 cups)
1   16-ounce container fresh strawberries, quartered (about 3 cups)
4   medium kiwifruit, peeled and cut into ¾-inch chunks (about 2½ cups)
3   tablespoons fresh lime juice
3   tablespoons fresh mint leaves, finely chopped
3   tablespoons honey
1   teaspoon freshly grated lime zest

Place all of the fruit in a large bowl. In a small bowl, whisk together the lime juice, mint, honey, and zest. Right before serving, pour the dressing over the fruit and toss gently to combine.

✱ DID YOU KNOW?
This fruit salad could help your skin look younger! That's because it is an excellent source of both vitamin C and beta carotene (a form of vitamin A), which can help shield skin from the aging effects of the sun and pollution.

banana splits with pineapple–brown sugar topping

The warm, sugared pineapple topping melts the ice cream just enough so it can mingle with the banana, bringing all the elements together as one scrumptious sundae. It's a fun, easy treat that's satisfaction guaranteed.

MAKES 6 SERVINGS

SERVING SIZE
1 BANANA SPLIT SUNDAE

PER SERVING
CALORIES 170
TOTAL FAT 2 G
  SAT FAT 1 G
  MONO FAT 0.4 G
  POLY FAT 0 G
PROTEIN 2 G
CARB 37 G
FIBER 2 G
CHOLESTEROL 10 MG
SODIUM 30 MG

EXCELLENT SOURCE OF
VITAMIN C

GOOD SOURCE OF
VITAMIN B6

1	15-ounce can crushed pineapple in natural juice
¼	cup fresh lemon juice
2	tablespoons light brown sugar
⅛	teaspoon ground cinnamon
3	ripe but firm bananas
1½	cups light vanilla ice cream or frozen yogurt
6	fresh mint leaves

Combine the pineapple and its juice with the lemon juice, sugar, and cinnamon in a medium saucepan. Cook over medium heat, stirring occasionally, until the sugar is dissolved and the juice is reduced somewhat, about 3 minutes. Set aside to cool slightly.

Cut the bananas in half crosswise, then cut each banana half lengthwise. Arrange two pieces of banana cut side up on a small dessert plate. Top each serving with a ¼-cup-size scoop of ice cream, then add about 2½ tablespoons of the warm pineapple mixture. Top each with a mint leaf and serve.

grilled peaches **with ice cream**

Grilling fruit makes it more decadent by intensifying its flavor, warming and plumping it. A little ice cream and a sprig of mint where the pit once was make these peaches a lovely finish to a summer meal.

MAKES 4 SERVINGS

SERVING SIZE
2 PEACH HALVES

PER SERVING
CALORIES 90
TOTAL FAT 3.5 G
   SAT FAT 0.5 G
   MONO FAT 1.75 G
   POLY FAT 0.75 G
PROTEIN 2 G
CARB 14 G
FIBER 1 G
CHOLESTEROL 5 MG
SODIUM 10 MG

GOOD SOURCE OF
VITAMIN C

4   ripe but firm peaches
2   teaspoons canola oil
½   cup light vanilla ice cream or frozen yogurt
8   small sprigs fresh mint

Preheat a grill or nonstick grill pan over medium heat.

Cut each peach in half and remove the pits. Brush the cut side of each peach half with oil. Place the peaches cut side down on the grill or grill pan and cook until the peaches soften slightly and grill marks are formed, 2 to 3 minutes.

Place a tablespoon-size scoop of ice cream in the center of each peach half. Garnish with mint and serve.

angel food cake with mango sauce

This vibrant yellow mango sauce is the perfect balance of sweet and tangy. Here it turns ordinary store-bought cake into a magnificent dessert, but it also happens to be delicious over ice cream. All it takes is a quick whir of the blender.

MAKES 12 SERVINGS

SERVING SIZE
1 SLICE CAKE,
1 TABLESPOON SAUCE,
AND 1 TABLESPOON
MANGO CHUNKS

PER SERVING
CALORIES 110
TOTAL FAT 0 G
  SAT FAT 0 G
  MONO FAT 0 G
  POLY FAT 0 G
PROTEIN 2 G
CARB 25 G
FIBER 1 G
CHOLESTEROL 0 MG
SODIUM 230 MG

GOOD SOURCE OF
RIBOFLAVIN, VITAMIN C

2 medium ripe mangoes, peeled, pitted, and cut into chunks, or one 10-ounce bag frozen mango, thawed
2 tablespoons fresh lime juice
1 tablespoon sugar
2 teaspoons Cointreau or other orange liqueur, optional
1 store-bought angel food cake (about 13 ounces)
¼ cup fresh mint leaves

In a blender or food processor, process half the mangoes with the lime juice, sugar, and Cointreau until smooth. Dice the rest of the mangoes.

Slice the cake, pour 1 tablespoon of the mango sauce over each slice, and toss some diced mango on top. Garnish with the mint leaves and serve.

desserts— extra special

* **THERE IS SOMETHING TO BE SAID FOR ANTICIPATION** — waiting for a cobbler to come out of the oven as the aroma teases you, looking forward to the glorious moment when **A SILKY PUDDING IS SET** or decadent chocolate pops are frozen. Something about the waiting makes the digging in even more satisfying. These **SCRUMPTIOUS DESSERTS** may ask you to wait a bit, but they won't ask you to do much more than that, except enjoy.

peanut butter crispy rice treats

Sticky sweet squares of crispy rice make you feel like a kid again—when you are making them and when you are eating them. Here the family favorite is updated, with whole-grain cereal and peanut butter and honey instead of marshmallow. I added chewy, tangy dried cherries to the mix here, but it works with any dried fruit—or even chocolate chips.

MAKES 15 SERVINGS

SERVING SIZE
1 SQUARE

PER SERVING
CALORIES 200
TOTAL FAT 7 G
  SAT FAT 1.5 G
  MONO FAT 3 G
  POLY FAT 1.5 G
PROTEIN 4 G
CARB 32 G
FIBER 2 G
CHOLESTEROL 0 MG
SODIUM 65 MG

¾   cup chunky natural-style peanut butter
¾   cup honey
6   cups crispy brown rice cereal
⅔   cup (3 ounces) dried cherries, chopped
    Cooking spray

Combine the peanut butter and honey in a large pot and heat over medium-low heat until melted, 2 to 3 minutes. Add the brown rice cereal and cherries and stir to combine until the mixture is sticky. Press into a 9x13-inch pan sprayed with cooking spray. Chill in the refrigerator for 40 minutes. Cut into fifteen 2½x3-inch squares.

fig and ginger truffles

Fig and ginger are a fabulous duo, with ginger adding just the right zing to the earthy sweet fruit. But when you envelop those flavors in rich dark chocolate—look out! Because then you have "fabulous" plus chocolate. Need I say more?

MAKES 8 SERVINGS

SERVING SIZE
2 TRUFFLES

PER SERVING
CALORIES 200
TOTAL FAT 3.5 G
  SAT FAT 2 G
  MONO FAT 0 G
  POLY FAT 0 G
PROTEIN 2 G
CARB 45 G
FIBER 6 G
CHOLESTEROL 0 MG
SODIUM 5 MG

EXCELLENT SOURCE OF
FIBER

GOOD SOURCE OF
MANGANESE

2	cups dried black Mission figs or other dried figs (about 8 ounces)
¼	cup crystallized ginger (about 2 ounces)
1	tablespoon honey
½	teaspoon ground cinnamon
2½	ounces dark chocolate (60% to 70% cocoa solids), chopped

Remove the stems from the figs and discard. Put the figs, ginger, honey, and cinnamon in a food processor and process for about 45 seconds, until the ingredients are finely chopped and begin to stick together. Roll the fig mixture with your hands into heaping teaspoon-size balls and set them on a baking sheet or plate lined with wax paper.

Place a small bowl over a saucepan containing barely simmering water over low heat. Make sure the water is at least 2 inches from the bottom of the bowl. Place half the chocolate in the bowl and stir until it is melted. Remove the saucepan from the heat and add the remaining chocolate. Stir until all the chocolate is melted. Remove the bowl containing the chocolate from the pan.

Roll the fig balls in the melted chocolate, one or two at a time, until they are all covered. Place them back on the wax paper and then chill in the refrigerator until set, about 15 minutes. Serve at room temperature.

* DID YOU KNOW?
Dried fruit, like figs, are among the foods most closely linked with less skin wrinkling. How ironic that a wrinkly fruit can help keep your skin smooth.

no-cook lemon bars

If you love cheesecake and you love lemon, you will double-love these delicious bars. They have a velvety, cream cheese filling with just the right citrus kick and that crave-able, classic graham cracker crust. All that and you don't even need an oven to make them.

MAKES 16 SERVINGS

SERVING SIZE
1 SQUARE

PER SERVING
CALORIES 150
TOTAL FAT 5 G
  SAT FAT 3 G
  MONO FAT 1.5 G
  POLY FAT 0.5 G
PROTEIN 4 G
CARB 22 G
FIBER 0 G
CHOLESTEROL 20 MG
SODIUM 160 MG

CRUST

14	whole-grain graham cracker squares (7 full sheets)
2	tablespoons melted unsalted butter
1	tablespoon dark brown sugar
¼	teaspoon salt
	Cooking spray

FILLING

1	8-ounce package Neufchâtel cheese (reduced-fat cream cheese), softened at room temperature
1	14-ounce can fat-free sweetened condensed milk
¼	cup pasteurized egg product (such as Egg Beaters)
½	cup fresh lemon juice
1	teaspoon finely grated lemon zest
2	teaspoons powdered gelatin
3	tablespoons boiling water

Place the graham crackers in a food processor and pulse until crumbs are formed. Add the butter, brown sugar, and salt and pulse until crumbs resemble wet sand. Coat an 8-inch-square pan with cooking spray and pack the crumbs firmly into the bottom of it. Refrigerate while you prepare the filling.

In a large bowl, combine the cream cheese, condensed milk, and pasteurized egg product and beat on high with an electric mixer until smooth and creamy, about 2 minutes. Add the lemon juice and zest and beat until fully incorporated, another 30 seconds. In a small bowl, combine the gelatin and boiling water and whisk until the gelatin is entirely dissolved; let cool for 2 to 3 minutes. Using a spoon, stir the gelatin into the cream cheese mixture until incorporated. Pour the filling over the crust. Refrigerate for at least 8 hours. Slice into 2-inch squares using a chilled knife coated with cooking spray.

mixed berry cobbler

When this down-home dessert comes out of the oven just watch the faces of those around you light up. They'll see flakey golden biscuits sitting proudly atop a bubbling mix of sweetened berries, bursting with juice that has thickened just enough to form a luscious fruit sauce. Eating it will satisfy body and soul. You gotta love a recipe that gives so much for so little effort.

MAKES 6 SERVINGS

SERVING SIZE
¾ CUP

PER SERVING
CALORIES 220
TOTAL FAT 9 G
   SAT FAT 3 G
   MONO FAT 4 G
   POLY FAT 1.5 G
PROTEIN 3 G
CARB 34 G
FIBER 5 G
CHOLESTEROL 10 MG
SODIUM 210 MG

EXCELLENT SOURCE OF
VITAMIN C

GOOD SOURCE OF
FIBER, MANGANESE,
SELENIUM

FILLING

    Cooking spray
2   12-ounce bags frozen mixed berries,
      thawed (about 6 cups)
¼   cup whole-wheat flour
¼   cup sugar
    Finely grated zest of 1 orange
      (about 2 teaspoons)

TOPPING

¼   cup whole-wheat flour
¼   cup all-purpose flour
2   tablespoons plus 1 teaspoon sugar
½   teaspoon baking powder
¼   teaspoon baking soda
¼   teaspoon salt
2   tablespoons chilled unsalted butter,
      cut into small pieces
⅓   cup low-fat buttermilk
2   tablespoons canola oil

Preheat the oven to 400°F. Coat an 8x8-inch baking dish with cooking spray.

In a large bowl, toss the berries with the whole-wheat flour, sugar, and zest. Transfer the berry mixture to the baking dish and set aside.

In a medium bowl, whisk together the flours, 2 tablespoons of the sugar, baking powder, baking soda, and salt. Cut in the butter using 2 knives or a pastry cutter until many small pebble-size pieces are formed.

In a small bowl or pitcher, whisk together the buttermilk and oil. Add the mixture to the dry ingredients and mix until just moistened. Do not over mix. Drop the batter onto the fruit, forming 6 mounds. Sprinkle with the remaining teaspoon of sugar. Bake for 30 minutes, until the fruit is bubbly and the top is golden. Let stand for at least 10 minutes before serving.

apple brown betty

With a sweet, tender apple "filling" and a golden buttery crust made from fresh bread crumbs, this dish gives you all the homey flavors and aromas of an apple pie, but without the fuss.

MAKES 6 SERVINGS

SERVING SIZE
1 CUP

PER SERVING
CALORIES 230
TOTAL FAT 7 G
  SAT FAT 3 G
  MONO FAT 1.5 G
  POLY FAT 2 G
PROTEIN 3 G
CARB 42 G
FIBER 6 G
CHOLESTEROL 10 MG
SODIUM 75 MG

EXCELLENT SOURCE OF
FIBER, MANGANESE

GOOD SOURCE OF
VITAMIN C

5   large Golden Delicious apples
      (about 2 pounds), peeled and thinly sliced
1   cup apple cider
3   tablespoons brown sugar
1   teaspoon vanilla extract
1   teaspoon ground cinnamon
2   tablespoons unsalted butter
3   slices whole-wheat bread (1 ounce each;
      crusts included), or enough to make about
      2¼ cups crumbs
3   tablespoons chopped walnuts

Preheat the oven to 350°F.

Combine the apples, apple cider, 1 tablespoon of the brown sugar, the vanilla, and ½ teaspoon of the cinnamon in a large saucepan over medium-high heat. Cook, stirring occasionally, until the apples are tender but still retain their shape, about 10 minutes. Stir in 1 tablespoon of the butter until melted, remove from the heat, and transfer the apple mixture to a 9-inch pie plate or a ceramic dish.

Place the bread in the food processor and process until crumbs are formed, about 15 seconds. Melt the remaining 1 tablespoon butter in the microwave for 20 seconds. Toss the crumbs with the melted butter, walnuts, remaining 2 tablespoons of brown sugar, and remaining ½ teaspoon of cinnamon. Scatter the crumb mixture on top of the apples and bake for 30 minutes, until the topping is crisped and lightly browned.

raspberry clafoutis

Clafoutis is a thick dessert pancake that is chock-full of fruit. It looks so special in its golden brown splendor, studded with plump raspberries and dusted with sugar, your guests will never guess how easy it is to whip up.

MAKES 6 SERVINGS

SERVING SIZE
1 WEDGE

PER SERVING
CALORIES 120
TOTAL FAT 3.5 G
  SAT FAT 1.5 G
  MONO FAT 0.5 G
  POLY FAT 0 G
PROTEIN 5 G
CARB 18 G
FIBER 2 G
CHOLESTEROL 45 MG
SODIUM 140 MG

GOOD SOURCE OF
IODINE, THIAMIN,
VITAMIN C

Cooking spray
1 tablespoon plus ⅓ cup whole-wheat pastry flour
1½ cups fresh or frozen (unthawed) raspberries (6 ounces)
1 large egg and 2 large egg whites, lightly beaten
1 cup low-fat (1%) milk
¼ cup granulated sugar
1 tablespoon melted butter, cooled
1 teaspoon vanilla extract or raspberry liqueur
¼ teaspoon salt
1 tablespoon turbinado sugar (such as Sugar in the Raw)

Preheat the oven to 350°F.

Spray a 9-inch pie plate or ceramic dish with cooking spray and coat with 1 tablespoon of the flour, shaking off the excess. Scatter the raspberries on the surface of the dish and reserve.

In a medium-size bowl, combine the egg and egg whites, milk, granulated sugar, butter, vanilla or liqueur, and salt and whisk to blend. Add the remaining ⅓ cup of flour and stir to incorporate, making sure not to over-work the batter. Pour the batter over the raspberries. Bake until the clafoutis is golden brown and the center is set, 45 to 50 minutes. Sprinkle with the turbinado sugar and serve immediately.

THE SCOOP ON SUGAR

Let's keep things in perspective, folks. Sugar isn't the demon it's made out to be. But we Americans seem to have a mouthful of sweet teeth, consuming an average of 23 teaspoons of added sugars (368 calories' worth) each day! That's a bit overboard, don't you think? Especially considering that the recommended cap is eight teaspoons a day.

I am not counting the sugar inherent in whole foods like fruit, 100% fruit juices, vegetables, and dairy foods. I am talking about the stuff you (and food companies) add to food to make it taste sweeter—white or brown sugar, honey, maple syrup, agave syrup, evaporated cane juice, high-fructose corn syrup—it all adds up. Here are a few ideas for getting back in balance.

AVOID SUGARY DRINKS

One 12-ounce can of regular soda packs a whopping 10 teaspoons of added sugar. Lemonade, energy drinks, and sweet teas have nearly as much.

SWEETEN YOURSELF

Buy the unsweetened versions of foods like yogurt and breakfast cereal and add sweetener at home to taste. Chances are you will put in a lot less than the food manufacturers do, and this way you can gradually wean yourself, using less over time.

GO UNREFINED

Whenever possible go for unrefined sweeteners like honey, maple syrup, and molasses. They are not tremendously different from the plain white stuff, but they do contain some antioxidants and minerals. And they have a richer flavor, so you'll likely use less.

SWEETEN SMARTLY

Use your daily eight-teaspoon allotment to enhance the deliciousness of good-for-you foods. Sprinkle some on your berries or grapefruit, stir it into your oatmeal, add some to balance the flavor of a salad dressing or marinade, or use it to make one of the fabulous desserts here.

pumpkin rice pudding

This dessert is the magic that happens when creamy rice pudding meets aromatic, deeply flavorful pumpkin pie. It is the best of both familiar favorites, and it practically makes itself in the oven.

MAKES 8 SERVINGS

SERVING SIZE
½ CUP RICE PUDDING
AND 1½ TABLESPOONS
WHIPPED CREAM

PER SERVING
CALORIES 240
TOTAL FAT 6 G
  SAT FAT 3.5 G
  MONO FAT 1.5 G
  POLY FAT 0 G
PROTEIN 4 G
CARB 42 G
FIBER 1 G
CHOLESTEROL 20 MG
SODIUM 120 MG

EXCELLENT SOURCE OF
VITAMIN A

GOOD SOURCE OF
CALCIUM, IODINE,
PHOSPHORUS,
RIBOFLAVIN, VITAMIN D

2	cups water
1	cup arborio rice
3	cups reduced-fat (2%) milk
1	cup solid-pack pure pumpkin (not pumpkin pie filling)
¾	cup honey
1	teaspoon vanilla extract
¾	teaspoon ground cinnamon plus more for garnish
¼	teaspoon ground ginger
¼	teaspoon ground nutmeg
¼	teaspoon salt
⅓	cup heavy whipping cream, whipped

Preheat the oven to 375°F.

Bring the water to a boil in an ovenproof 4-quart saucepan. Stir in the rice and cover. Reduce the heat to low and simmer until the rice is nearly cooked, about 20 minutes.

In a large bowl, whisk together the milk, pumpkin, honey, vanilla, cinnamon, ginger, nutmeg, and salt. While the rice is still hot, add the pumpkin mixture to the saucepan and stir well to combine. Cover and transfer to the oven. Bake until the liquid has reduced by about a third and the mixture is foamy and bubbling, 45 to 50 minutes. Remove from the oven and stir well to combine all the ingredients. Transfer to a large bowl, then cover and chill in the refrigerator for at least 8 hours or overnight. The pudding will keep for up to 4 days in an airtight container in the refrigerator. Serve with a dollop of whipped cream and a sprinkling of cinnamon.

✳ EATING WELL TIP
Canned pumpkin is one of the top sources of beta carotene, and it is packed with potassium and fiber. Once opened, it will last up to a week in an airtight container in the refrigerator. Add it to smoothies or pancake batter or stir some into your morning oatmeal.

balsamic strawberries with ricotta cream

Ricotta cheese fits just as well in the world of sweet as it does in savory. Whip it up with a little honey and you get the most magnificent, rich cream, which is fantastic topped with juicy strawberries in a sweet balsamic syrup. Ribbons of basil add a fresh perfume, proving it too is delightful in dessert.

MAKES 4 SERVINGS

SERVING SIZE
⅓ CUP CREAM AND
½ CUP BERRIES

PER SERVING
CALORIES 180
TOTAL FAT 5 G
  SAT FAT 3 G
  MONO FAT 1.5 G
  POLY FAT 0 G
PROTEIN 8 G
CARB 27 G
FIBER 2 G
CHOLESTEROL 20 MG
SODIUM 80 MG

EXCELLENT SOURCE OF
MANGANESE, VITAMIN C

GOOD SOURCE OF
CALCIUM, PHOSPHORUS,
PROTEIN, SELENIUM,
VITAMIN K

1   cup part-skim ricotta cheese
2   tablespoons honey
½   teaspoon vanilla extract
3   tablespoons balsamic vinegar
2   tablespoons sugar
1   16-ounce container fresh strawberries,
      stems removed and quartered
2   tablespoons fresh basil leaves, cut into ribbons

Put the ricotta cheese, honey, and vanilla extract into the small bowl of a food processor and process until smooth, about 1 minute. Transfer to a small bowl and refrigerate for at least 2 hours.

In a small saucepan, combine the vinegar and sugar and bring to a boil. Simmer over medium heat for 2 minutes, stirring occasionally. Allow to cool completely. In a medium-size bowl, toss the berries with the basil and the balsamic syrup.

Divide the ricotta mixture among 4 cocktail glasses or dessert bowls, top with the berry mixture, and serve.

sparkling basil peaches

Maybe it's the bubbly, but this dessert makes me giddy. It's effervescent, exciting, and practically poetic in its elegant simplicity. Just four little ingredients with big power to impress.

MAKES 6 SERVINGS

SERVING SIZE
⅔ CUP PEACHES AND
½ CUP LIQUID

PER SERVING
CALORIES 200
TOTAL FAT 0 G
  SAT FAT 0 G
  MONO FAT 0 G
  POLY FAT 0 G
PROTEIN 1 G
CARB 30 G
FIBER 2 G
CHOLESTEROL 0 MG
SODIUM 0 MG

GOOD SOURCE OF
VITAMIN A, VITAMIN C,
VITAMIN K

5	large ripe peaches, or two 10-ounce bags unsweetened frozen sliced peaches
1	750-ml bottle Prosecco or other sparkling wine (not an extra-dry variety)
⅓	cup superfine sugar
½	cup packed basil leaves, sliced into ribbons

If using fresh peaches, bring a 4-quart pot of water to a boil and fill a large bowl with ice water. With a paring knife, slice through each peach skin from end to end, but leave the peach intact. Gently place the peaches in the boiling water and boil for 30 seconds. Transfer the peaches into the ice water for 30 seconds, and then remove them using a slotted spoon. Gently remove the skins from the peaches, then split the peaches in half and remove the pits. Cut each peach into 8 slices.

Pour the Prosecco into a large bowl. Add the sugar and stir gently until dissolved. Add the peach slices and basil and stir to combine. Cover and refrigerate for at least 2 hours and up to 8 hours. Serve the peaches in a bowl with some liquid and basil leaves.

✳ EATING WELL TIP
If you don't have superfine sugar, you can make it yourself by processing regular granulated sugar in the food processor until fine.

choco-coco pops

Chocolate and coconut are one of my all-time favorite combinations. Here they meet as an indulgent ice pop, ready to save the day whenever the craving for cool, sweet, and creamy strikes.

MAKES 6 SERVINGS

SERVING SIZE
1 POPSICLE

PER SERVING
CALORIES 140
TOTAL FAT 8 G
  SAT FAT 6 G
  MONO FAT 1.5 G
  POLY FAT 0 G
PROTEIN 3 G
CARB 18 G
FIBER 1 G
CHOLESTEROL 0 MG
SODIUM 35 MG

1   13.5-ounce can unsweetened light
      coconut milk
1   cup low-fat (1%) milk
3   ounces dark or bittersweet chocolate
      (60% to 70% cocoa solids), chopped
2   tablespoons sugar
1   teaspoon vanilla extract

Combine all the ingredients in a saucepan and bring to a boil over medium heat. Reduce to a simmer and whisk until the chocolate is melted. Remove from the heat and allow to cool for about 15 minutes. Distribute among six 8-ounce Popsicle molds or paper cups and place in the freezer. If using paper cups, place a Popsicle stick in the center of each cup after a ½ hour in the freezer. Allow to freeze completely, about 4 hours.

* EATING WELL TIP
Coconut is the one fruit I consider a "rarely" because it is high in saturated fat. The type of saturated fat it contains may not be as damaging as others, but the jury isn't yet in. Until it is, I recommend the light version of coconut milk, which has a third of the calories and a quarter of the fat of regular.

watermelon blueberry pops

I came up with this recipe as a kitschy red, white, and blue tribute to Independence Day. They were such a hit with kids and adults alike and so easy to prepare that I wound up making them all summer long. They are the perfect refreshment on a hot day.

MAKES 6 SERVINGS

SERVING SIZE
1 POP

PER SERVING
CALORIES 45
TOTAL FAT 0 G
  SAT FAT 0 G
  MONO FAT 0 G
  POLY FAT 0 G
PROTEIN 0 G
CARB 13 G
FIBER 1 G
CHOLESTEROL 0 MG
SODIUM 0 MG

GOOD SOURCE OF
VITAMIN C

3   cups cubed seeded watermelon
      (from about 2 pounds with the rind)
2   tablespoons fresh lime juice
2   tablespoons confectioner's sugar
1   cup blueberries

Puree the watermelon, lime juice, and sugar in a blender. Distribute the blueberries among six 8-ounce Popsicle molds or paper cups, then fill each with the watermelon mixture and place in the freezer. If using paper cups, place a Popsicle stick in the center of each cup after a ½ hour in the freezer. Allow to freeze completely, about 4 hours.

CRAVING SWEETS? NIBBLE ON THIS.

Listening to your sugar cravings and satisfying them smartly can be a key part of living a balanced life. Here are some ways to get your fix without overdoing it.

INDULGE MINDFULLY. We've all been there: in front of the fridge with a carton of ice cream guiltily shoveling it in. Before we know it the pint is gone. It's OK to indulge, just do so mindfully. Scoop a portion into a dish, sit down, and savor every luscious bite. This way you'll enjoy more, eat less, and there will be no room left over for guilt.

STAY ON SCHEDULE. Next time you're hit with a sugar-craving tsunami, consider the last time you ate a balanced meal or snack. Your urge for sugar may be a result of having gone too long without eating or not eating enough throughout the day. So before you reach for the sweets, try a healthier snack like some nuts and fruit, and get into the habit of fueling up regularly.

DON'T COMPROMISE. Too often, in an earnest effort to conquer cravings healthfully, we choose a tasteless fat-free, sugar-free substitute for what we really want. On the flip side, there are times when we eat a sweet just because it is in front of us, whether it is truly appealing or not. Both scenarios leave us full but unsatisfied. For maximum dessert satisfaction, be picky. Go for a little of the real thing and make sure it's absolutely delicious.

CHEW AWAY. Research shows that chewing gum can help curb sweet cravings. So keep a stick on hand for when the sugar urge strikes. It just might do the trick.

TAKE STOCK AND TUNE IN. Paying attention to when and why you reach for sweets can help you get a handle on cravings. Whether you reach for a bag of candy after a tough day at work or plop down each night in front of the TV with a box of cookies, learning what turns these cravings on is the best way to satisfy them. A relaxing bath, a walk in the park, or a chat with a friend could be what you really need.

mini ice cream sandwiches

What's more fun than an ice cream sandwich? Mini ice cream sandwiches! They are cold, creamy, crunchy morsels you can eat in two bites. A whimsical treat that is great for a party, or when you just feel like you need one.

MAKES 4 SERVINGS

SERVING SIZE
3 ICE CREAM SANDWICHES

PER SERVING
CALORIES 220
TOTAL FAT 8 G
  SAT FAT 3 G
  MONO FAT 0 G
  POLY FAT 0 G
PROTEIN 4 G
CARB 35 G
FIBER 1 G
CHOLESTEROL 10 MG
SODIUM 170 MG

½ cup light vanilla ice cream or frozen yogurt, softened at room temperature
24 vanilla wafer cookies (1½ inches in diameter)
1 ounce dark or bittersweet chocolate (60% to 70% cocoa solids), finely chopped

Line a shallow storage container with wax paper. Put a small scoop of ice cream (about 2 teaspoons) on a cookie and top with another cookie. Roll the ice cream sandwich in the chopped chocolate so the chocolate adheres to the ice cream. Place in the wax paper-lined container. Repeat with the remaining ingredients until you have 12 ice cream sandwiches.

    Cover and place in the freezer to set for at least 30 minutes, or freeze for up to 1 week.

recipe nutritional data index

* **IN CASE YOU WANT TO MAKE ANY OF THE RECIPES "A LA CARTE"**
  (not as part of the suggested meal), here is the nutrition information for them individually.

SALMON, EGGS, AND ONION (PAGE 50)

PER SERVING CALORIES 220; TOTAL FAT 9 G (SAT FAT 2.5 G, MONO FAT 2 G, POLY FAT 1.5 G); PROTEIN 28 G; CARB 6 G; FIBER 1 G; CHOLESTEROL 260 MG; SODIUM 140 MG
EXCELLENT SOURCE OF NIACIN, PHOSPHORUS, PROTEIN, SELENIUM, VITAMIN B12, VITAMIN D
GOOD SOURCE OF IODINE, POTASSIUM, RIBOFLAVIN, THIAMIN, VITAMIN A, VITAMIN B6, VITAMIN C, VITAMIN K

PUMPERNICKEL CRISPS (PAGE 50)

PER SERVING: CALORIES 150; TOTAL FAT 1 G (SAT FAT 0 G, MONO FAT 0 G, POLY FAT 0 G); PROTEIN 5 G; CARB 31 G; FIBER 2 G; CHOLESTEROL 0 MG; SODIUM 280 MG
GOOD SOURCE OF PROTEIN, NIACIN, THIAMIN

DUTCH BABY PANCAKE (PAGE 57)

PER SERVING CALORIES 200; TOTAL FAT 7 G (SAT FAT 3.5 G, MONO FAT 1 G, POLY FAT 0 G); PROTEIN 10 G; CARB 26 G; FIBER 1 G; CHOLESTEROL 120 MG; SODIUM 380 MG
EXCELLENT SOURCE OF THIAMIN
GOOD SOURCE OF IODINE, PROTEIN, RIBOFLAVIN

PEACH COMPOTE (PAGE 58)

PER SERVING CALORIES 110; TOTAL FAT 0 G (SAT FAT 0 G, MONO FAT 0 G, POLY FAT 0 G); PROTEIN 1 G; CARB 27 G; FIBER 2 G; CHOLESTEROL 0 MG; SODIUM 150 MG
EXCELLENT SOURCE OF MANGANESE
GOOD SOURCE OF VITAMIN C

WHOLE-WHEAT APPLE PANCAKES (PAGE 61)

PER SERVING CALORIES 240; TOTAL FAT 2.5 G; (SAT FAT 1 G, MONO FAT 0.1 G, POLY FAT 0 G); PROTEIN 8 G; CARB 48 G; FIBER 3 G; CHOLESTEROL 75 MG; SODIUM 446 MG
EXCELLENT SOURCE OF MANGANESE, PROTEIN, SELENIUM
GOOD SOURCE OF CALCIUM, FIBER, IRON, PHOSPHO-RUS, THIAMIN

NUTTY TOPPING (PAGE 62)

PER SERVING CALORIES 160; TOTAL FAT 9 G (SAT FAT 1.5 G, MONO FAT 2.5 G, POLY FAT 2.5 G); PROTEIN 7 G; CARB 15 G; FIBER 2 G; CHOLESTEROL 0 MG; SODIUM 0 MG
EXCELLENT SOURCE OF MANGANESE
GOOD SOURCE OF COPPER, IRON, MAGNESIUM, PHOS-PHORUS, PROTEIN, ZINC

WHEAT BERRY SALAD (PAGE 69)

PER SERVING CALORIES 360; TOTAL FAT 17 G (SAT FAT 2 G, MONO FAT 6 G, POLY FAT 8 G); PROTEIN 9 G; CARB 47 G; FIBER 8 G; CHOLESTEROL 0 MG; SODIUM 40 MG
EXCELLENT SOURCE OF FIBER, MANGANESE, VITAMIN A, VITAMIN K
GOOD SOURCE OF COPPER, IRON, PROTEIN, VITAMIN C

LEMON-CUMIN GRILLED CHICKEN BREAST (PAGE 70)

PER SERVING CALORIES 180; TOTAL FAT 6 G (SAT FAT 1.5 G, MONO FAT 3 G, POLY FAT 1 G); PROTEIN 29 G; CARB 1 G; FIBER 0 G; CHOLESTEROL 80 MG; SODIUM 360 MG
EXCELLENT SOURCE OF NIACIN, PHOSPHORUS, PROTEIN, SELENIUM, VITAMIN B6

LAMB AND FETA PITA PIZZAS (PAGE 97)

PER SERVING CALORIES 420; TOTAL FAT 22 G (SAT FAT 8 G, MONO FAT 8 G, POLY FAT 3 G); PROTEIN 19 G; CARB 41 G; FIBER 6 G; CHOLESTEROL 55 MG; SODIUM 950 MG
EXCELLENT SOURCE OF FIBER, MANGANESE, NIACIN, PHOSPHORUS, PROTEIN, SELENIUM, THIAMIN, VITAMIN B12, VITAMIN K, ZINC
GOOD SOURCE OF CALCIUM, COPPER, FOLATE, IRON, MAGNESIUM, PANTOTHENIC ACID, POTASSIUM, RIBOFLAVIN, VITAMIN A, VITAMIN B6, VITAMIN C

FENNEL-ARUGULA SALAD (PAGE 98)

PER SERVING CALORIES 90; TOTAL FAT 7 G (SAT FAT 1 G, MONO FAT 5 G, POLY FAT 1 G); PROTEIN 2 G; CARB 7 G; FIBER 2 G; CHOLESTEROL 0 MG; SODIUM 180 MG
EXCELLENT SOURCE OF VITAMIN C, VITAMIN K
GOOD SOURCE OF FOLATE, MANGANESE, POTASSIUM, VITAMIN A

SPAGHETTI FRITTATA (PAGE 100)

PER SERVING CALORIES 320; TOTAL FAT 13 G (SAT FAT 4 G, MONO FAT 3 G, POLY FAT 1 G); PROTEIN 22 G; CARB 32 G; FIBER 6 G; CHOLESTEROL 275 MG; SODIUM 790 MG
EXCELLENT SOURCE OF CALCIUM, FIBER, MANGANESE, PROTEIN, SELENIUM, VITAMIN A
GOOD SOURCE OF IODINE, IRON, RIBOFLAVIN, VITAMIN C

SALAD PRESTO (PAGE 101)
PER SERVING CALORIES 60; TOTAL FAT 7 G (SAT FAT 1 G, MONO FAT 5 G, POLY FAT 1 G); PROTEIN 1 G; CARB 1 G; FIBER 1 G; CHOLESTEROL 0 MG; SODIUM 20 MG
EXCELLENT SOURCE OF VITAMIN A
GOOD SOURCE OF VITAMIN C

CRAB AND AVOCADO DUET (PAGE 109)
PER SERVING CALORIES 150; TOTAL FAT 8 G (SAT FAT 1 G, MONO FAT 5 G, POLY FAT 1 G); PROTEIN 15 G; CARB 5 G; FIBER 3 G; CHOLESTEROL 65 MG; SODIUM 390 MG
EXCELLENT SOURCE OF PROTEIN
GOOD SOURCE OF FIBER, FOLATE, POTASSIUM, VITAMIN C, VITAMIN K

COOL CUCUMBER SOUP (WITHOUT BREAD) (PAGE 110)
PER SERVING CALORIES 130; TOTAL FAT 2.5 G (SAT FAT 0 G, MONO FAT 1.5 G, POLY FAT 0 G); PROTEIN 11 G; CARB 17 G; FIBER 2 G; CHOLESTEROL 5 MG; SODIUM 140 MG
EXCELLENT SOURCE OF CALCIUM, PROTEIN, VITAMIN A, VITAMIN C, VITAMIN K

SHRIMP ROLL (PAGE 113)
PER SERVING CALORIES 340; TOTAL FAT 14 G (SAT FAT 2.5 G, MONO FAT 5 G, POLY FAT 6.5 G); PROTEIN 29 G; CARB 24 G; FIBER 3 G; CHOLESTEROL 225 MG; SODIUM 540 MG
EXCELLENT SOURCE OF IRON, MANGANESE, NIACIN, PHOSPHORUS, PROTEIN, SELENIUM, VITAMIN B12, VITAMIN D
GOOD SOURCE OF CALCIUM, COPPER, FIBER, MAGNESIUM, POTASSIUM, VITAMIN B6, ZINC

CRACKED PEPPER POTATO CHIPS (PAGE 114)
PER SERVING CALORIES 190; TOTAL FAT 5 G (SAT FAT 0.5 G, MONO FAT 3 G, POLY FAT 0.75 G); PROTEIN 4 G; CARB 32 G; FIBER 4 G; CHOLESTEROL 0 MG; SODIUM 20 MG
EXCELLENT SOURCE OF POTASSIUM, VITAMIN B6, VITAMIN C
GOOD SOURCE OF FIBER, MAGNESIUM, MANGANESE, NIACIN, PHOSPHORUS

BEEF STROGANOFF (PAGE 120)
PER SERVING CALORIES 520; TOTAL FAT 15 G (SAT FAT 3.5 G, MONO FAT 6.5 G, POLY FAT 2.5 G); PROTEIN 40 G; CARB 51 G; FIBER 2 G; CHOLESTEROL 85 MG; SODIUM 560 MG
EXCELLENT SOURCE OF COPPER, FOLATE, IRON, MANGANESE, NIACIN, PANTOTHENIC ACID, PHOSPHORUS, POTASSIUM, PROTEIN, RIBOFLAVIN, SELENIUM, THIAMIN, VITAMIN B6, VITAMIN B12, VITAMIN K, ZINC
GOOD SOURCE OF FIBER, MAGNESIUM

GREEN BEANS AND GRAINY MUSTARD (PAGE 121)
PER SERVING CALORIES 40; TOTAL FAT 0 G (SAT FAT 0 G, MONO FAT 0 G, POLY FAT 0 G); PROTEIN 2 G; CARB 9 G; FIBER 4 G; CHOLESTEROL 0 MG; SODIUM 25 MG
EXCELLENT SOURCE OF VITAMIN C, VITAMIN K
GOOD SOURCE OF FIBER, FOLATE, MANGANESE, VITAMIN A

STEAK CHIMICHURRI (PAGE 125)
PER SERVING CALORIES 270; TOTAL FAT 16 G (SAT FAT 3.5 G, MONO FAT 9.5 G, POLY FAT 2 G); PROTEIN 32 G; CARB 1 G; FIBER 0 G; CHOLESTEROL 50 MG; SODIUM 370 MG
EXCELLENT SOURCE OF NIACIN, PHOSPHORUS, PROTEIN, SELENIUM, VITAMIN B6, VITAMIN B12, VITAMIN K, ZINC
GOOD SOURCE OF IRON, POTASSIUM, RIBOFLAVIN, THIAMIN, VITAMIN C

GRILLED GARLIC BREAD (PAGE 126)
PER SERVING CALORIES 160; TOTAL FAT 6 G (SAT FAT 1 G, MONO FAT 3 G, POLY FAT 1.5 G); PROTEIN 7 G; CARB 22 G; FIBER 4 G; CHOLESTEROL 0 MG; SODIUM 350 MG
EXCELLENT SOURCE OF MANGANESE, SELENIUM
GOOD SOURCE OF FIBER, NIACIN, PHOSPHORUS, PROTEIN

GRILLED TOMATOES (PAGE 126)
PER SERVING CALORIES 60; TOTAL FAT 4 G (SAT FAT 0.5 G, MONO FAT 2.5 G, POLY FAT 0.5 G); PROTEIN 2 G; CARB 7 G; FIBER 2 G; CHOLESTEROL 0 MG; SODIUM 150 MG
EXCELLENT SOURCE OF VITAMIN A, VITAMIN C
GOOD SOURCE OF MANGANESE, POTASSIUM, VITAMIN K

BETTER BURGER WITH GREEN OLIVES (PAGE 127)

PER SERVING CALORIES 280; TOTAL FAT 9 G (SAT FAT 2 G, MONO FAT 4 G, POLY FAT 2 G); PROTEIN 26 G; CARB 25 G; FIBER 4 G; CHOLESTEROL 60 MG; SODIUM 510 MG
EXCELLENT SOURCE OF MANGANESE, NIACIN, PROTEIN, SELENIUM, VITAMIN B12, VITAMIN K, ZINC
GOOD SOURCE OF FIBER, IRON, MAGNESIUM, PHOSPHORUS, VITAMIN A, VITAMIN C

CREAMY BROCCOLI SLAW (PAGE 128)

PER SERVING CALORIES 180; TOTAL FAT 12 G (SAT FAT 1.5 G, MONO FAT 3.5 G, POLY FAT 7 G); PROTEIN 6 G; CARB 12 G; FIBER 3 G; CHOLESTEROL 5 MG; SODIUM 400 MG
EXCELLENT SOURCE OF VITAMIN A, VITAMIN C
GOOD SOURCE OF COPPER, FIBER, FOLATE, MAGNESIUM, MANGANESE, PHOSPHORUS, PROTEIN, THIAMIN, VITAMIN B6

PORK PICCATA (PAGE 131)

PER SERVING CALORIES 310; TOTAL FAT 11 G (SAT FAT 2 G, MONO FAT 7 G, POLY FAT 1 G); PROTEIN 32 G; CARB 10 G; FIBER 1 G; CHOLESTEROL 90 MG; SODIUM 660 MG
EXCELLENT SOURCE OF NIACIN, PHOSPHORUS, PROTEIN, RIBOFLAVIN, SELENIUM, THIAMIN, VITAMIN B6, SELENIUM
GOOD SOURCE OF IRON, MAGNESIUM, PANTOTHENIC ACID, POTASSIUM, VITAMIN B12, VITAMIN C, ZINC

EXPRESS "STEAMED" SPINACH (PAGE 132)

PER SERVING CALORIES 10; TOTAL FAT 0 G (SAT FAT 0 G, MONO FAT 0 G, POLY FAT 0 G); PROTEIN 1 G; CARB 1 G; FIBER 1 G; CHOLESTEROL 0 MG; SODIUM 30 MG
EXCELLENT SOURCE OF VITAMIN A, VITAMIN K
GOOD SOURCE OF FOLATE, MANGANESE, VITAMIN C

GARLIC MASHED POTATOES (PAGE 133)

PER SERVING CALORIES 140; TOTAL FAT 4 G (SAT FAT 0.5 G, MONO FAT 2.5 G, POLY FAT 0.5 G); PROTEIN 3 G; CARB 24 G; FIBER 3 G; CHOLESTEROL 0 MG; SODIUM 190 MG
EXCELLENT SOURCE OF VITAMIN C
GOOD SOURCE OF FIBER, MANGANESE, PHOSPHORUS, POTASSIUM, VITAMIN B6

CHIPOTLE ORANGE GLAZED PORK CHOPS (PAGE 135)

PER SERVING CALORIES 270; TOTAL FAT 9 G (SAT FAT 3.5 G, MONO FAT 4 G, POLY FAT 0 G); PROTEIN 34 G; CARB 10 G; FIBER 0 G; CHOLESTEROL 90 MG; SODIUM 360 MG
EXCELLENT SOURCE OF NIACIN, PHOSPHORUS, PROTEIN, RIBOFLAVIN, SELENIUM, THIAMIN, VITAMIN B6, VITAMIN C, ZINC
GOOD SOURCE OF MANGANESE, POTASSIUM, VITAMIN B12

MAPLE SQUASH PUREE (PAGE 136)

PER SERVING CALORIES 150; TOTAL FAT 3 G (SAT FAT 2 G, MONO FAT 0.75 G, POLY FAT 0 G); PROTEIN 3 G; CARB 31 G; FIBER 2 G; CHOLESTEROL 10 MG; SODIUM 5 MG
EXCELLENT SOURCE OF MANGANESE, VITAMIN A
GOOD SOURCE OF FOLATE, POTASSIUM, THIAMIN, VITAMIN C

SPINACH-GREEN APPLE SALAD (PAGE 137)

PER SERVING CALORIES 150; TOTAL FAT 13 G (SAT FAT 1.5 G, MONO FAT 6 G, POLY FAT 5 G); PROTEIN 2 G; CARB 9 G; FIBER 2 G; CHOLESTEROL 0 MG; SODIUM 60 MG
EXCELLENT SOURCE OF MANGANESE, VITAMIN A, VITAMIN C, VITAMIN K
GOOD SOURCE OF FOLATE, MAGNESIUM

PULLED BBQ CHICKEN SANDWICHES (PAGE 141)

PER SERVING CALORIES 440; TOTAL FAT 12 G (SAT FAT 2.5 G, MONO FAT 5 G, POLY FAT 3.5 G); PROTEIN 36 G; CARB 47 G; FIBER 5 G; CHOLESTEROL 95 MG; SODIUM 400 MG
EXCELLENT SOURCE OF COPPER, FIBER, IRON, MAGNE-SIUM, MANGANESE, NIACIN, PHOSPHORUS, POTASSIUM, PROTEIN, SELENIUM, VITAMIN B6, VITAMIN C, ZINC
GOOD SOURCE OF CALCIUM, PANTOTHENIC ACID, RIBO-FLAVIN, THIAMIN, VITAMIN A, VITAMIN K

CLASSIC COLESLAW (PAGE 142)

PER SERVING CALORIES 110; TOTAL FAT 7 G (SAT FAT 1 G, MONO FAT 1.8 G, POLY FAT 4 G); PROTEIN 3 G; CARB 10 G; FIBER 2 G; CHOLESTEROL 5 MG; SODIUM 280 MG
EXCELLENT SOURCE OF VITAMIN A, VITAMIN C

FLOUNDER WITH ALMOND TOPPING (PAGE 148)

PER SERVING CALORIES 230; TOTAL FAT 8 G (SAT FAT 1 G, MONO FAT 4 G, POLY FAT 2 G); PROTEIN 35 G; CARB 4 G; FIBER 2 G; CHOLESTEROL 80 MG; SODIUM 430 MG

EXCELLENT SOURCE OF MAGNESIUM, NIACIN, PHOSPHORUS, POTASSIUM, PROTEIN, SELENIUM, VITAMIN B12, VITAMIN D

GOOD SOURCE OF MANGANESE, RIBOFLAVIN, THIAMIN, VITAMIN B6, VITAMIN C

SAFFRON RICE (PAGE 149)

PER SERVING CALORIES 190; TOTAL FAT 1 G (SAT FAT 0 G, MONO FAT 0 G, POLY FAT 0 G); PROTEIN 6 G; CARB 38 G; FIBER 1 G; CHOLESTEROL 0 MG; SODIUM 330 MG

EXCELLENT SOURCE OF FOLATE, MANGANESE

GOOD SOURCE OF IRON, NIACIN, PROTEIN, SELENIUM, THIAMIN

LEMON BROCCOLINI (PAGE 149)

PER SERVING CALORIES 80; TOTAL FAT 3.5 G (SAT FAT 0 G, MONO FAT 2.5 G, POLY FAT 0.5 G); PROTEIN 4 G; CARB 8 G; FIBER 1 G; CHOLESTEROL 0 MG; SODIUM 180 MG

EXCELLENT SOURCE OF VITAMIN A, VITAMIN C

GOOD SOURCE OF POTASSIUM

PROSCIUTTO-WRAPPED COD (PAGE 154)

PER SERVING CALORIES 170; TOTAL FAT 2.5 G (SAT FAT 0.5 G, MONO FAT 0 G, POLY FAT 0 G); PROTEIN 34 G; CARB 1 G; FIBER 0 G; CHOLESTEROL 85 MG; SODIUM 620 MG

EXCELLENT SOURCE OF PHOSPHORUS, POTASSIUM, PROTEIN, SELENIUM

GOOD SOURCE OF MAGNESIUM, NIACIN, VITAMIN B6, VITAMIN B12, VITAMIN D

PESTO POTATOES AND GREEN BEANS (PAGE 155)

PER SERVING CALORIES 240; TOTAL FAT 6 G (SAT FAT 1 G, MONO FAT 0 G, POLY FAT 0 G); PROTEIN 7 G; CARB 43 G; FIBER 7 G; CHOLESTEROL 5 MG; SODIUM 130 MG

EXCELLENT SOURCE OF FIBER, FOLATE, MANGANESE, POTASSIUM, VITAMIN A, VITAMIN B6, VITAMIN C, VITAMIN K

GOOD SOURCE OF COPPER, IRON, MAGNESIUM, NIACIN, PHOSPHORUS, PROTEIN, RIBOFLAVIN, THIAMIN

MUSSELS PROVENÇAL (WITHOUT BREAD) (PAGE 156)

PER SERVING CALORIES 240; TOTAL FAT 7 G (SAT FAT 1 G, MONO FAT 4 G, POLY FAT 1 G); PROTEIN 13 G; CARB 22 G; FIBER 2 G; CHOLESTEROL 25 MG; SODIUM 730 MG

EXCELLENT SOURCE OF MANGANESE, PHOSPHORUS, PROTEIN, SELENIUM, VITAMIN A, VITAMIN B12, VITAMIN C

GOOD SOURCE OF FOLATE, MAGNESIUM, POTASSIUM, RIBOFLAVIN, THIAMIN, VITAMIN B6, ZINC

BLT FRISÉE SALAD (PAGE 157)

PER SERVING CALORIES 200; TOTAL FAT 15 G (SAT FAT 2.5 G, MONO FAT 9.5 G, POLY FAT 1.5 G); PROTEIN 11 G; CARB 8 G; FIBER 4 G; CHOLESTEROL 20 MG; SODIUM 770 MG

EXCELLENT SOURCE OF FOLATE, MANGANESE, PROTEIN, THIAMIN, VITAMIN A, VITAMIN C, VITAMIN K

GOOD SOURCE OF FIBER, NIACIN, PANTOTHENIC ACID, PHOSPHORUS, POTASSIUM, SELENIUM, VITAMIN B6

SIRLOIN STEAK WITH GRAINY MUSTARD SAUCE (PAGE 169)

PER SERVING CALORIES 220; TOTAL FAT 9 G (SAT FAT 2 G, MONO FAT 4.5 G, POLY FAT 2 G); PROTEIN 25 G; CARB 10 G; FIBER 1 G; CHOLESTEROL 35 MG; SODIUM 510 MG

EXCELLENT SOURCE OF NIACIN, PHOSPHORUS, POTASSIUM, PROTEIN, SELENIUM, VITAMIN B6, VITAMIN C, ZINC

GOOD SOURCE OF IRON, RIBOFLAVIN, VITAMIN A, VITAMIN B12, VITAMIN K

PARMESAN STEAK "FRIES" (PAGE 170)

PER SERVING CALORIES 200; TOTAL FAT 6G; (SAT FAT 1.5 G, MONO FAT 2 G, POLY FAT 1 G); PROTEIN 7 G; CARB 31 G; FIBER 2 G; CHOLESTEROL 5 MG; SODIUM 135 MG

EXCELLENT SOURCE OF POTASSIUM, VITAMIN B6

GOOD SOURCE OF CALCIUM, MANGANESE, PROTEIN, VITAMIN C

PORCINI CRUSTED FILET MIGNON (PAGE 172)

PER SERVING CALORIES 160; TOTAL FAT 5 G (SAT FAT 2 G, MONO FAT 2 G, POLY FAT 0 G); PROTEIN 28 G; CARB 1 G; FIBER 0 G; CHOLESTEROL 75 MG; SODIUM 210 MG

EXCELLENT SOURCE OF IRON, PROTEIN, VITAMIN B12, VITAMIN D, ZINC

GOOD SOURCE OF NIACIN

CREAMED SPINACH (PAGE 175)

PER SERVING CALORIES 130 ; TOTAL FAT 5 G (SAT FAT 1.5 G, MONO FAT 2 G, POLY FAT 0.5 G); PROTEIN 9 G; CARB 16 G; FIBER 4 G; CHOLESTEROL 5 MG; SODIUM 170 MG
EXCELLENT SOURCE OF CALCIUM, FOLATE, MAGNESIUM, MANGANESE, POTASSIUM, PROTEIN, RIBOFLAVIN, VITAMIN A, VITAMIN K
GOOD SOURCE OF COPPER, FIBER, IODINE, IRON, PHOSPHORUS, SELENIUM, THIAMIN, VITAMIN B6, VITAMIN C, VITAMIN D

HERBED MASHED POTATOES (PAGE 174)

PER SERVING CALORIES 160; TOTAL FAT 4.5 G (SAT FAT 2.5 G, MONO FAT 1 G, POLY FAT 0 G); PROTEIN 4 G; CARB 26 G; FIBER 3 G; CHOLESTEROL 10 MG; SODIUM 170 MG
EXCELLENT SOURCE OF VITAMIN B6, VITAMIN C
GOOD SOURCE OF FIBER, MANGANESE, PHOSPHORUS, POTASSIUM

BAKED BEANS WITH HAM (PAGE 179)

PER SERVING CALORIES 430; TOTAL FAT 8 G (SAT FAT 1.5 G, MONO FAT 4 G, POLY FAT 1 G); PROTEIN 31 G; CARB 58 G; FIBER 14 G; CHOLESTEROL 45 MG; SODIUM 910 MG
EXCELLENT SOURCE OF FIBER, IRON, MAGNESIUM, NIACIN, PHOSPHORUS, POTASSIUM, PROTEIN, SELENIUM, THIAMIN, VITAMIN A, VITAMIN B6, VITAMIN C, ZINC
GOOD SOURCE OF CALCIUM, IODINE, MANGANESE, RIBOFLAVIN

GREEN APPLE AND CABBAGE SALAD (PAGE 180)

PER SERVING CALORIES 130; TOTAL FAT 5 G (SAT FAT 0 G, MONO FAT 3 G, POLY FAT 1.5 G); PROTEIN 2 G; CARB 23 G; FIBER 4 G; CHOLESTEROL 0 MG; SODIUM 350 MG
EXCELLENT SOURCE OF VITAMIN A, VITAMIN C, VITAMIN K
GOOD SOURCE OF FIBER, MANGANESE, POTASSIUM, VITAMIN B6

HAM WRAPPED ENDIVE AU GRATIN (WITHOUT BREAD) (PAGE 181)

PER SERVING CALORIES 240; TOTAL FAT 10 G (SAT FAT 6 G, MONO FAT 2.5 G, POLY FAT 0.5 G); PROTEIN 22 G; CARB 18 G; FIBER 5 G; CHOLESTEROL 50 MG; SODIUM 750 MG
EXCELLENT SOURCE OF CALCIUM, FIBER, PHOSPHORUS, PROTEIN
GOOD SOURCE OF FOLATE, IODINE, POTASSIUM, RIBOFLAVIN, THIAMIN, VITAMIN B12, VITAMIN D

GREEN SALAD WITH SHALLOT VINAIGRETTE (PAGE 180)

PER SERVING CALORIES 80; TOTAL FAT 7 G (SAT FAT 1 G, MONO FAT 5 G, POLY FAT 1 G); PROTEIN 1 G; CARB 3 G; FIBER 1 G; CHOLESTEROL 0 MG; SODIUM 180 MG
EXCELLENT SOURCE OF VITAMIN A, VITAMIN C

MARINATED CHICKEN AND GRAPE SKEWERS (PAGE 185)

PER SERVING CALORIES 210; TOTAL FAT 8 G (SAT FAT 1.5 G, MONO FAT 4 G, POLY FAT 1 G); PROTEIN 24 G; CARB 13 G; FIBER 1 G; CHOLESTEROL 65 MG; SODIUM 350 MG
EXCELLENT SOURCE OF NIACIN, PROTEIN, SELENIUM, VITAMIN B6, VITAMIN C
GOOD SOURCE OF PHOSPHORUS, VITAMIN K

GARDEN LENTIL PILAF (PAGE 186)

PER SERVING CALORIES 230; TOTAL FAT 8 G (SAT FAT 1 G, MONO FAT 5 G, POLY FAT 1 G); PROTEIN 11 G; CARB 33 G; FIBER 9 G; CHOLESTEROL 0 MG; SODIUM 330 MG
EXCELLENT SOURCE OF FIBER, IRON, PROTEIN, VITAMIN A, VITAMIN C, VITAMIN K
GOOD SOURCE OF POTASSIUM

LEMON-GARLIC ROAST TURKEY BREAST (PAGE 187)

PER SERVING CALORIES 350, TOTAL FAT 4 G (SAT FAT 1 G, MONO FAT 2 G, POLY FAT 1 G); PROTEIN 73 G; CARB 2 G; FIBER 0 G; CHOLESTEROL 200 MG; SODIUM 430 MG
EXCELLENT SOURCE OF IRON, NIACIN, PHOSPHORUS, POTASSIUM, PROTEIN, SELENIUM, VITAMIN B6, ZINC
GOOD SOURCE OF COPPER, MAGNESIUM, PANTOTHENIC ACID, RIBOFLAVIN, VITAMIN B12

ROASTED ROSEMARY POTATOES (PAGE 188)

PER SERVING CALORIES 160; TOTAL FAT 3.5 G (SAT FAT 0.5 G, MONO FAT 2.5 G, POLY FAT 0.5 G); PROTEIN 3 G; CARB 28 G; FIBER 3 G; CHOLESTEROL 0 MG; SODIUM 160 MG
EXCELLENT SOURCE OF POTASSIUM, VITAMIN C
GOOD SOURCE OF COPPER, FIBER, MAGNESIUM, MANGANESE, NIACIN, PHOSPHORUS, VITAMIN B6

ROASTED BRUSSELS SPROUTS (PAGE 188)

PER SERVING CALORIES 80; TOTAL FAT 4 G (SAT FAT 0.5 G, MONO FAT 2.5 G, POLY FAT 0.5 G); PROTEIN 4 G; CARB 10 G; FIBER 4 G; CHOLESTEROL 0 MG; SODIUM 170 MG
EXCELLENT SOURCE OF VITAMIN C, VITAMIN K
GOOD SOURCE OF FIBER, FOLATE, MANGANESE, POTASSIUM, THIAMIN, VITAMIN A, VITAMIN B6

RATATOUILLE WITH RED SNAPPER (PAGE 192)

PER SERVING CALORIES 310; TOTAL FAT 13 G (SAT FAT 2 G, MONO FAT 8 G, POLY FAT 2 G); PROTEIN 33 G; CARB 17 G; FIBER 7 G; CHOLESTEROL 50 MG; SODIUM 580 MG
EXCELLENT SOURCE OF FIBER, MAGNESIUM, MANGANESE, PHOSPHORUS, POTASSIUM, PROTEIN, SELENIUM, VITAMIN B6, VITAMIN B12, VITAMIN C, VITAMIN K
GOOD SOURCE OF COPPER, FOLATE, IRON, PANTOTHENIC ACID, RIBOFLAVIN, THIAMIN, VITAMIN A

HERBED GOAT CHEESE CROSTINI (PAGE 194)

PER SERVING CALORIES 110; TOTAL FAT 4 G (SAT FAT 2.5 G, MONO FAT 1 G, POLY FAT 0 G); PROTEIN 6 G; CARB 12 G; FIBER 2 G; CHOLESTEROL 5 MG; SODIUM 190 MG
EXCELLENT SOURCE OF MANGANESE
GOOD SOURCE OF COPPER, PROTEIN, SELENIUM

SALMON FLORENTINE (PAGE 197)

PER SERVING CALORIES 330; TOTAL FAT 13 G (SAT FAT 3 G, MONO FAT 5 G, POLY FAT 3 G); PROTEIN 43 G; CARB 11 G; FIBER 5 G; CHOLESTEROL 100 MG; SODIUM 600 MG
EXCELLENT SOURCE OF CALCIUM, COPPER, FOLATE, IRON, MAGNESIUM, MANGANESE, NIACIN, PHOSPHORUS, POTASSIUM, PROTEIN, RIBOFLAVIN, SELENIUM, THIAMIN, VITAMIN A, VITAMIN B6, VITAMIN B12, VITAMIN D
GOOD SOURCE OF PANTOTHENIC ACID, ZINC

QUINOA PILAF WITH PINE NUTS (PAGE 198)

PER SERVING CALORIES 270; TOTAL FAT 13 G (SAT FAT 1 G, MONO FAT 5 G, POLY FAT 5 G); PROTEIN 6 G; CARB 32 G; FIBER 4 G; CHOLESTEROL 0 MG; SODIUM 40 MG
EXCELLENT SOURCE OF FOLATE, MAGNESIUM, MANGANESE, PHOSPHORUS, VITAMIN K
GOOD SOURCE OF FIBER, IRON, NIACIN, POTASSIUM, PROTEIN, RIBOFLAVIN, THIAMIN, VITAMIN B6, VITAMIN C, ZINC

FOUR-CHEESE BAKED PENNE (PAGE 201)

PER SERVING CALORIES 400; TOTAL FAT 10 G (SAT FAT 5 G, MONO FAT 3 G, POLY FAT 0.5 G); PROTEIN 24 G; CARB 55 G; FIBER 7 G; CHOLESTEROL 25 MG; SODIUM 670 MG
EXCELLENT SOURCE OF CALCIUM, FIBER, PHOSPHORUS, PROTEIN, VITAMIN C, VITAMIN K
GOOD SOURCE OF IODINE, IRON, MANGANESE, POTASSIUM, RIBOFLAVIN, SELENIUM, VITAMIN A, VITAMIN B6, VITAMIN B12

ROMAINE HEARTS MEDITERRANEAN (PAGE 202)

PER SERVING CALORIES 100; TOTAL FAT 10 G (SAT FAT 1.5 G, MONO FAT 7 G, POLY FAT 1 G); PROTEIN 1 G; CARB 3 G; FIBER 1 G; CHOLESTEROL 0 MG; SODIUM 230 MG
GOOD SOURCE OF VITAMIN A, VITAMIN C

ROASTED TOMATO AND BLACK BEAN SOUP (PAGE 205)

PER SERVING CALORIES 390; TOTAL FAT 12 G (SAT FAT 2.5 G, MONO FAT 6 G, POLY FAT 1 G); PROTEIN 21 G; CARB 52 G; FIBER 13 G; CHOLESTEROL 10 MG; SODIUM 730MG
EXCELLENT SOURCE OF FIBER, IRON, MAGNESIUM, NIACIN, PHOSPHORUS, POTASSIUM, PROTEIN, VITAMIN C
GOOD SOURCE OF CALCIUM, IODINE, PHOSPHORUS, RIBOFLAVIN, THIAMIN, VITAMIN A, ZINC

AVOCADO-MANGO SALAD (PAGE 206)

PER SERVING CALORIES 120; TOTAL FAT 8 G (SAT FAT 1 G, MONO FAT 5 G, POLY FAT 1 G); PROTEIN 1 G; CARB 14 G; FIBER 5 G; CHOLESTEROL 0 MG; SODIUM 150 MG
EXCELLENT SOURCE OF VITAMIN C, VITAMIN K
GOOD SOURCE OF FIBER, FOLATE, VITAMIN A, VITAMIN B6

index